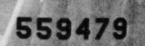
559479

Jet Fighters & Bombers

CHARTWELL
BOOKS INC.

in association with Phoebus

Written by David A. Anderton
Illustrated by John Batchelor
Edited by Bernard Fitzsimons

Published by Chartwell Books Inc
A Division of Book Sales Inc
110 Enterprise Avenue
Secaucus, New Jersey 07094

Library of Congress Catalog
Card Number 76-14638

This edition © 1976
Phoebus Publishing Company
BPC Publishing Limited
169 Wardour Street
London W1A 2JX
This material first appeared in Purnell's History
of the World Wars Specials © 1975/6 Phoebus
Publishing Company

Made and printed in Great Britain by
Waterlow (Dunstable) Limited

ISBN 0 7026 0010 5

David Anderton's professional and technical
qualifications are too numerous to list in detail. He
graduated in aeronautical engineering in 1941, and
during World War II worked for Grumman on, among
other projects, the F8F-1 Bearcat and F9F-1 Panther,
before being appointed Consultant to Grumman on
unconventional powerplants. Later, with General
Electric, he was Project Engineer for the Hermes B
missile programme. In 1950 he joined McGraw Hill as
an Associate Editor of 'Aviation Week', eventually
becoming Technical Editor of the magazine. Since 1963
he has run his own technical consultancy on
aerospace, his forte being the forecasting of trends in
technical developments.

John Batchelor, after serving in the RAF, worked in
the technical publications departments of several
British aircraft firms, and went on to contribute on a
freelance basis to many technical magazines. Since
then, his work for Purnell's Histories of the World Wars,
and subsequently the Purnell's World War Specials,
has established him as one of the most outstanding
artists in his field. A total enthusiast, he takes every
opportunity to fly, sail, drive or shoot with any piece of
military equipment he can find.

ABOUT THIS BOOK

From the pioneering efforts of Heinkel and Whittle which led to the first operational jets of World War II to the technological wonders which equip the air forces of today, this book tells the fascinating story of the development and operational use of the world's jet fighters and bombers. Each aircraft is discussed in chronological order, the reference date being that of the first flight of the prototype or of the development aircraft immediately preceding it.

The forerunner of all jet fighters, the Heinkel 178, took off on its maiden flight on August 27, 1939. Since then each decade has seen the introduction of a new breed of fighter, characterised by such outstanding successes as the Messerschmitt Me 262 of the war years, the F-86 Sabre and MiG-15 of the Korean War, and after that by such famous names as the Phantom, the MiG-21 and the Mirage IIIC.

The first jet bomber, the Arado Ar 234, saw action only in the last months of World War II. But it showed the way to bigger and better things, and before long the jet bomber was the key weapon in the Cold War arsenal. The need for a credible global deterrent gave rise to such aircraft as the B-47, B-52 and B-58 in the USA, the V-Bombers in Britain and the Tu-16 in Russia. Today, however, missiles are the prime strategic weapons, and bombers have become more specialised and complex, incorporating such features as inertial navigation, terrain-following radar, electronic-counter-measures and cruise missiles.

This history of jet fighters and bombers combines the talents of David Anderton, a writer whose involvement with the subject has been long and intense, and John Batchelor, whose dazzling full-colour illustrations complement the lavish use of photographs to show virtually every important jet fighter and bomber ever built.

CONTENTS

Jet Fighters: The First Steps 6
Wartime Developments: Too Fast to Fight 12
Postwar Developments:
   The Sweep Towards Mach 1 20
War in Korea:
   The First Jet Fighter Aces 28
Dead End Developments 42
The Sixties: Lessons From Small Wars 44
The Present:
   Soaring Cost and Complexity 53

The Future: Where Do We Go From Here?............56
Ejector Seats 60
Fighter Armament:
    Choose Your Weapon..............................63
Jet Bombers: The Starting Place 66
Postwar Developments: The Class of '47 70
Boeing B-47 Stratojet:
    In a Class by Itself 78
Europe Joins In:
    Light Twins and Losers 82

New Programmes:
    Two New, Two for Insurance......................86
Boeing B-52 Stratofortress:
    Heavyweight Warrior 92
End of an Era:
    The Last of the Subsonic Bombers................98
New Technology:
    The Supersonic Generation 110
Attack Bombers...122
Bomb Loads: Plutonium to Iron 126

The first half of this book deals with that prince of modern aircraft, the jet fighter. Here a fighter is defined as an aircraft designed to destroy other aircraft as its primary role. This rules out the plane designed mainly for the strike or ground attack role, even though it may have some remaining capability as a fighter to claw its way back from the target area.

The chapters that deal with the development of the jet fighter are divided to follow that development in one country at a time. Further, the arrangement is chronological, with the key time being the date of the first flight of either a fighter prototype or of the research aircraft that immediately preceded development of a jet fighter.

Two types of basic jet propulsion powerplants are considered here. One is the rocket engine, a self-contained motor burning a liquid fuel and oxidiser, and generating its thrust by combustion of the two in a suitably shaped chamber and exhaust nozzle. The other is the aircraft gas turbine for jet propulsion, an engine which takes in outside air, mixes it with fuel, burns the mixture, and exhausts the hot gases at high speed through a suitable nozzle.

Neither engine type was new when it was first applied to aircraft. The rocket engine, albeit in the form of a solid-propellant system, had been known for years, and was familiar to millions in the form of fireworks. Rockets had been used in warfare and, in the daring years of flight during the 1920s, they had been adapted to launch a glider into the air in the first recorded flight of any aircraft anywhere using jet propulsion of any type.

But that experiment, demonstrated by the Opel-Sander Rakete 1 on 30 September 1929 at Frankfurt, led to a dead end. Neither the state of the solid-propellant rocket art nor that of aeroplane design was ready then for the use of such a novel form of propulsion.

The gas turbine is also an old form of powerplant. The first patent for such an engine

JET FIGHTERS THE FIRST STEPS

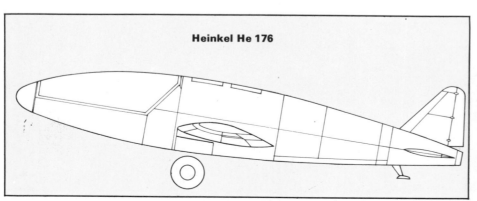

Heinkel He 176

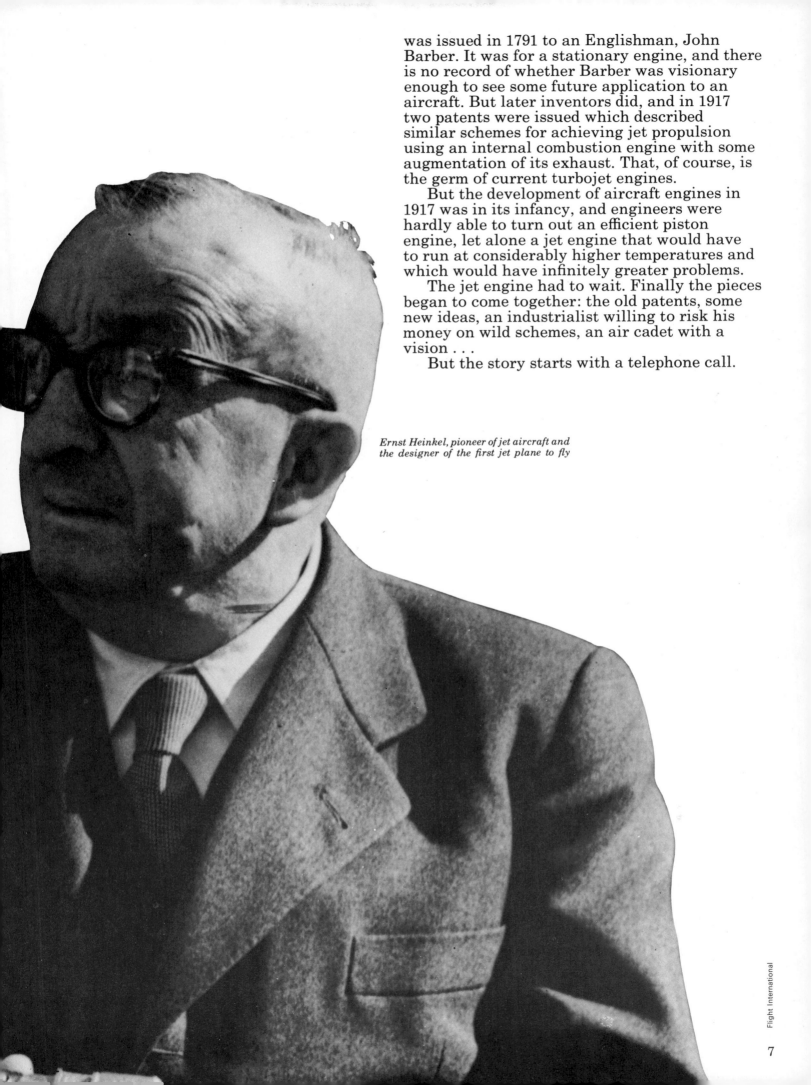

was issued in 1791 to an Englishman, John Barber. It was for a stationary engine, and there is no record of whether Barber was visionary enough to see some future application to an aircraft. But later inventors did, and in 1917 two patents were issued which described similar schemes for achieving jet propulsion using an internal combustion engine with some augmentation of its exhaust. That, of course, is the germ of current turbojet engines.

But the development of aircraft engines in 1917 was in its infancy, and engineers were hardly able to turn out an efficient piston engine, let alone a jet engine that would have to run at considerably higher temperatures and which would have infinitely greater problems.

The jet engine had to wait. Finally the pieces began to come together: the old patents, some new ideas, an industrialist willing to risk his money on wild schemes, an air cadet with a vision . . .

But the story starts with a telephone call.

Ernst Heinkel, pioneer of jet aircraft and the designer of the first jet plane to fly

At half-past four on the morning of 27 August 1939, the telephone's insistent ringing woke Ernst Udet, the top-ranking living ace of the former German Imperial Air Service, and head of the new Luftwaffe's Technical Department.

Udet growled into the phone, still sleepy. The voice from the distance was jubilant. 'This is Heinkel. We've just flown the world's first jet airplane!'

'Fine,' said Udet, grumbling. 'Now let me get back to sleep.'

Germany was only a few days from its invasion of Poland; and Udet could reasonably be expected to be on edge, wondering if each phone call would bring news of the march to the East. But the news that he

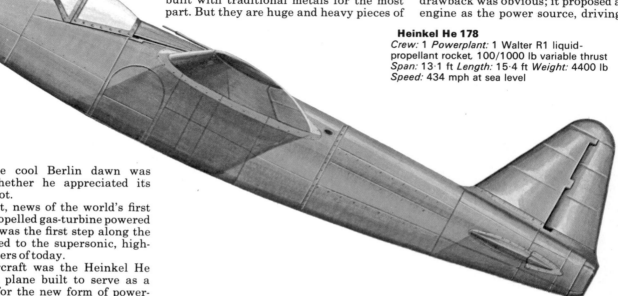

Heinkel He 178
Crew: 1 *Powerplant:* 1 Walter R1 liquid-propellant rocket, 100/1000 lb variable thrust
Span: 13·1 ft *Length:* 15·4 ft *Weight:* 4400 lb
Speed: 434 mph at sea level

received in the cool Berlin dawn was electrifying, whether he appreciated its importance or not.

It was, in fact, news of the world's first flight by a jet-propelled gas-turbine powered aircraft, and it was the first step along the path that has led to the supersonic, high-altitude jet fighters of today.

That first aircraft was the Heinkel He 178, a research plane built to serve as a flying test-bed for the new form of powerplant. It was tiny, spanning less than 24 ft and weighing less than two tons, fully loaded with fuel. Its turbojet engine produced about 1000 lb of thrust. Its performance was modest; it probably never flew faster than 350 mph, and never got very far out of sight of the aerodrome at Marienehe. It was overtaken by events. The German Air Ministry ignored it, and eventually it was dropped from active development only a few months after its historic first flight.

In a way, the German Air Ministry couldn't be blamed then for its lack of interest. There were other tasks of a higher priority. Hitler was about to invade Poland, and the air support needed for the job was marginal. If the Polish resistance lasted longer than planned, if the offensive strikes did not knock out enough of the Polish air force, if another country should side with the Poles, there was serious doubt about the ability of the Luftwaffe to maintain its part of the push eastward.

Further, the concept of war held by Hitler and his staff was built around the Blitzkrieg – lightning war – which would move so fast and so powerfully that it would steam-roller the opposition before any countering forces had time to realise what was happening. There was no time for development that might take years to come to fruition. New weapons were needed, yes; but they were needed tomorrow. The jet fighter was an interesting new idea, but of no immediate practical value.

It is not exactly correct to speak of jet propulsion as a new idea. The idea of

propulsion by reaction is as old as propulsion itself. The classical example is the aeolipile, which is supposed to have been demonstrated by the Alexandrian philosopher Hero before the time of Christ. His little sphere, whirled on its bearings by two steam jets driven by the boiling of water inside the sphere, was what we would now call an interesting laboratory experiment. It served to illustrate the principle, but did nothing else.

Jet propulsion was an idea that had to wait for its time to come, primarily because it depended on the generation of high temperatures within an engine. High temperatures and the attendant high pressures required containment in shells that were strong when red-hot. And that required new lightweight metals. True, it could be done with the old ones; steam turbines have been built with traditional metals for the most part. But they are huge and heavy pieces of stationary machinery, hardly suitable for powering aircraft in flight.

And that was the toughest requirement of all. Whatever form of engine was to be built, if it were to fly it had to be light as well as strong. There was no way the jet engine could have been built and flown by the Wright brothers. The state of the art in 1903 simply would not have permitted it.

Jet propulsion is a very general term, because everything that flies under power is propelled by a jet. A propeller, a helicopter rotor, a turbojet or a rocket engine all move an aircraft by jet propulsion. Each of those engines generates a mass of air moving at a higher speed than its surroundings. The difference in momentum is applied as thrust to the airframe, and the aircraft moves through the air, propelled by a jet of faster air.

Toughest problems
The gas turbine for jet propulsion presents some of the toughest design problems ever faced by engineers. The basic problem is to increase the momentum – the mass times the velocity – of the air going through the engine. That is done by burning fuel and adding its energy to that of the incoming air, which is not too difficult to accomplish, in engineering terms. But it is difficult to accomplish with economy of fuel, with safety of operation, and with long life of the moving and stationary parts of the engine.

Building jet engines and getting them to

work was, in retrospect, the simple part. The hard part was getting them to stand up to high performance for hour after hour, while a white-hot exhaust roared out of the tailpipe and the engine glowed from orange to dull red.

The story of today's jet fighters starts, truly, with a young British air cadet, Frank Whittle, studying at the RAF College at Cranwell preparatory to getting his commission. In his fourth term, Whittle wrote a paper, 'Future Developments in Aircraft Design', pointing out some of the possibilities of rockets and of gas turbines driving propellers, but not of the gas turbine producing only a jet of hot air for propulsion.

That came later, about 18 months into his RAF career. Whittle's research had found a basic patent, dated 1917, that covered the principles of jet propulsion for aircraft. Its drawback was obvious; it proposed a piston engine as the power source, driving a fan, or a shrouded propeller within the fuselage, and with the addition of afterburning for additional thrust from the engine.

The principle was sound, but its failings were obvious to Whittle. He hit on the idea of using a gas turbine instead of the piston engine, proposed it to the Air Ministry, and was politely turned down. Materials just didn't exist that could do the job, said the Ministry rejection. Whittle persisted, and filed a patent application for an aircraft gas turbine on 16 January 1930. Because the Air Ministry was not officially interested, the patent was openly published after it was granted about 18 months later. The secret was out.

Another jet pioneer was German aircraft designer Ernst Heinkel, a brilliant innovator. Heinkel was always looking for ways to improve performance, to go faster and higher.

He had become interested in jet propulsion while doing research for an article he was writing in 1935, called 'An Inquiry into Engine Development'. It was a look at future trends desirable for aircraft powerplants. Heinkel saw 500 mph as a practical limit to the speed of propeller-driven aircraft. To get over that hurdle, he reasoned, it would be necessary to have some new kind of propulsion, and he thought in terms of jet engines, primarily those driven by gas turbines.

Late in 1935, Heinkel met Wernher von Braun, then a young engineer testing rocket engines of his own design and longing for an airplane with which to do flight tests. Heinkel loaned von Braun a fuselage from an He 112 fighter, and eventually supported experiments in flight with a modified He 112 driven by an auxiliary rocket engine.

In early 1936, Heinkel's interest was further sparked by a letter from a colleague, Professor Pohl, head of the Science Institute at the University of Göttingen. Pohl's

Caproni-Campini N 1
Crew: 2 *Powerplant:* 900 hp Isotta-Fraschini piston engine driving 3-stage ducted fan with afterburner *Span:* 50·3 ft *Length:* 42·9 ft *Weight:* 9229 lb *Speed:* 233 mph at 9800 ft

assistant was a 24-year old scientist named Pabst von Ohain, who had been working on a new kind of aeroplane engine, said Pohl, which did not need a propeller. Pohl believed in the young man and his ideas, and urged Heinkel to investigate.

Heinkel met von Ohain, hired him and his assistant Hahn, and set the team to work in a special building across the aerodrome at Marienehe, a former Mecklenburg state park which Heinkel had bought as the site of a new factory for Luftwaffe production.

Marienehe is rolling country, lying along the Warnow river in the north of Mecklenburg province, now part of the German Democratic Republic. There were farms and estates in the vicinity, and it was a quiet backwater of rural Germany in the years before the war.

But in September 1937 the stillness of the night was disturbed by a low humming that built quickly to a scream and then to a sudden roar. A tongue of flame shot out of the building at the Heinkel field, hot and red, jutting toward the river, scattering the first leaves of fall, lighting the area around the hangar. Von Ohain's strange engine had just been fired for the first time. Hahn telephoned Heinkel with the news, and within a few minutes Heinkel himself was at the building to see and hear the birth of the jet age.

By the next spring the engine was advanced enough to produce repeatable performance. Its fuel was gasoline, instead of the hydrogen used during development work. It produced about 1100 lb of thrust, and it seemed to Heinkel to be ready to power an aircraft.

The design of the aircraft began, with engineers, draftsmen and technicians sworn to secrecy. With that project in capable hands, Heinkel turned back to rocket aircraft, and to experiments aimed at getting one into the air. The first flight of the modified He 112 lent to von Braun's team had been made in April 1937, with the rocket engine operated during flight only. On later tests, pilot Erich Warsitz made takeoffs on the combined power of the He 112's Junkers Jumo piston engine and the von Braun rocket engine in the tail.

Finally, in the summer of 1937, Warsitz made the takeoff on rocket power alone, climbed to altitude, circled the field and landed, using only the rocket engine for propulsion during the entire flight. The point had been proven; Heinkel now was keen to build a special aeroplane for rocket propulsion instead of attempting to modify the He 112 or any other aircraft.

He and Warsitz agreed that the design should aim for the round number of 1000 kilometres per hour speed (621 mph). The airplane was designed around Warsitz. It had a tiny wing span, only 13·1 ft, and the top of the fuselage came up to Warsitz' waist. The nose was detachable in the event of an accident, and used a drogue parachute to cut its speed to a point where Warsitz would have been able to bail out and use his own parachute.

Design and construction of the He 176, as the rocket research aircraft was designated, took about one year. It was trucked to the experimental airfield at Peenemünde, later to become world-famous for its development of the A-4 rocket weapon under von Braun. But it was to take another year of slow development before the He 176 was ready for flight. Meanwhile, Warsitz made taxi runs, extending the speed range and distance covered. The Peenemünde runway was lengthened by nearly one mile to accommodate the tests, and Warsitz occasionally took advantage of the long runway to lift the little plane into the air for a few seconds.

Official interference
Meanwhile the Air Ministry did develop some interest in the He 176. They saw it as a potential rocket-powered interceptor, heavily armed and able to slash through bomber formations with great effectiveness. Their insistence on that role for the He 176 caused Heinkel to install small blisters on the fuselage, alleging they were the provisions for armament, but actually filling them with test instrumentation.
Finally Warsitz and the He 176 were ready. On 30 June 1939 the tiny plane blasted off the runway on its first full flight. It lasted less than one minute, but Warsitz and the rest of the Heinkel team were

jubilant. Rocket-powered aircraft had flown before, for short distances and times; but they had been modified aircraft, flying testbeds for the rocket and only a means for getting in-flight data on the powerplant. But none had been considered as a candidate for development into a fighter, although that thought was not exactly uppermost in Heinkel's mind.

On 1 July, Heinkel himself saw the He 176 fly. So did Udet, Milch and others in the Air Ministry. After Warsitz landed, Udet shook his hand and then forbade any further flying with the He 176. 'That's no aeroplane' was his verdict. Warsitz and Heinkel argued for continuance of the tests, and eventually they were successful. Then they were refused permission again. That was rescinded, and permission reinstated, because there was to be a demonstration of new aircraft for Hitler, and the Air Ministry wanted to include the He 176.

Hitler saw it fly, passed a few compliments around, and left the field. Warsitz later had a personal talk with Hitler, during which the subject of the He 176 never came up. Obviously there was to be no official support for the project.

The He 176 and He 178 had been hangar mates, both having been built in a special hangar erected for the purpose away from the rest of the Marienehe plant. Now work concentrated on the He 178, aiming for an early flight.

On the morning of 27 August 1939, Warsitz climbed into the He 178 and started the engine. It whined up to speed; he taxied out, roared down the runway and lifted off. The undercarriage could not be retracted and Warsitz, after trying every trick in the trade, finally resigned himself to circling the field about 1500 ft altitude with the gear hanging. After about six minutes in the air, he swung into the approach pattern, sideslipped on final, and touched lightly down on the grass, rumbling across the field to a stop.

For Heinkel and the rest of his design team, it was the justification for the hours of work on two pioneering aircraft, both jet-propelled, one by a rocket and one by a gas turbine. Under the circumstances, the Heinkel organisation would have had a tremendous technological lead on the rest of industry. But the events of September 1939 caught up with them. After only a few flights by both airplanes, and despite long hours of arguing, cajoling and pleading by Heinkel, both aircraft projects were stopped

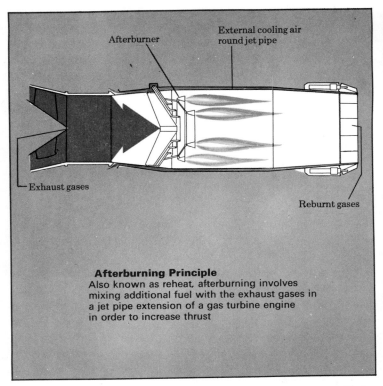

Afterburner

External cooling air round jet pipe

Exhaust gases

Reburnt gases

Afterburning Principle
Also known as reheat, afterburning involves mixing additional fuel with the exhaust gases in a jet pipe extension of a gas turbine engine in order to increase thrust

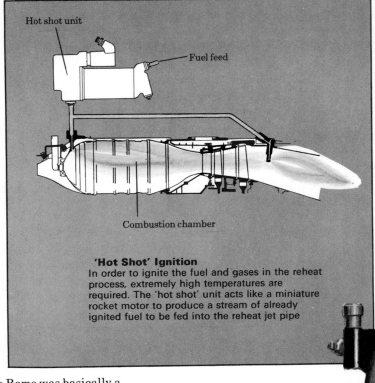

Hot shot unit

Fuel feed

Combustion chamber

'Hot Shot' Ignition
In order to ignite the fuel and gases in the reheat process, extremely high temperatures are required. The 'hot shot' unit acts like a miniature rocket motor to produce a stream of already ignited fuel to be fed into the reheat jet pipe

dead. The word was production, and there was no time for research and development. Besides, they would not be needed for the short war that would be over before winter.

Sadly Heinkel saw both the He 176 and He 178 crated and sent off for display in the Berlin Air Museum. Their fate was predictable from the day they left Marienehe. In 1943, one of the many bombing raids that were to destroy Berlin pounded the Air Museum and its priceless collection of aeronautical history into rubble.

Soon after the pioneering flights of the two Heinkel jet-propelled aircraft in 1939, an Italian research aircraft flew from Milan to Rome under jet power. It was the first cross-country flight of any length by a jet-propelled aircraft, and even though the run included a stop for fuel, the flight was epochal.

The airplane was the Caproni-Campini N 1, a low-winged monoplane with a cylindrical fuselage. A circular inlet at the nose and an exhaust nozzle at the tail gave the only clues to the internal arrangement, which was unusual. In some ways, it predated the most advanced jet engines operational today; but it was then only a makeshift approach to jet propulsion.

Inside the N 1, an Isotta-Fraschini piston engine, which developed about 900 hp, drove a three-stage variable-pitch fan in an application of the principle of the ducted fan, today the most economical and advanced type of turbojet development. Downstream of the ducted fan discharge was a ring burner fed with fuel to augment the thrust of the engine-driven fan; it was, in essence, an afterburner.

Designer Secondo Campini had been working on the idea of a jet-propelled aeroplane for eight years, and had hit upon this particular scheme, perhaps as a result of finding earlier research and patents along this line.

The N 1 made its first flight on 27 August 1940 from Forlanini aerodrome near Milan, and was airborne for about ten minutes. The

cross-country flight to Rome was basically a ferry flight to get the aircraft to the Italian aeronautical test establishment at Guidonia. With maximum publicity planned, the N 1 took off from Forlanini and headed south. A fuelling stop was made at Pisa, and the final landing at Rome.

It was found to be a not very efficient method of achieving jet propulsion. The programme was abandoned about two years after the first flight, although Campini continued to press for adoption of his basic ideas as a possible auxiliary powerplant for fighter aircraft.

Frank Whittle, British pioneer of jet aircraft who patented his first jet engine in 1930

THE WHITTLE ENGINE

Whittle W 1 Turbojet: 2-sided centrifugal compressor, 10 reverse-flow interconnected combustion chambers *Fuel:* Paraffin with atomised burners *Specific fuel consumption:* 1·4 lb/lb thrust/hour *Performance:* 850 lb static thrust at 16,500 rpm *Thrust/Weight ratio:* 1:0·66

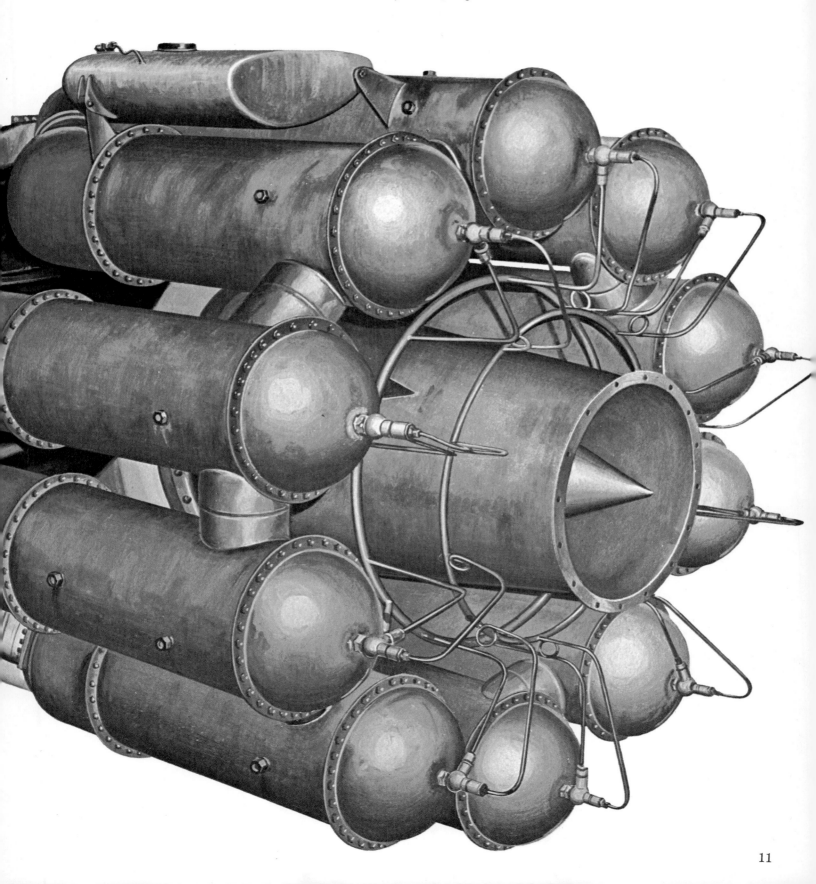

TOO FAST TO FIGHT

The early experiments with jet engines and aircraft led to both Britain and Germany having jet fighters operational during the Second World War. Me 262s terrorised British bombers, while Gloster Meteors brought down several V-1 flying bombs. But against conventional aircraft the jet planes' superior speed could also be a handicap, hindering accurate fire

The real impetus to the development of jet aircraft was the start of the Second World War in September 1939. As country after country realised the ugly truth, industry, science and engineering teams girded for their parts in the struggle to come.

Germany had a head start, thanks to the pioneering work by Ernst Heinkel. So it should not be surprising that the world's first turbojet aircraft to be designed as a fighter from the beginning was yet another Heinkel effort, the He 280. It was also the world's first twin-jet aircraft.

Heinkel visualised a twin-engined jet fighter, with engines slung in individual nacelles under the wing, minimising the length of the intake and exhaust ducting. For ground clearance, and to avoid blasting loose huge chunks of the runway surface, he decided on tricycle landing gear, the first on a German aircraft.

Design of the He 280 started in late 1939. In March 1940, the Air Ministry awarded a contract to the Messerschmitt organisation for prototypes of a twin-engined aircraft. A few days later, Heinkel got essentially the same sort of contract.

The first prototype He 280 was completed

by September, lacking only airworthy engines. Heinkel had the prototype flown first as a glider, testing basic aerodynamic characteristics. When the Heinkel HeS 8A engines were ready for flight the following spring, the airplane was already well understood.

On 2 April 1941, at Marienehe airfield, Fritz Schaefer climbed into the cockpit of the He 280. He taxied out and took off, climbing to 900 ft or so for a circle of the field. He did not attempt to retract the landing gear, or to do anything exceptional with the aircraft.

Three days later it was flown again, and demonstrated to Udet and others from the Air Ministry. Their indifference was annoying to Heinkel, who could not understand why his advanced ideas were continually rejected.

He thought the He 280 had proved .its point and that it should be considered for production. So he arranged a series of tests against the Luftwaffe's top fighter of the time, the Focke-Wulf 190. It was no contest; the jet-propelled fighter outperformed the Fw 190 in every way. The Ministry bent a little, and awarded Heinkel a contract for 13 pre-production aircraft.

His designers put together a further development, with the unusually heavy armament of six 20-mm cannon, and proposed it to the Air Ministry. To everybody's surprise, the Ministry awarded a contract for the production of 300, but Heinkel's facilities, strained as they were by existing production programmes, were bypassed by this order and the He 280 was scheduled to be built by another firm.

But by then the Me 262 had flown under jet power; it appeared so promising that the Ministry cancelled the He 280.

The rocket-powered jet fighter arrived, in prototype form, in 1941. On 13 August

Messerschmitt test pilot Heini Dittmar strapped himself into a prototype Me 163A, started the rocket engine, and blasted across the turf at Peenemünde-West, the experimental Luftwaffe airfield. The Me 163A was held in a climb until the fuel was burned; then Dittmar turned and began a circling letdown to a landing. It was the first flight by a rocket-powered interceptor prototype, and it began a long, frustrating and ultimately unsuccessful development programme.

It had begun some years earlier, as a project to power a tailless glider designed by Dr Alexander Lippisch. Working at the German Research Institute for Soaring (DFS), Lippisch's team had brought along the design of their DFS 194 to the point where it obviously required industrial support.

Messerschmitt was designated, and Lippisch's team went to Augsburg. The aircraft turned out well, but its rocket powerplant did not, and the DFS 194 was never flown under power. It was used instead for ground tests of the rocket.

The baulky rocket was replaced by a new design with controllable thrust, other changes were made, and the result was the Me 163A series, prototypes used for development of the interceptor version.

It was one of this first batch of 13 that Dittmar first flew in August 1941. But there was a long time between that first flight and the first operational sortie. The Me 163 did not see action until 13 May 1944, and even that attempt to seek combat was made in a development aircraft, one of the Me 163B prototypes. By the time the Luftwaffe had production versions of the Me 163B in service, the war was running down and the visions of hundreds of the tiny rocket fighters slashing through disrupted bomber formations had been reduced to the actual-

Messerschmitt Me 163
Crew: 1 *Powerplant:* 1 Walter RII liquid-propellant rocket *Span:* 30·5 ft *Length:* 17·8 ft
Weight: 5291 lb *Speed:* 558 mph

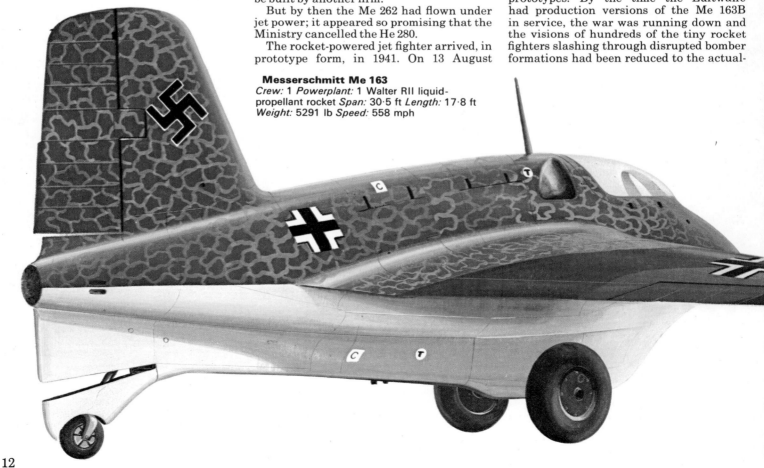

ity of a few sporadic intercepts and some hideous operational accidents.

A dispassionate examination of the concept led to one conclusion: it was possible to be too fast for effective combat. The Me 163s were designed to be used as interceptors of daylight bombing raids. They were to take off and climb rapidly (they could get to bomber height in less than three minutes), attack the bombers with their paired 30-mm cannon, and break away for the return to base.

In practice, the speed of the rocket fighter was so much greater than that of

its bomber target that a pilot only had two or three seconds to aim and fire. It proved to be nearly impossible. The Me 163 was not suitable for combat against slow-flying bombers.

Those that did get into combat managed to shoot down a few bombers, but it was too late. The factory producing one of the essential fuel components was bombed in

May 1973: 'Vintage Pair' of the RAF's Historic Flight, a De Havilland Vampire T 11, the last Vampire still flying with the RAF, and a Gloster Meteor T 7.

August 1944. Ground transportation was under constant attack, and several complete shipments of rocket fuel were lost to Allied gunnery. As winter neared, the weather worsened – and the Me 163 was not suitable for bad weather or night operations. The whole programme ground to a halt, with only a few intercepts flown against special targets such as high-altitude photo flights.

There was only one truly successful jet fighter developed and brought to operational status during the Second World War: the Messerschmitt Me 262. In spite of setbacks to the smooth development of the programme caused by such diverse factors as Hitler's dreams and bombing realities, the project maintained and even gained momentum.

It began in late 1938 with an Air Ministry contract with Messerschmitt for a twin-engine jet fighter. By March 1940, both Messerschmitt and Heinkel were told to go ahead with the development of their respective twin-jet fighters.

The first Messerschmitt prototype was completed well before its jet engines were ready for flight. The first alternative, to fit

rocket engines in the nacelles for flight tests, was ruled out because the engines weren't considered safe enough.

So Messerschmitt installed a standard Junkers Jumo piston engine in the nose, and the first flight of an Me 262 was made on 18 April 1941, with a piston engine and propeller providing propulsion, and empty jet nacelles under the wings. By March of the following year airworthy jet engines were available, and on 25 March the prototype was flown on the combined power of its piston engine and the two new jets. It nearly ended in disaster for the pilot, Fritz Wendel, because both turbojets failed shortly after takeoff, and he had a tough time keeping the Me 262 in the air.

Wendel made the first flight on jet power only with the third prototype, which had been fitted with a pair of Junkers Jumo 004A-0 turbojets producing about 1850 lb of thrust each. On 18 July 1942 he took off from the hard-surfaced runway at Leipheim for a flight of about twelve minutes. He completed a second flight that day, and was delighted with the way the plane handled.

But he had had to use brakes momentarily during the takeoff roll, in order to get the tail up into the slipstream so that the elevators would be effective. The braking served to rotate the aircraft nose down and had to be done carefully, gently and at exactly the right time.

This must have been one of the reasons that Messerschmitt decided to redesign the Me 262 with a new type of landing gear – the tricycle type with nosewheel – that became the standard for all subsequent Me 262s.

Happily for the Allied cause, the decision-making machinery broke down on the Me 262 programme. Production schedules were changed almost monthly. Variations on the theme were developed on request and the Me 262 was built as a fighter, an all-weather fighter, a reconnaissance aircraft, a ground-attack aircraft, a fighter with reconnaissance capabilities, a fighter-bomber, and an interceptor with rocket booster engines in the nacelles, all in a single-seat version. Two-seat models were developed as trainers and night fighters. They were built in small batches of only a few of most of the versions, and only one model was produced in any quantity.

It was July 1944 before the Me 262 engaged in combat, the first recorded instance being an encounter with a reconnaissance Mosquito flown by Flt Lt Wall, RAF. Wall reported that an Me 262 made five passes at his Mosquito, but in each case he was able to break away and finally dove into clouds to escape his persistent adversary.

Time and the losing position of Germany caught up with the Me 262. By tremendous industrial effort, mass production of the aircraft had been achieved under mountains of difficulties. The first production aircraft had been delivered in March 1944, and by February 1945 production had peaked at 300 completed aircraft per month. Factory delivery data show that 1320 were rolled out of the doors for delivery to the Luftwaffe during the 13-month production programme.

The most famous unit to operate the Me 262 was JV 44, formed and commanded by General Adolf Galland. The unit arrived

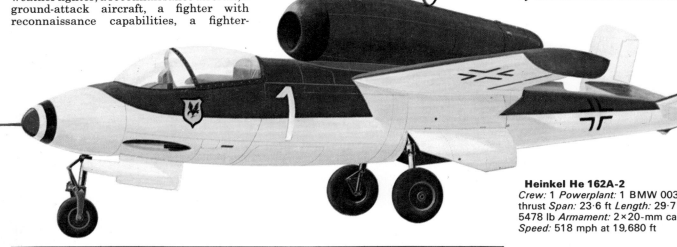

Heinkel He 162A-2
Crew: 1 *Powerplant:* 1 BMW 003E-1, 1760 lb thrust *Span:* 23·6 ft *Length:* 29·7 ft *Weight:* 5478 lb *Armament:* 2×20-mm cannon *Speed:* 518 mph at 19,680 ft

Heinkel He 280
Crew: 1 *Powerplant:* 2 HeS 8, 1100 lb thrust each *Span:* 40 ft *Length:* 34·1 ft *Weight:* 9500 lb *Armament:* 3×20-mm cannon *Speed:* 558 mph at 19,680 ft

Cockpit is a totally enclosed unit for pressurisation purposes, although no service machines were ever pressurised

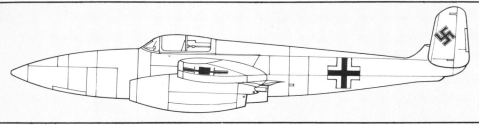

Tank filler cap

Radio loop

Stabiliser adjusting motor

238-gallon tank

132-gallon auxiliary tank

Radio

Master compass

Flaps

Variable orifice 'bullet' moves in and out to vary exit area

at its base near Munich on the last day of March 1945, and operated for only about one month, finally making its sorties from the autobahn between Munich and Augsburg. But in that time, they terrorised bomber crews, made about 50 kills, and established once and for all the value of the jet fighter.

As Germany's position grew more desperate, so did attempts to develop new weapons to stave off the inevitable. One of these was the Heinkel 162, a tricky single-engined jet fighter. Its specification, issued in September 1944, called for a lightweight fighter, using an absolute minimum of strategic materials, and capable of being put into rapid mass production. It was to be flown into combat by the loyal Hitler Youth, after they had been given a brief training period on gliders.

Heinkel was awarded the contract on 30 September. By 29 October the He 162 had been designed, and construction had begun. The first prototype was flown on 6 December, with Flugkapitän Peter at the controls. One month later, the first He 162s were delivered to a test unit, and in February 1945 I/JG-1 began conversion to the type.

Few German records remain of those frantic last days, but there is at least one reported incident of combat between an He 162 and a USAAF P-51 Mustang. The jet was able to turn and climb with the Mustang, but it was much faster and had greater acceleration. The combat was inconclusive; neither claimed victory.

By the end of the war, about 275 had been built and another 800 were in various stages of assembly. It was a formidable accomplishment by the Heinkel organisation. They designed a contemporary jet fighter in one month, flew it nine weeks after starting design, and delivered 275 in less than seven months.

There was one more last-gasp defence effort to fly: the Bachem 349 Natter. Work had begun in the spring of 1944, to a specification for a target defence interceptor. Bachem's first proposal was rejected in

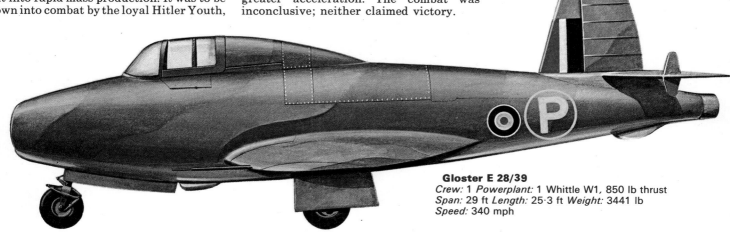

Gloster E 28/39
Crew: 1 *Powerplant:* 1 Whittle W1, 850 lb thrust
Span: 29 ft *Length:* 25·3 ft *Weight:* 3441 lb
Speed: 340 mph

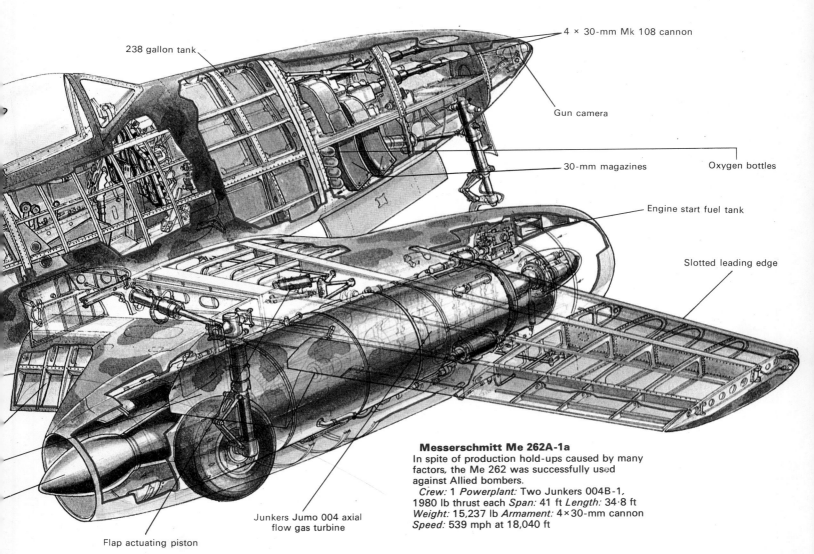

238 gallon tank

4 × 30-mm Mk 108 cannon

Gun camera

30-mm magazines

Oxygen bottles

Engine start fuel tank

Slotted leading edge

Messerschmitt Me 262A-1a
In spite of production hold-ups caused by many factors, the Me 262 was successfully used against Allied bombers.
Crew: 1 *Powerplant:* Two Junkers 004B-1, 1980 lb thrust each *Span:* 41 ft *Length:* 34·8 ft *Weight:* 15,237 lb *Armament:* 4×30-mm cannon *Speed:* 539 mph at 18,040 ft

Junkers Jumo 004 axial flow gas turbine

Flap actuating piston

15

favour of a Heinkel design; but Erich Bachem knew the sources of power and had an interview with Heinrich Himmler. The decision of the Ministry was immediately changed to support the Bachem proposal as well.

It was a tiny wooden airframe powered by a single rocket engine, boosted by four solid-propellant rockets, launched from a vertical tower, and armed by a nose full of air-to-air rockets. The attack over, the pilot was expected to bail out. He and the valuable engine were to be saved by parachutes.

The Natter was tested as a glider in November 1944, launched unmanned in December under boost power only, and was successful in both tests. But the first piloted flight ended in disaster. On 28 February 1945 Oberleutnant Lothar Siebert, a volunteer for the test flight, was killed when the canopy came off during launch, ap-

parently knocking him unconscious as it left. The Natter crashed out of control. But the next three manned launches were successful, and the programme moved ahead. Seven manned flights were made in all, and the production programme continued to grind out the wooden airframes which took only a few hundred man-hours each to build.

In April 1945, a squadron of 10 Natters was set up ready to launch near Stuttgart, waiting for the next bomber raid for its initiation into combat. But before the aerial assault, Allied armoured units rolled into the area, and the Natter crews destroyed their aircraft to keep them from falling into enemy hands. That was the effective end of the Natter programme.

The turbulence of war was a major factor in the establishment and cancellation of aircraft programmes. It was the beginning of war that must have been one of the events prompting the issuing of a British Air Ministry specification, E 28/39, for a single-seat fighter prototype aircraft powered by a gas turbine for jet propulsion.

Earlier, the Ministry had contracted with Power Jets, a firm headed by Frank Whittle, for development of an airworthy jet engine. Power Jets received its first Ministry support in March 1938; the engine contract was received on 7 July 1939.

The aircraft contract, issued to Gloster Aircraft on 3 February 1940, described a design based on the need for an interceptor. Top speed was to be about 380 mph, and armament was to be four machine-guns. The primary purpose of the aircraft was to obtain flight data on the engine, but it was also to be a prototype fighter.

The first run of an engine in the E 28/39 airframe was made on 6 April 1941, using an unairworthy engine. The next day, Flt Lt P E G Sayer began taxi tests at Brockworth. The plane rolled across the green field, picking up speed and slowing again as Sayer felt out the handling. Three times during the taxi runs, Sayer lifted the plane off the ground briefly. It seemed ready to fly.

The first prototype was trucked to the airfield at Cranwell, home of the RAF College where Whittle had spent his cadet days. There were practical as well as sentimental reasons for selecting that field. It had a long runway, with clear approaches, and was one of the best available fields for test work.

On 14 May Sayer repeated some of the taxi tests and planned to fly the following day. Low clouds hid the sky on the morning of May 15, but towards evening they began to lift. The camouflaged E 28/39 with Sayer in the cockpit trundled out to the starting area. There was a rising howl from the

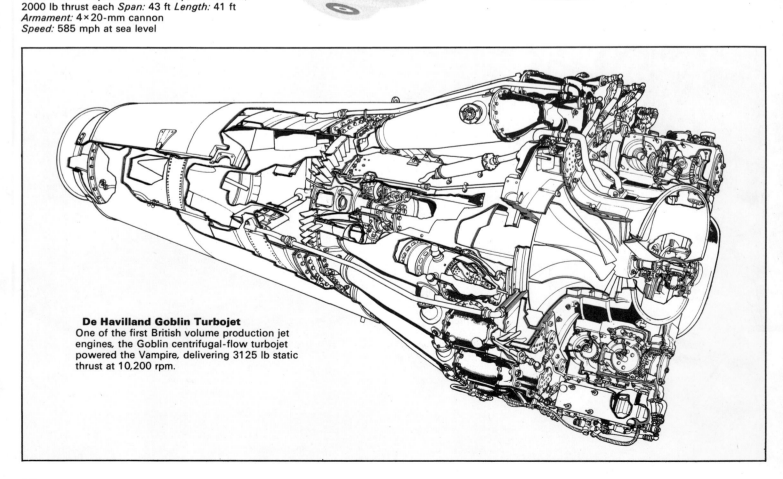

Gloster Meteor F 3
Meteors were the only Allied jet fighters to see operational service during the Second World War.
 Crew: 1 *Powerplant:* 2 Rolls-Royce Derwents, 2000 lb thrust each *Span:* 43 ft *Length:* 41 ft
Armament: 4×20-mm cannon
Speed: 585 mph at sea level

De Havilland Goblin Turbojet
One of the first British volume production jet engines, the Goblin centrifugal-flow turbojet powered the Vampire, delivering 3125 lb static thrust at 10,200 rpm.

engine, the plane began to move, and with darkness already gathering, Sayer lifted the plane off on its first flight.

He stayed aloft 17 minutes. It was the first flight ever made by a British jet-propelled aircraft.

Official support came soon. The flight programme was pushed to learn more about this new form of propulsion. Gradually the aircraft was taken to 25,000 ft and 300 mph in less than 10 hours flying.

Later, Rolls-Royce took over development of the engine, and raised its basic thrust to 1400 lb. Then the plane was flown to a maximum speed of 466 mph, and to an altitude above 42,000 ft. Gloster completed its portion of the programme in late June 1943, and turned the E 28/39 over to the care of the Royal Aircraft Establishment at Farnborough.

Britain's first true jet fighter was the Gloster Meteor, begun as an answer to specification F 9/40. It was planned as a twin-engine craft, because one engine of the type then available was hardly sufficient to obtain performance better than that of contemporary piston-engined fighters. Further, there was a supposed advantage of twin-engine reliability and safety.

and action near the end of the war. Issued to 616 Squadron RAF, based at Culmhead and later at Manston, they first saw action on 27 July 1944, on 'Diver' patrol against the German V-1 buzz-bombs. Sqdn Ldr Watts was the first Meteor pilot to contact one; but his guns jammed and the flying bomb continued on course. First kill of a V-1 was made on 4 August by F/O Dean, whose guns also jammed. So Dean closed the distance, eased the Meteor's wingtip under that of the V-1, and banked sharply away. The Meteor's wingtip slammed against the V-1's wing and sent it into a spiral dive and a crash in open country.

F/O Rogers, almost at the same time, was having more conventional success. His guns fired, and he became the first RAF pilot to shoot down an enemy aircraft from a jet fighter.

Britain's only other jet fighter of the war years, the de Havilland DH 100 Vampire, was very different from the Meteor. Designed to specification E 6/41, which defined an experimental aircraft rather than

the fighter required by the Gloster Meteor specification of F 9/40, the Vampire started to take shape on the drawing boards at Hatfield in May 1942.

The single jet engine was enclosed in an egg-shaped fuselage, with inlets for the air at the root of each wing, and the exhaust discharging directly aft on the centre line of the egg. De Havilland designers used twin tail booms, perhaps borrowing the idea from the piston-engined Lockheed P-38 Lightning.

The Vampire was all metal, but there was one holdover from earlier DH designs; the cockpit section was constructed of a plywood and balsa sandwich material.

It was an all-DH project. The engine was the Halford H 1, designed by Maj Frank Halford and built by de Havilland. Geoffrey de Havilland, Jr, made the first flight on 30 September 1943, at Hatfield, six months after the Meteor had flown. The time differential was critical; the Meteor just barely saw action near the end of the war, but the Vampire was too late to be tested under combat conditions.

About a year earlier, the first flight of the first US jet fighter, the Bell XP-59A, had taken place. The site was a remote desert area, part of the USAAF Muroc Bombing and Gunnery Range located on a dry lake bed about 100 miles north of Los Angeles, California. (That site later became Edwards Air Force Base.)

Robert M Stanley, then chief pilot for Bell, fired up the twin General Electric I-A turbojets, which had been closely but not completely copied from the British W 2B engines. A few minutes later, on the after-

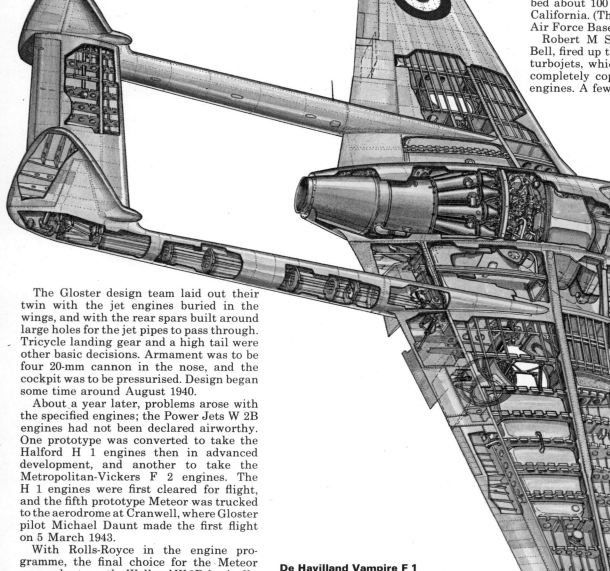

The Gloster design team laid out their twin with the jet engines buried in the wings, and with the rear spars built around large holes for the jet pipes to pass through. Tricycle landing gear and a high tail were other basic decisions. Armament was to be four 20-mm cannon in the nose, and the cockpit was to be pressurised. Design began some time around August 1940.

About a year later, problems arose with the specified engines; the Power Jets W 2B engines had not been declared airworthy. One prototype was converted to take the Halford H 1 engines then in advanced development, and another to take the Metropolitan-Vickers F 2 engines. The H 1 engines were first cleared for flight, and the fifth prototype Meteor was trucked to the aerodrome at Cranwell, where Gloster pilot Michael Daunt made the first flight on 5 March 1943.

With Rolls-Royce in the engine programme, the final choice for the Meteor powerplant was the Welland W 2B, basically the Whittle/Power Jets engine. Wellands powered the first 20 production F Mk 1 Meteors, a fighter rushed into production

De Havilland Vampire F 1
Crew: 1 *Powerplant:* DH Goblin, 3125 lb thrust
Span: 40 ft *Length:* 30·8 ft
Armament: 4×20-mm cannon
Speed: 525 mph at 25,000 ft

noon of 1 October 1942, the XP-59A lifted off the dry lake bed into the California sky.

It would not have made such progress without British help. Major General Henry H Arnold, then Chief of the USAAC, visited Britain in the spring of 1941, saw the Whittle engine and the E 28/39, and was impressed. After follow-up meetings, it was agreed that the US should copy the Whittle engine and develop a twin-engine fighter around it. Bell were chosen as the airframe company to be responsible, and General Electric were chosen to build the engines. Bell were given eight months from the date of the contract approval to have their first aircraft ready for flight.

Construction stayed on schedule, but the timetable for GE engine deliveries slipped. They were not ready until August 1942, and they were never trouble-free. Their performance did not meet expectations, because

Smithsonian Institution Photo No A516A

Bell XP-59A Airacomet
More of a research aircraft than a service fighter, the XP-59A first flew in October 1942

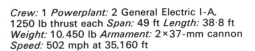

Crew: 1 *Powerplant:* 2 General Electric I-A, 1250 lb thrust each *Span:* 49 ft *Length:* 38·8 ft *Weight:* 10,450 lb *Armament:* 2×37-mm cannon *Speed:* 502 mph at 35,160 ft

the British data used as the basis for their design proved optimistic. Neither the original nor later production engines ever developed the predicted thrust. Consequently, the P-59 Airacomet never served with front-line units; it served instead with a squadron training pilots and mechanics on the new aircraft.

It was obvious early in the Bell programme that its performance was not going to be earth-shaking. Everybody had ideas about what to do, but Lockheed's Clarence L (Kelly) Johnson was to see his ideas take tangible form.

Lockheed had done earlier work on a jet fighter proposal, had been rejected, but had persisted. On one of Johnson's periodic visits to Wright Field, then the technical headquarters of the USAAF, he was asked to consider designing a jet fighter around a British engine. Within a few days the first sketches were ready, and Johnson got the go-ahead in June 1943. At the far side of the Lockheed airport at Burbank, California, a temporary building was erected, the 'Skunk Works', named after a mythical factory in the popular comic strip, 'Li'l Abner'.

The contract gave Lockheed 180 days to design, build and fly the XP-80. They beat the construction deadline and had the plane ready to go in 143 days. But the first flight was delayed by engine availability, and it was not until 9 January 1943, that Lockheed chief test pilot Milo Burcham made the first flight with the XP-80 from the dry lake bed at Muroc.

Then Lockheed had to repeat the whole performance. It was decided that the production P-80 would be powered by the new General Electric I-40 engine, based on British designs. Back to the Skunk Works went Johnson's team, to emerge 139 days later with another prototype, the XP-80A. It first flew on 11 June 1944, and by the time the war ended, 45 had been delivered to USAAF squadrons. A few had even been tested at operational bases in England and Italy, but had been kept from any area where combat might have been possible.

Early in the development of the jet fighter, the navies of Great Britain and the US had studied the new type and wondered how best to adapt it to carrier operations. In the US, the Navy Bureau of Aeronautics were sponsoring the development of a series of axial-flow turbojets by Westinghouse Electric Corp. These small-diameter engines promised much better overall installed performance than did the bulkier centrifugal-flow engines pioneered by Whittle, Rolls-Royce, and General Electric.

The Navy, Westinghouse and the McDonnell Aircraft Corp got together in early 1943 to discuss the design of a Naval fighter built around two or more of the Westinghouse engines. McDonnell designers investigated a wide range of possibilities, guided by basically conservative design policies. They checked eight-, six-, four- and twin-engined schemes and settled on the twin as the basis for their design of the XFD-1. It was to be a fighter

with a defensive mission of combat air patrol at 15,000 ft above a carrier task force. Two years and a few days after the contract was signed, the first prototype XFD-1 took to the air on 26 January 1945. Two months later McDonnell received a production order.

But the war was to be over by almost two years when the first McDonnell Phantoms, redesignated FH-1, were delivered to the fleet. By then, it was apparent that the Phantoms were only an interim type serving to accumulate some fleet experience with jet fighters.

To the East, the Russians had been working for several years to develop their own rocket-powered interceptor. Two designers – Bereznyak and Isaev – planned a tiny aircraft around a single rocket engine rated at 2420 lb of thrust. They designed a conventional fighter, armed with a pair of 20-mm cannon in the nose, and intended for the same kind of mission as the Me 163.

The expected bomber raids against Russia never happened; the rocket-powered interceptor would not have been needed. But it was a fatal accident during a test flight that put an end to the development programme. The first flight had been successful. Test pilot Grigori Bakhchivandzhe flew the BI for a little longer than three minutes on its maiden trip on 15 May 1942.

It was slow development. A second plane was added, but the rocket engine proved troublesome. Only six flights were logged in ten months. Bakhchivandzhe was killed

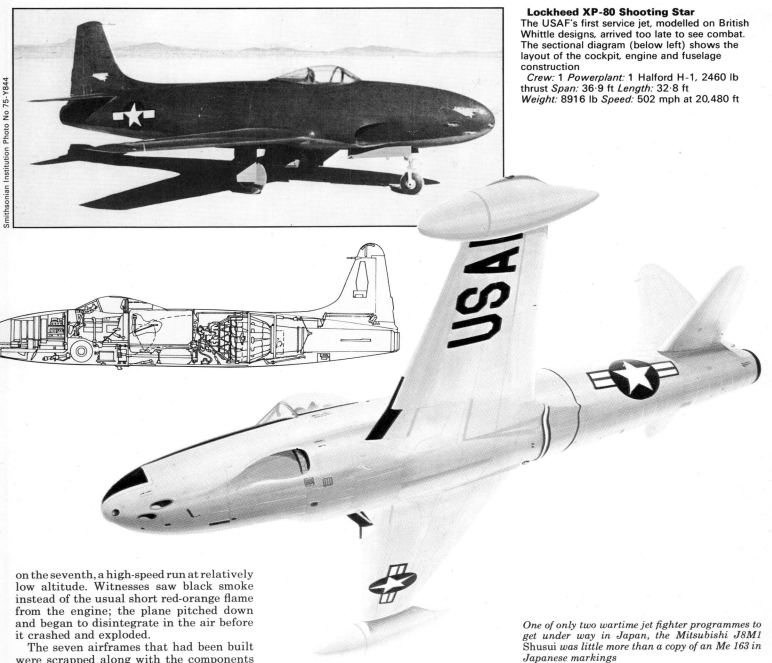

Smithsonian Institution Photo No 75-Y844

Lockheed XP-80 Shooting Star
The USAF's first service jet, modelled on British Whittle designs, arrived too late to see combat. The sectional diagram (below left) shows the layout of the cockpit, engine and fuselage construction
Crew: 1 *Powerplant:* 1 Halford H-1, 2460 lb thrust *Span:* 36·9 ft *Length:* 32·8 ft
Weight: 8916 lb *Speed:* 502 mph at 20,480 ft

One of only two wartime jet fighter programmes to get under way in Japan, the Mitsubishi J8M1 Shusui was little more than a copy of an Me 163 in Japanese markings

Maru Magazine/Orion Press

on the seventh, a high-speed run at relatively low altitude. Witnesses saw black smoke instead of the usual short red-orange flame from the engine; the plane pitched down and began to disintegrate in the air before it crashed and exploded.

The seven airframes that had been built were scrapped along with the components for another 20 or so, on orders from the Kremlin banning all further work on rocket fighters.

Only two jet fighter projects ever got under way in Japan, and both were inspired by German developments. Japan acquired licence rights to the Me 163 and its rocket engine. But delivery of a sample Me 163 and a complete set of blueprints was not completed; the submarine carrying them to Japan was sunk. Japan received only a single rocket engine and an Me 163 manual a Japanese naval officer had brought back from a visit to Germany.

In July 1944 the Japanese Navy issued a specification for a rocket-powered interceptor. The Army joined the programme, and the first prototype of a training glider was completed by December 1944. It flew successfully, after being towed to altitude and released. But the aircraft itself, the Mitsubishi J8M1, was not as successful. The first prototype was finished in June 1945, and its first flight was scheduled for 7 July. The engine failed soon after takeoff, and the J8M1 smashed into the ground, killing Lt Cdr Toyohiko Inuzuka, the test pilot. Although production had started,

and other J8M1 aircraft were available, no more flights were made before the Japanese surrender.

The success of the Me 262 programme sparked Japanese interest in a twin-jet fighter, and the Navy issued an order to Nakajima for development of such a fighter, based on the German twin-jet craft but smaller. Data were limited. The turbojet engines were designed using, among other

sources, photographs of the German BMW 003 turbojet. The first prototype was completed in August 1945, just days before the final bell rang for Japan. On 7 August it made its first flight from the Naval air base at Kisarazu, with Lt Cdr Susumu Tanaoha at the controls. On his second flight, Tanaoha had to abort during the takeoff run because of engine failure. It was the last attempt to fly the Nakajima J8N1 *Kikka*.

Britain and Germany were the first countries to develop jet fighters. Unfortunately, Britain was slow to adapt to the development of jet aircraft technology. The USA and USSR adopted the axial flow engine and sweptback wing configuration (both based on German research) much earlier: seizing the lead in the postwar years, they never let it go

The victorious Allied armies that steam-rollered through Germany towards the end of the Second World War liberated filing cabinets and desk drawers crammed with documents on aerodynamic, structural and powerplant ideas, designs and tests. It was a bonanza, a major foundation for the postwar development of jet fighters.

In spite of the intense pressures of war, German scientists working in university and government research institutes were able to develop ideas at their own pace. They had time to calculate, sketch, build models and test them in flight or a wind tunnel. Combined with practical experience from operational use of a wide variety of unusual weapons and aircraft, this wealth of data fell almost intact into Allied hands at the end of the war.

Many of these ideas had been discovered or developed earlier by scientists in other countries. But in Great Britain and the United States, there was more pressure to produce aircraft in quantity than there was to improve the breed with new and revolutionary ideas, even though both countries did develop and produce jet fighters during the war. But they did not do so on the scale of Germany, and their operational experience was very limited compared to that of the Luftwaffe.

One major contribution made by the Germans was their standardisation of axial-flow jet engines of reduced diameters, compared to the centrifugal-flow types pioneered by Heinkel and Whittle. The axial-flow jets were better suited to installation in a slim fighter fuselage, or under the wings. It took several postwar years before other nations realised that the axial-flow engine was really the best way to do the job.

Another German contribution was sweep-back. Known as early as 1935, sweepback reduces the drag of the wing by aero-dynamically thinning the wing section. German wind tunnel tests proved and evaluated this, and almost every late wartime German design featured a swept-back wing.

The combination of these two basic concepts – the axial-flow engine and sweep-back – produced a long series of combat aircraft after the war, spilled over into civilian designs in the late 1950s, and remains as the basic configuration of many military and civil aircraft today.

The Germans spent a tremendous amount of their scientific resources on guided missiles. Even though they were not all applicable to fighter design, or to exploitation for fighter use, the basic technology developed for them furnished valuable background experience.

Unguided missiles and air-to-air rockets were developed and used operationally by

The Republic XF-91 mixed-powerplant (rocket and turbojet) sweptwing interceptor

POSTWAR DEVELOPMENTS
THE SWEEP TOWARDS MACH 1

the Germans, and that type of weapon was destined to become an important part of the striking power of fighters to come.

Airborne radar systems, primitive though they were, had been used by both sides during the war. Postwar, they blossomed as technology advanced. Combined with ground-based long-range radars and improved communications, they formed the beginnings of the highly effective command and control systems now in operation.

Gradually these developments began to come together. A new design might incorporate one or two new ideas; later designs might add a third or fourth. And, piece by piece, the unsophisticated jets of the war's end led on to advanced designs that broke through the speed of sound, and could fly and fight in an all-weather environment.

Those few postwar years were exciting. There was money to spend on unusual concepts, and designers had a wealth of data to draw on. The jet fighters we talk about here are only those that were

significant during that period. For every one of these, there were others that led only to a dead end in development.

During the five years between the end of the Second World War and the start of the Korean conflict, the design lead was seized and exploited by the United States and Russia, and they have never let go of it. The British, whose truly pioneering efforts contributed so much to the early development of the jet fighter, never exploited their position with advanced technology. They stayed too long with the straight wing and the centrifugal engine and – with one exception – never again became a technological competitor in fighter design.

This period of time also saw the emergence of strong jet fighter design teams in France and Sweden. Both countries continued to improve their position, the French more rapidly and on a broader scale because of their greater size and wealth. Today they stand on a technical par with the United

States and Russia in advanced aeronautics.

28 February 1946:
Republic XP-84 Thunderjet
This American aircraft was the first significant jet fighter to fly in the postwar years. Sleek, powered by a new General Electric axial-flow engine, the XP-84 was designed as an interceptor, but was destined to spend most of its long career in the USAF as a fighter-bomber. It was later blooded in the Korean war, and was the mainstay of tactical airpower for many Allied countries and the United States during the years of cold war.

24 April 1946:
Yakovlev Yak-15 and Mikoyan MiG-9
Both these Russian jet fighters, first of that country's postwar types to fly, were powered by originals or copies of German jet engines that had been captured in quantity by the Russians. The Yak-15 was a single-engined modification of a piston-engined interceptor that saw much service during the war. It was the first of the pair to fly, followed into the air within minutes by the MiG-9, a bulkier, twin-engined fighter. Both types went into production, although the MiG-9 faded from the scene early and the Yak-15 stayed on in service in Russia and some of its allied countries, and was later developed further.

27 July 1946:
Supermarine Attacker
This was the first jet fighter to serve with the Royal Navy on carriers, but it had started life as a land-based interceptor design for the Royal Air Force. Developed late in the war years, it was built around the ubiquitous centrifugal-flow engine and a straight wing adapted from the last of the piston-engined Spitfire line. With the Attacker, the Royal Navy learned the operational problems of jet fighters.

11 November 1946:
SNCASO 6000-01 Triton
French daring developed their first jet aircraft, designed under the noses of occupying German troops. Work began in 1943, in spite of the lack of contact with other countries developing jet aircraft, the systematic despoiling of the industry and German labour drafts that decimated its personnel. The Triton was a single-engined test-bed, built to be able to handle a variety of jet engines. The first prototype flew – on the anniversary of Armistice Day – under the power of a German jet Junkers 004B. It was the harbinger of dynamic French fighter designs to come.

27 November 1944:
North American XFJ-1 Fury
This stubby, straight-winged aircraft was North America's first jet fighter. It was designed as one of two successors to the Navy's first jet, the McDonnell Phantom, and was bought only in small quantity because other and newer developments were coming along rapidly. It served with only one squadron on one carrier, and might have been forgotten but for one thing: its rugged airframe was the basis that led to NAA's sweptwing XP-86 the following year.

11 January 1947:
McDonnell XF2H-1 Banshee
A bigger and more powerful brother-in-arms to the Phantom then in fleet service with the US Navy, the Banshee was a linear, almost scaled-up development of the earlier McDonnell jet fighter. It had more of

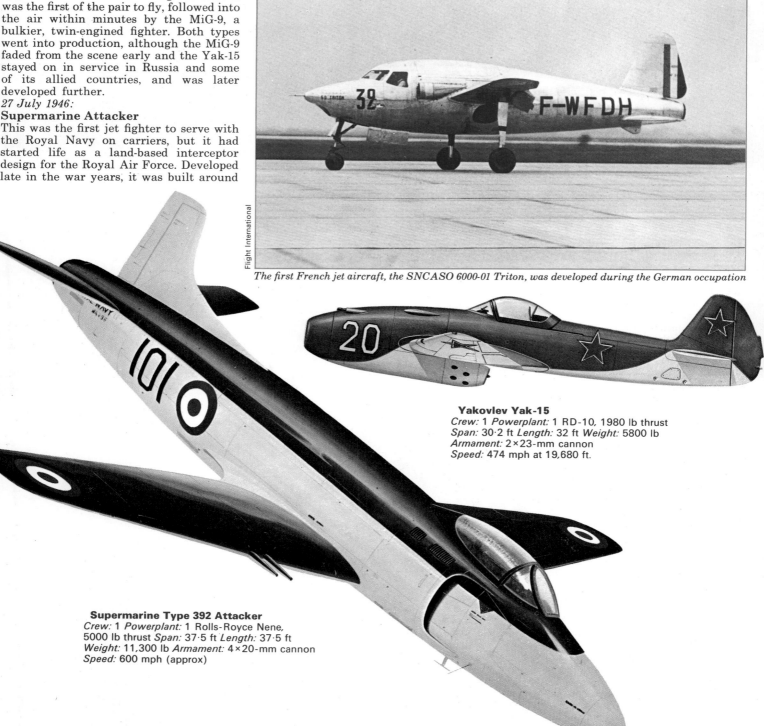

Flight International

The first French jet aircraft, the SNCASO 6000-01 Triton, was developed during the German occupation

Yakovlev Yak-15
Crew: 1 *Powerplant:* 1 RD-10, 1980 lb thrust
Span: 30·2 ft *Length:* 32 ft *Weight:* 5800 lb
Armament: 2×23-mm cannon
Speed: 474 mph at 19,680 ft.

Supermarine Type 392 Attacker
Crew: 1 *Powerplant:* 1 Rolls-Royce Nene,
5000 lb thrust *Span:* 37·5 ft *Length:* 37·5 ft
Weight: 11,300 lb *Armament:* 4×20-mm cannon
Speed: 600 mph (approx)

everything, including range – one of the more elusive performance characteristics of early, fuel-guzzling jets. That goal achieved, the Banshee stayed in the fleet to serve as a potent fighter-bomber during the Korean war some years later.

10 March 1947:
SAAB 21R
Sweden, later to become known for superlative combat aircraft, built its first jet fighter by converting a piston-engined type. This is the only known case where the same basic configuration served in both a piston-engined and jet-engined form. The SAAB J 21R could not have been a very efficient aircraft, and it was not produced in large quantity. But it served a very useful purpose, furnishing both industry and the Royal Swedish Air Force with valuable experience they could not get otherwise.

A McDonnell F2H Banshee of the US Navy, photographed in 1957 with an armament of Zuni missiles. The Banshee was virtually just a scaled up version of the earlier McDonnell Phantom

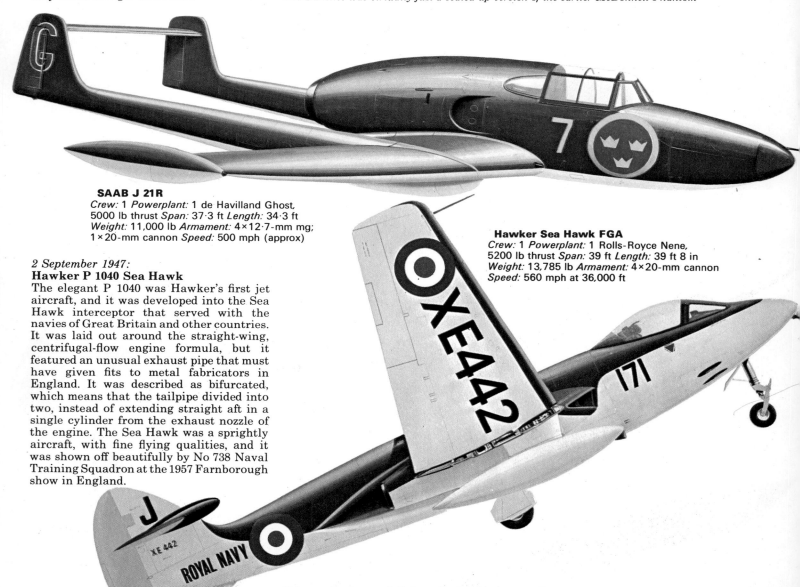

SAAB J 21R
Crew: 1 *Powerplant:* 1 de Havilland Ghost, 5000 lb thrust *Span:* 37·3 ft *Length:* 34·3 ft *Weight:* 11,000 lb *Armament:* 4×12·7-mm mg; 1×20-mm cannon *Speed:* 500 mph (approx)

Hawker Sea Hawk FGA
Crew: 1 *Powerplant:* 1 Rolls-Royce Nene, 5200 lb thrust *Span:* 39 ft *Length:* 39 ft 8 in *Weight:* 13,785 lb *Armament:* 4×20-mm cannon *Speed:* 560 mph at 36,000 ft

2 September 1947:
Hawker P 1040 Sea Hawk
The elegant P 1040 was Hawker's first jet aircraft, and it was developed into the Sea Hawk interceptor that served with the navies of Great Britain and other countries. It was laid out around the straight-wing, centrifugal-flow engine formula, but it featured an unusual exhaust pipe that must have given fits to metal fabricators in England. It was described as bifurcated, which means that the tailpipe divided into two, instead of extending straight aft in a single cylinder from the exhaust nozzle of the engine. The Sea Hawk was a sprightly aircraft, with fine flying qualities, and it was shown off beautifully by No 738 Naval Training Squadron at the 1957 Farnborough show in England.

1 October 1947:
North American XP-86 Sabre
The immortal Sabre started as a parallel design to the Fury, with a similar layout, including the straight wing. But the exciting wartime German data on swept wings led to a complete rethinking of the design concept and the alteration of the Sabre proposal to sweptwing geometry. The wings were angled back at 35°, measured at the quarter-chord line, the tail was matched to that sweep angle, and the Sabre was born.

It was an advanced fighter for its day, was built in Australia and Canada in licensed – and improved – versions, and later racked up an astonishing combat record in the high skies over MiG Alley in the Korean war.

24 November 1947:
Grumman XF9F-2 Panther
Grumman's first jet fighter followed the established and conservative formula of British jet fighters. Not that it was a bad formula to follow at that time; given the state of both engine and aerodynamic technology, the Grumman choice was as justifiable as that of North American.

Events were to prove that it was the conservative choice, but the Panther was built in quantity, maintained the Grumman reputation for fine and rugged combat aircraft, and acquitted itself well in Korea.

30 December 1947:
Mikoyan MiG-15
The thrust of an exported Nene engine from England urged this little Russian sweptwing jet fighter into the air on its first flight. Copied versions of that engine formed the basis for a later Russian industry and the powerplant for many thousands of the Red fighters. The MiG-15 became one

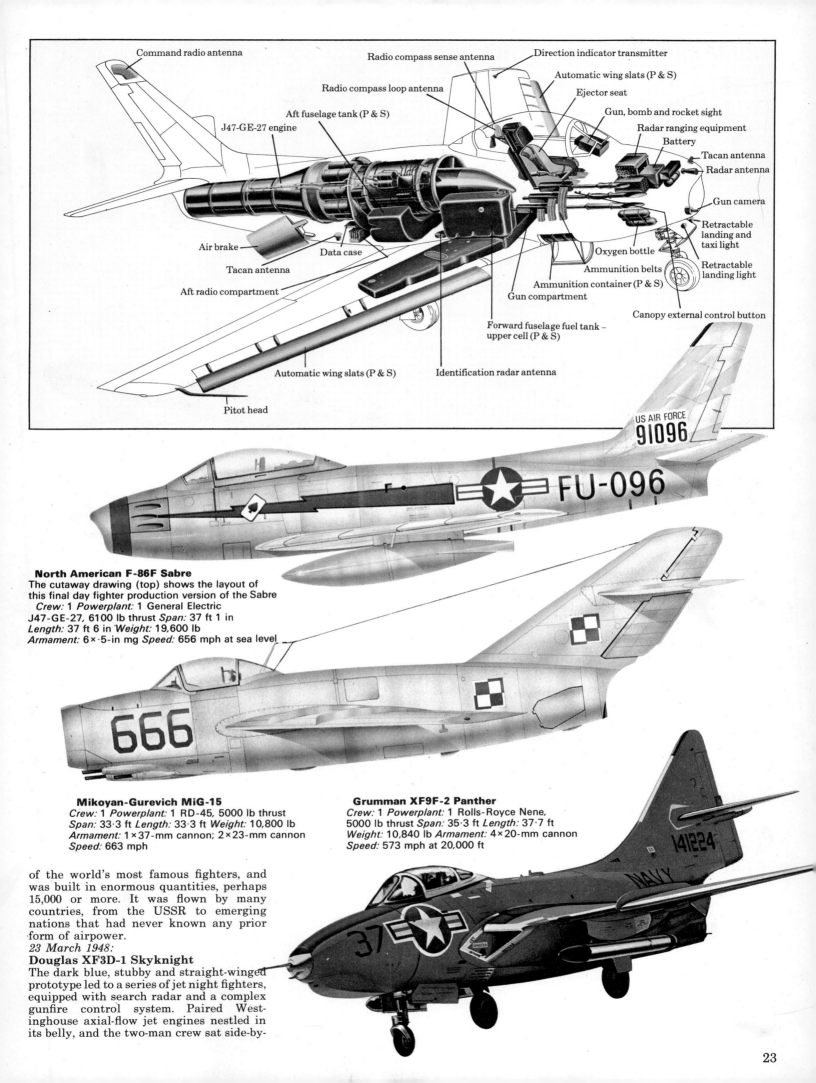

Command radio antenna

Radio compass sense antenna

Direction indicator transmitter

Radio compass loop antenna

Automatic wing slats (P & S)

Aft fuselage tank (P & S)

Ejector seat

J47-GE-27 engine

Gun, bomb and rocket sight

Radar ranging equipment

Battery

Tacan antenna

Radar antenna

Gun camera

Retractable landing and taxi light

Air brake

Data case

Oxygen bottle

Retractable landing light

Tacan antenna

Ammunition belts

Aft radio compartment

Ammunition container (P & S)

Gun compartment

Canopy external control button

Automatic wing slats (P & S)

Identification radar antenna

Forward fuselage fuel tank – upper cell (P & S)

Pitot head

US AIR FORCE
91096

FU-096

North American F-86F Sabre
The cutaway drawing (top) shows the layout of
this final day fighter production version of the Sabre
Crew: 1 *Powerplant:* 1 General Electric
J47-GE-27, 6100 lb thrust *Span:* 37 ft 1 in
Length: 37 ft 6 in *Weight:* 19,600 lb
Armament: 6×·5-in mg *Speed:* 656 mph at sea level

666

Mikoyan-Gurevich MiG-15
Crew: 1 *Powerplant:* 1 RD-45, 5000 lb thrust
Span: 33·3 ft *Length:* 33·3 ft *Weight:* 10,800 lb
Armament: 1×37-mm cannon; 2×23-mm cannon
Speed: 663 mph

Grumman XF9F-2 Panther
Crew: 1 *Powerplant:* 1 Rolls-Royce Nene,
5000 lb thrust *Span:* 35·3 ft *Length:* 37·7 ft
Weight: 10,840 lb *Armament:* 4×20-mm cannon
Speed: 573 mph at 20,000 ft

141224

NAVY

37

of the world's most famous fighters, and
was built in enormous quantities, perhaps
15,000 or more. It was flown by many
countries, from the USSR to emerging
nations that had never known any prior
form of airpower.
23 March 1948:
Douglas XF3D-1 Skyknight
The dark blue, stubby and straight-winged
prototype led to a series of jet night fighters,
equipped with search radar and a complex
gunfire control system. Paired Westinghouse axial-flow jet engines nestled in
its belly, and the two-man crew sat side-by-

23

side under the cockpit canopy. Like the Sabre, Panther and MiG, the Skyknight was to go on to gain combat laurels in the Korean war.

16 August 1948:
Northrop XF-89 Scorpion
The night fighter has always been a specialised weapon, working with a combination of electronic and human sensors to seek out and destroy its prey under cover of darkness or bad weather. It needs a two-man crew to fly and to operate the complex radar, plus endurance and heavy armament. Thus it tends to be big and heavy. The Northrop XF-89 featured the same basic layout as the Skyknight, except that its crew sat in tandem positions, and it dispensed with guns as the primary

The Douglas XF3D Skyknight was a radar-equipped night fighter. Two Westinghouse engines gave it a maximum speed of 500 mph, and its armament consisted of four 20-mm cannon

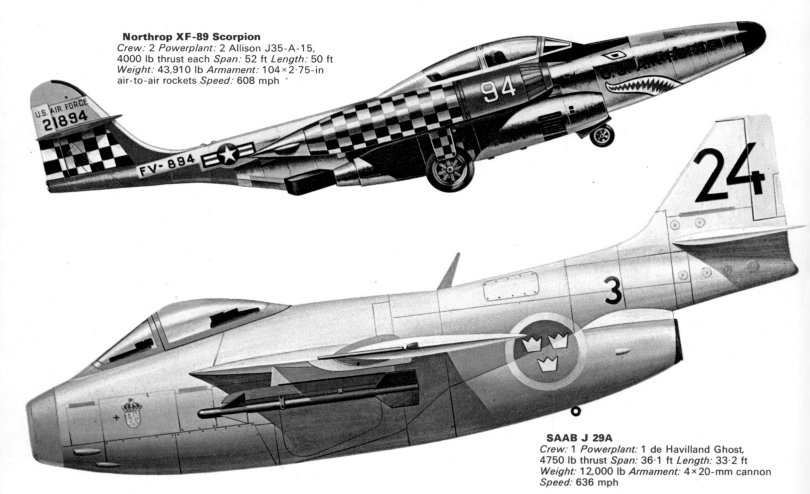

Northrop XF-89 Scorpion
Crew: 2 *Powerplant:* 2 Allison J35-A-15, 4000 lb thrust each *Span:* 52 ft *Length:* 50 ft *Weight:* 43,910 lb *Armament:* 104×2·75-in air-to-air rockets *Speed:* 608 mph

SAAB J 29A
Crew: 1 *Powerplant:* 1 de Havilland Ghost, 4750 lb thrust *Span:* 36·1 ft *Length:* 33·2 ft *Weight:* 12,000 lb *Armament:* 4×20-mm cannon *Speed:* 636 mph

weapons. It was armed with 104 small folding-fin air-to-air unguided rockets, housed in wingtip pods. They were fired in a devastating ripple pattern, rocket after rocket bursting from the pod at split-second intervals.

1 September 1948:
SAAB J 29
Europe's first sweptback wing fighter design, the barrel-shaped prototype was the first in a large quantity of the speedy Swedish fighters. Some were delivered as low-level reconnaissance aircrafts, with batteries of cameras in the forward fuselage. Many years later, the J 29s served in the Congo with a United Nations force.

18 September 1948:
Convair XF-92A
The delta wing, a major technical innovation based on German experiments, first flew on the Convair XF-92A. Since there was no previous flight research experience with the new wing form, the Convair design was developed as both a flight-test aircraft and the possible prototype for an interceptor. It featured trailing-edge elevons, control surfaces that combined the functions of elevators and ailerons. Experience with the XF-92A led to Convair's later successes with the more advanced F-102A and F-106A delta-winged supersonic interceptors.

29 September 1948:
Vought XF7U-1 Cutlass
Another tailless design, but based on German sweptback wing technology rather than that of the delta shape, the Cutlass was developed for the US Navy as a carrier-based, twin-engined interceptor. Its performance was based on the use of afterburners for its jet engines, which increased the thrust substantially by adding and burning additional fuel downstream of the engine in the tailpipe. Trouble dogged the series, and the Cutlass never achieved the expected performance, what with its problematic Westinghouse jet engines and its tricky aerodynamics.

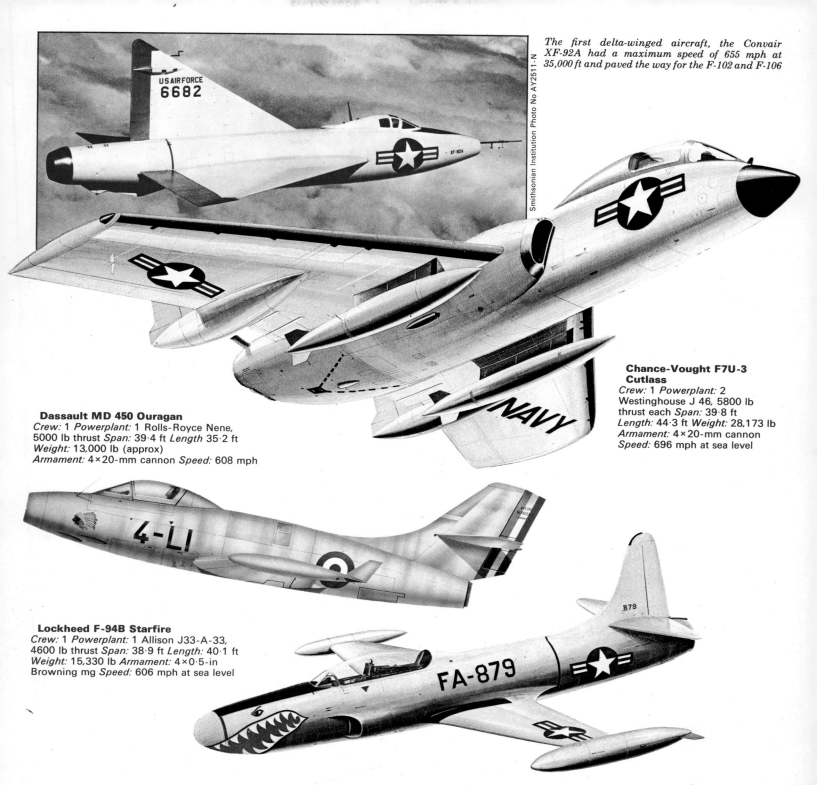

Smithsonian Institution Photo No AY2511-N

The first delta-winged aircraft, the Convair XF-92A had a maximum speed of 655 mph at 35,000 ft and paved the way for the F-102 and F-106

Dassault MD 450 Ouragan
Crew: 1 *Powerplant:* 1 Rolls-Royce Nene, 5000 lb thrust *Span:* 39·4 ft *Length* 35·2 ft *Weight:* 13,000 lb (approx) *Armament:* 4×20-mm cannon *Speed:* 608 mph

Chance-Vought F7U-3 Cutlass
Crew: 1 *Powerplant:* 2 Westinghouse J 46, 5800 lb thrust each *Span:* 39·8 ft *Length:* 44·3 ft *Weight:* 28,173 lb *Armament:* 4×20-mm cannon *Speed:* 696 mph at sea level

Lockheed F-94B Starfire
Crew: 1 *Powerplant:* 1 Allison J33-A-33, 4600 lb thrust *Span:* 38·9 ft *Length:* 40·1 ft *Weight:* 15,330 lb *Armament:* 4×0·5-in Browning mg *Speed:* 606 mph at sea level

28 December 1948:
Supermarine Type 510
This experimental prototype led directly and eventually to Britain's first sweptwing service fighter, but there were to be other prototypes with many changes before the final production configuration had been adopted. Then more than five years were to elapse between the first flight of the prototype and the early deliveries to Royal Air Force squadrons. In the end, the Swift – as the service fighter development was named – never achieved a full measure of success. It was outpaced by the advances of technology and the complexities of high-speed aircraft design.

28 February 1949:
Dassault MD 450 Ouragan
After more than two years of experimentation and trial of a variety of designs, the

French produced the first in a long series of jet fighters that were to establish that country as a major exporter of aircraft. Like so many early jet designs, the Ouragan had a straight wing and a centrifugal-flow engine. But it was a major breakthrough for the French, and particularly for Marcel Dassault himself, then and still the leading exponent of private enterprise in the nationalised French aircraft industry. The Ouragan was the first French jet fighter to go into large-scale production, and was also sold abroad.

16 April 1949:
Lockheed XF-94 Starfire
The USAF sponsored continuing development of night- and all-weather fighters, hoping to counter the trend toward larger, heavier and more costly aircraft of this type. One of the successful attempts was

the Starfire. Single-engined, using its afterburner for bursts of power during takeoff and at altitude, the F-94 had excellent performance for its time. Its design was an adaptation of the basic Lockheed F-80/T-33 series, so its cost was lower than it would have been if developed as a new type. Its unusual feature was the rocket armament. Like the F-89, it was also armed with folding-fin rockets, named 'Mighty Mouse' after a cartoon character of the day, and they were housed in mid-wing pods and in an annulus around the blunt nose radome.

9 May 1949:
Republic XF-91
Designed as a mixed-powerplant interceptor, the XF-91 was built around the combined thrust of a turbojet engine and a powerful four-barrelled liquid-propellant rocket engine. The theory was that the

rocket engine would provide super-performance at high altitudes, long after the thrust of the turbojet had fallen off to a fraction of its sea-level value. The Republic design was the first aircraft to fly with such a combined powerplant, although it was not until much later in the programme that it did so, and then not with the proposed production engine. Among the unusual technical features of the design were the inverse-taper wings, broader at the tips than at the root. This improved the low-speed performance. Additionally, the wings had variable incidence. Tandem landing gear was another innovative feature. The XF-91 was both the first and last attempt in the United States

to follow the mixed-powerplant formula, and it never progressed beyond the experimental prototype.

2 September 1949:
De Havilland DH 112 Venom
Britain's first all-weather interceptor came out of this successful fighter-bomber design. It was rather like an enlarged Vampire, with its twin tail boom layout and the egg-shaped fuselage carrying the jet engine. Its bulbous radome housed airborne intercept radar, and the two-man crew sat side by side under the broad canopy. It pioneered the use of wingtip fuel tanks in the RAF. Its wings had a modest degree of sweepback to give a straight-across trailing edge.

22 December 1949:
North American YF-95A Sabre
Originating as a modification of the Sabre line, the YF-95A (later redesignated F-86D) was designed as a night- and all-weather fighter, armed only with rockets. It required an entirely new fuselage to house a more powerful engine with an afterburner, and the nose radome changed the contours of the straight-in nose inlet of the standard Sabres. Wings, tail and landing gear came unchanged from the Sabre production line.

The single-place F-86D carried 24 Mighty Mouse rockets and had an advanced radar and gunfire control system. A simplified system and a battery of four cannon were the major changes made on the F-86K, a special version developed for export and NATO use which was produced in Italy as well as by North American.

19 January 1950:
Avro Canada CF-100
Canadian engineering developed this twin-engined, two-place all-weather fighter-

Republic XF-91
Crew: 1 *Powerplant:* 1 General Electric J47-GE-3 5200 lb thrust, plus 1 × 6000-lb thrust liquid-propellant rocket *Span:* 31·3 ft
Length: 43·3 ft *Weight:* 28,300 lb
Speed: 984 mph at 47,500 ft

interceptor with very long range to defend the extended northern borders of the country. With powerful airborne intercept radar hidden behind the nose radome, and a battery of six ·50-cal machine-guns, the CF-100 was a formidable weapon. It served in Canada and overseas with the (then) Royal Canadian Air Force, and some were exported to the Belgian air force.

3 June 1950:
Republic YF-96A Thunderstreak
This sweptwing version of the F-84 Thunderjet became a quite different aeroplane, and therefore began life under a new desig-

Westland Wyvern
The Wyvern was the highest development of the torpedo strike fighter concept, but with a turbo-prop driving contra-rotating propellors it could not compete with the pure-jet naval fighter

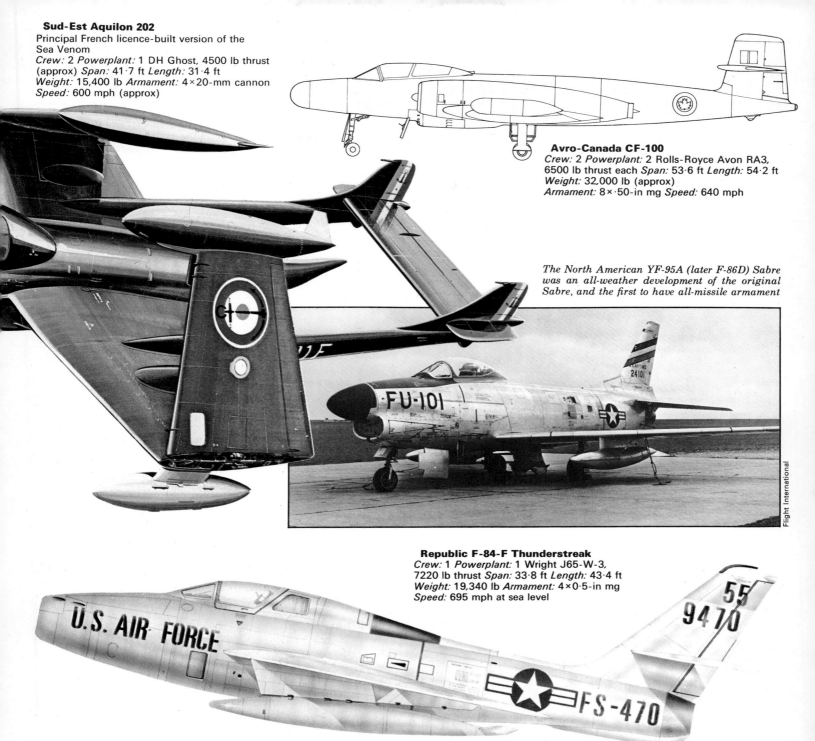

Sud-Est Aquilon 202
Principal French licence-built version of the
Sea Venom
Crew: 2 *Powerplant:* 1 DH Ghost, 4500 lb thrust
(approx) *Span:* 41·7 ft *Length:* 31·4 ft
Weight: 15,400 lb *Armament:* 4×20-mm cannon
Speed: 600 mph (approx)

Avro-Canada CF-100
Crew: 2 *Powerplant:* 2 Rolls-Royce Avon RA3,
6500 lb thrust each *Span:* 53·6 ft *Length:* 54·2 ft
Weight: 32,000 lb (approx)
Armament: 8×·50-in mg *Speed:* 640 mph

*The North American YF-95A (later F-86D) Sabre
was an all-weather development of the original
Sabre, and the first to have all-missile armament*

Flight International

Republic F-84-F Thunderstreak
Crew: 1 *Powerplant:* 1 Wright J65-W-3,
7220 lb thrust *Span:* 33·8 ft *Length:* 43·4 ft
Weight: 19,340 lb *Armament:* 4×0·5-in mg
Speed: 695 mph at sea level

nation, later changed to F-84F. It was powered by an American-built model of a British jet engine, the Armstrong Siddeley Sapphire. But the Sapphire must have suffered in the translation, because it took an abnormally long time before the F-84F was accepted for service. This author remembers a visit to Edwards AFB during the accelerated service testing of the early production Thunderstreaks, and hearing the almost uniformly bad comments from pilots and technicians alike about the short-lived engines (as much as 25 hours between overhauls, when they were lucky) and its flying qualities (it was called the Hog, the Lead Sled, and other uncomplimentary names). But eventually the troubles were licked, and the F-84F went on to serve well in the tactical air arms of many countries as well as that of the United States.

The F-84F, like many of the aircraft developed since the end of the Second World War, was a basis for a major export programme. It happened, in almost every case, because somebody's air force wanted to convert from old-fashioned piston-engined fighters to the new jet breed, and didn't have a local industry that could develop the relatively complex airplanes. In fact, their local industry often could hardly cope with simpler types, and many a jet was to be delivered later, flown a few times until something went wrong, and left to stand on the ramp, deteriorating, unfixed and unfixable by the local talent.

The export pattern solidified early. It was clear that exporting was one way of recovering some of the high development costs of these new jet fighters and, at the same time, of exerting a powerful political and military influence on the customer country. The early postwar years saw British dominance in the marketplace with its Meteor and Vampire fighter and trainer lines. Between the two companies, they sold aircraft to 26

countries, alphabetically beginning with Argentina and ending with Venezuela. The planes were manufactured under licence in eight other countries besides Great Britain.

The United States did not, at first, sell its new jet aircraft abroad, preferring to unload some of its vast stock of piston-engined Mustangs and Thunderbolts. It was to be a while before the US industry began to take the export market very seriously.

The postwar years were characterised, then, by the maturing of wartime designs into a number of basic types of operational jet fighters. The discoveries and wild ideas of wartime were exploited in new designs and used as the foundation for further advances in technology, and the advantages of an export market became very apparent.

But the events of June 1950 were to play a very important part in the future development of jet fighters, and in the concepts of their design and operational use by opposing air forces.

THE FIRST JET FIGHTER ACES

The experiments with jet aircraft in the years after the Second World War, and the planes that were developed, did not have to wait long to be put to the test. In 1950 the Korean War began, and soon Russian and American Jet fighters were mixing it over war-torn Asia – not for the last time

When the North Koreans struck across their borders against South Korea early on the morning of 25 June 1950, they set in motion events that became major factors in the maturing of military jet aircraft design.

In the conflict that followed, the aerial warfare quickly became a war of interdiction, with primary roles assigned to bombers and fighter-bombers. Whatever fighter-to-fighter combat resulted was subordinate to those primary missions. This is not to downgrade the extremely valuable role of fighters in that war, but to emphasise that their missions rose out of the USAF's need to protect its bomber forces, and the North Korean and Chinese need to destroy those forces.

Some significant milestones of the jet fighter war in Korea should be recorded here. Within a week of the invasion of South Korea, USAF jets scored their first victories. Four Lockheed F-80Cs from the 35th Fighter-Bomber Squadron tangled with eight Ilyushin piston-engined attack aircraft, and shot down four of the Russian-built planes.

The first-ever combat between jet fighters was on 8 November 1950. Lt Russell J Brown, pilot of an F-80C from the USAF's 51st Fighter-Interceptor Wing, blasted a Russian-built MiG-15 that unwisely tried to out-dive the Lockheed plane.

The first victory by a North American F-86A Sabre over a MiG took place on 17 December, gained by Lt Col Bruce H Hinton. On 20 May 1951, USAF Capt James Jabara became history's first jet ace, downing his fifth and sixth MiG-15s during a single combat.

The first jet night victory was achieved by a USMC Douglas F3D-2 Skyknight, vectored by ground radar to locate a Yak-15 in the night skies over Sinui-ju.

Near the end of the war, United Nations air superiority had been established without challenge. During June 1953, USAF Sabres sighted 1268 MiG-15s, and engaged 501 of them in battle. They destroyed 77, probably destroyed another 11, and damaged 41, without losing a single Sabre all month. Those kinds of scores helped increase the highly publicised kill ratio which, near the end of the war, averaged out to better than ten to one. USAF pilots gunned down 792 MiG-15s for the loss of 78 Sabres, according to final official US figures.

What was learned? Early in the fighting, the Sabre pilots wanted more thrust – they were tired of being bounced from above by MiGs with superior altitude performance. They wanted heavier-calibre guns with a high firing rate; the ·50-cal machine-guns, so effective against German and Japanese designs during the Second World War, often failed to destroy a MiG because of the lack of striking power. And they wanted a radar-ranging gunsight, because the gyro types in the Sabres were not suitable for holding the large leads required during deflection shooting in turning combat.

Conceptually, the idea of air superiority was again tested in the skies, and the final ability of the UN air forces to fly almost anywhere without serious challenge was proof of the value, and the attainment, of that concept. Jet fighters also made good fighter-bombers, it was found, able to deliver their ordnance loads with speed and accuracy.

The end of a MiG-15, photographed with a camera mounted in the nose of an F-86 Sabre

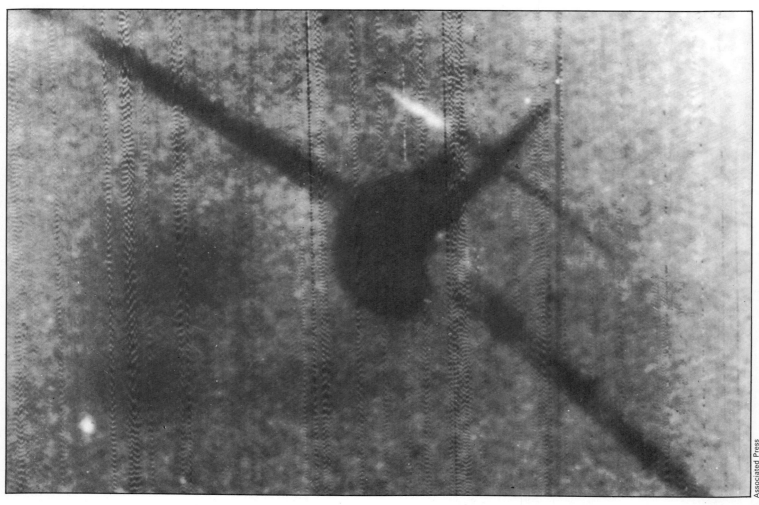

Associated Press

The idea of the long-range escort fighter grew out of early experience of the accompanied bomber raids. The B-29s operated by Strategic Air Command were slow; they were escorted by a top cover of F-86 Sabres and lower elements of Thunderjets. Typically, the attacking MiGs would streak through the top cover and go after the bombers; they were able to avoid combat with the Thunderjets by virtue of superior speed and manoeuvrability. One answer seemed to be a supersonic long-range fighter that could both escort and fight.

By the time the Korean war was seriously under way, one basic form of future air action had been further emphasised. Long-range bomber forces would continue to be one component of any future threat. The defence would be by a mix of interceptor aircraft and missiles, able to reach out with electronic sensors to see, attack and destroy the bombers at either long or short range and in all kinds of weather.

This scenario, born during the Second World War, gave rise to a continuing series of fighter-interceptor designs during the decade which began with the Korean war. In the sequential descriptions that follow, note how many of the new aircraft fit into this single category.

23 January 1951:
Douglas XF4D-1 Skyray
This tailless interceptor was designed for Fleet defence under the conditions of the last months of the Second World War. It emphasised climb performance at the expense of range. Although it demonstrated its potential by setting a series of world

US jets scored heavily over MiGs in Korea, in spite of atrocious climatic conditions

Major James Jabara (with cigar), first ace of the Korean War, with two fellow pilots at their base

records, it was delayed from operational use by engine problems. Later, with those problems solved, it served well as a fighter on US carriers.

23 February 1951:
Dassault MD 452-01 Mystère
Basically a sweptwing version of the Ouragan, the Mystère prototype was the first of a series that went through extensive development, including major aerodynamic, structural and powerplant changes. It was built in quantity under off-shore procure-ment contracts from the US, and became one of Europe's top fighter aircraft. An advanced version, the Mystère IVA, saw service in the combat in the Suez war of 1956.

20 July 1951:
Hawker P 1067
The pale green prototype was an aircraft of classic beauty. It was developed into the Hawker Hunter, first-line Royal Air Force interceptor and later ground-attack fighter. It was widely used in a variety of roles by many countries, and is regarded by many as the peak development of the subsonic jet fighter. Originating as an interceptor study built around the then-new Rolls-Royce Avon engine, it featured heavy armament and outstanding flying qualities.

7 August 1951:
McDonnell XF3H-1 Demon
The US Navy wanted this high-performance interceptor to give its carrier forces the same kind of defensive protection that land-based interceptors afforded. But the dismal failure of its Westinghouse engine to live up to requirements hamstrung the Demon from the start. It was only after long and trouble-filled delays that the type was cleared for Fleet service. The developed models served on carriers as night-fighters and as missile-armed interceptors.

20 September 1951:
Grumman F9F-6 Cougar
First sweptwing fighter in the US Navy, the Cougar was essentially a sweptwing Panther with a new horizontal tail. Development time was shortened by this fairly simple modification of the straight-winged F9F series, and the Cougars went on to serve with the Navy and the Marines as a fighter, a reconnaissance aircraft, and a trainer.

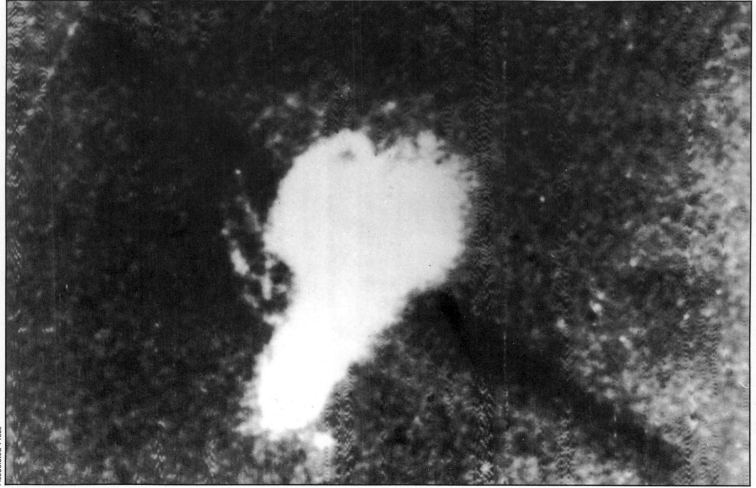

26 September 1951:
De Havilland DH 110
This twin-engined, two-place, twin-boomed, trans-sonic all-weather fighter was developed in response to a Royal Air Force requirement. After the structural failure and crash of the first prototype during the 1952 Farnborough show, the DH 110 was rejected in favour of the Gloster Javelin. The Royal Navy then funded the development programme and, after major redesign, the modified DH 110 was named the Sea Vixen. The first production version of that Naval all-weather interceptor flew in March 1957. It was the first British gunless interceptor, armed instead with four DH Firestreak missiles and 28 unguided rockets.

3 November 1951:
SAAB 32 Lansen
Swedish defence policy requirements for a strike fighter were the origin of this graceful and efficient two-place aircraft. Developed for a multi-role mission, the Lansen was produced as a night- and all-weather fighter in addition to its attack and reconnaissance versions. It was the first Swedish aircraft to attain supersonic speeds, flying in shallow dives to reach them for brief periods.

26 November 1951:
Gloster GA 5 Javelin
Conservatively designed as a tailed delta to improve its landing characteristics for night operations, the Javelin was the first twin-jet delta-winged aircraft to fly. It had a huge wing, in area and volume, and could

performance was to get a similar airplane. The XFJ-2, first of the Fury line, was a modified and navalised standard F-86E Sabre. Changes included arresting gear and heavier armament. But its production was slowed by increasing demands of higher priority for the F-86s, which were being built on the same production lines in the same factories. Eventually, the Fury was modified to a strike fighter with nuclear capability.

16 October 1952:
SNCASO SO 4050 Vautour
This versatile, twin-engined, two-place aircraft was produced in three versions, but

Dassault Super Mystère B-2
Last production version of the Mystère
Crew: 1 *Powerplant:* SNECMA Atar 101G, 7480 lb thrust *Span:* 34·5 ft *Length:* 46·1 ft
Weight: 19,840 lb *Armament:* 2×30-mm cannon; 35×68-mm air-to-air rockets
Speed: Mach 1·25 at altitude

November 1952: prototype of the Hawker Hunter, probably the best subsonic jet fighter ever built

carry a large load of fuel as well as the bulky and heavy radar needed for its mission. It went through a long development period and several production versions, used both British and American radars, and lasted in service with the Royal Air Force until 1967.

27 December 1951:
North American XFJ-2 Fury
With Sabres matching and beating MiG-15 performance in Korea, the US Navy concluded that its fastest way to get similar

Smithsonian Institution Photo No 75-Y841

Above: Grumman F9F-6 Cougar, a sweptwing development of the F9F-2 Panther, and the US Navy's first sweptwing fighter. Armed with four 20-mm cannon, it had a speed of about 550 mph

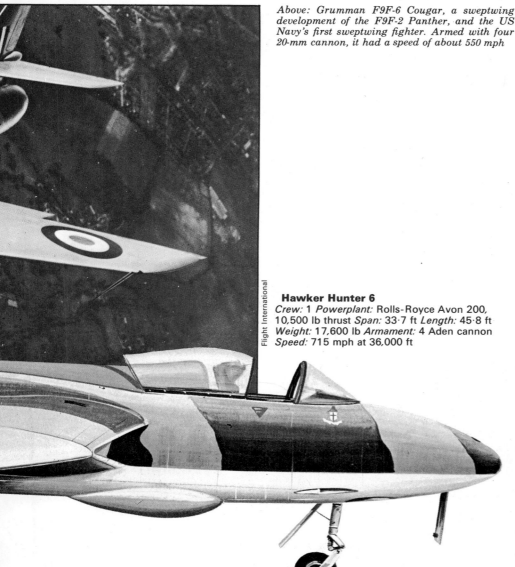

Flight International

Hawker Hunter 6
Crew: 1 *Powerplant:* Rolls-Royce Avon 200, 10,500 lb thrust *Span:* 33·7 ft *Length:* 45·8 ft *Weight:* 17,600 lb *Armament:* 4 Aden cannon *Speed:* 715 mph at 36,000 ft

the greatest number were night and all-weather fighters. They were armed with a powerful battery of four 30-mm cannon and 232 air-to-air rockets in paired belly trays. This was France's only all-weather fighter for several years, and it also served that country's defences as a two-place light bomber and a single-seat strike aircraft. Some of the latter were exported to Israel, and fought with the Israeli air force in the Suez war.

2 March 1953:
SNCASO SO Trident I
Another in the periodic appearances of the super-performance manned interceptor, the Trident was a mixed-powerplant aircraft with turbojets at the wingtips and a powerful rocket motor in the fuselage. Its rate of climb was comparable to that of contemporary guided missiles, and it had high supersonic speed in level flight. Pre-production aircraft were built, but the planned production programme never materialised because of the lack of French government support.

19 May 1953:
Grumman XF10F-1 Jaguar
The date was eagerly anticipated and now is happily forgotten by senior personnel at Grumman. The Jaguar was the world's first variable-sweep aircraft and – in that respect – it performed very well, without any trouble during the entire flight-test programme. But the Jaguar was another casualty of the Westinghouse jet engine fiasco. There is one former Grumman engineering test pilot who wears a pair of Jaguar cufflinks, given by his wife to remind him that whenever things seem bad, they once were worse.

25 May 1953:
North American YF-100A Super Sabre
First of the Century Series of fighters for the USAF, the Super Sabre was designed as a tactical day fighter based on the lessons of Korea. The first approach had been to plan a new wing for the old Sabre; but a powerful new engine – the Pratt & Whitney J57 – became available, and it was decided to design around it. The combination was a winner: it was the world's first supersonic combat aircraft, and the progenitor of a long-lived line of fighters and fighter-bombers. It pioneered the low-set horizontal tail to eliminate a disastrous form of instability appearing on high-speed aircraft. Other innovations included the one-piece 'slab' horizontal tail, and the use of titanium metal for some components.

September 1953:
Mikoyan MiG-19
Opposite number to the Super Sabre, this Russian fighter became the second supersonic combat aircraft in the world. It used a twin-engined layout and contemporary aerodynamic features to develop a high-performance fighter and night-fighter that served well and long with the Soviet Union and their allied countries and friends.

24 October 1953:
Convair YF-102A Delta Dagger
Designed as an all-weather interceptor, the Delta Dagger did not, at first, meet its expected supersonic speed performance because of high drag. Happily, a development at the laboratories of the National Advisory Committee for Aeronautics (now NASA) produced a way of reducing trans-sonic drag. The YF-102 was speedily redesigned to take advantage of the 'area rule' developed by NASA's Richard T Whitcomb, and it easily slipped through the speed of sound in

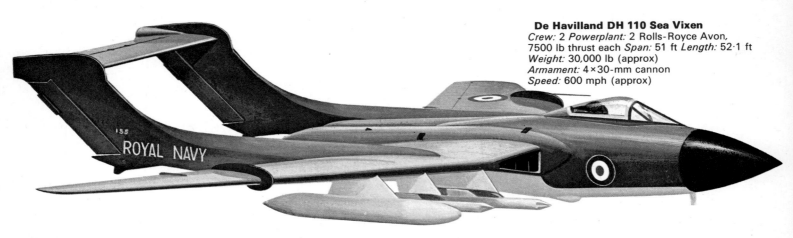

De Havilland DH 110 Sea Vixen
Crew: 2 *Powerplant:* 2 Rolls-Royce Avon,
7500 lb thrust each *Span:* 51 ft *Length:* 52·1 ft
Weight: 30,000 lb (approx)
Armament: 4×30-mm cannon
Speed: 600 mph (approx)

SAAB A32-A Lansen
Crew: 1 *Powerplant:* 1 SFA RM 5, 8050 lb thrust
Span: 42·7 ft *Length:* 48 ft *Weight:* 16,535 lb
(empty) *Armament:* 4×20-mm cannon
Speed: 700 mph at sea level

Gloster Javelin FAW 8 (foot of page)
The FAW 8 was the final production version of
the Javelin, and was equipped with American
radar equipment. Below left: Gloster Javelin
taking off
  (FAW 8) *Crew:* 2 *Powerplant:* 2 Bristol
Siddeley Sapphire 203/204, 11,000 lb thrust each
Span: 52 ft *Length:* 56·3 ft *Weight:* 38,000 lb
Armament: 2×30-mm cannon; 4 Firestreak
missiles *Speed:* 695 mph at 10,000 ft

Above: The SNCASO SO 4050 Vautour was France's only all-weather fighter for several years, and was powerfully armed with four 30-mm cannon plus 232 68-mm unguided rockets. Above right: Engine trouble with the Grumman XF10F-1 Jaguar made it a major disappointment to its sponsors. Right: The SNCASO SO Trident was powered by two Armstrong Siddeley Vipers and a 6600-lb thrust liquid-fuel rocket. It was France's first plane capable of supersonic speeds in level flight, but in spite of its exceptionally good performance it never achieved production status

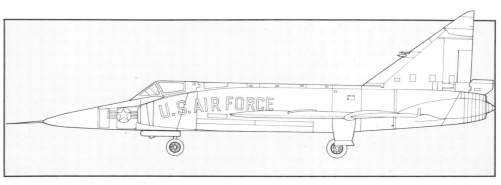

Convair YF-102 Delta Dagger
Above, and, left, in flight
  Crew: 1 *Powerplant:* 1 Pratt & Whitney
J57-P-11, 9700 lb thrust *Span:* 37 ft
Length: 52·5 ft *Weight:* 25,000 lb (approx)
Armament: 6 Falcon guided missiles; 12×2·75-in
rockets *Speed:* 780 mph

North American F-100D Super Sabre
Crew: 1 *Powerplant:* 1 Pratt & Whitney
J57-P-21A, 11,700 lb thrust *Span:* 38·8 ft
Length: 54·3 ft *Weight:* 29,762 lb
Armament: 4×20-mm cannon
Speed: 864 mph at 35,000 ft

Flight International

F-100D Super Sabres, final production version of the F-100 Sabre, at the point of takeoff

Mikoyan MiG-19
Crew: 1 *Powerplant:* 2 AM-5, 4850 lb thrust
each *Span:* 29·5 ft *Length:* 42·9 ft
Weight: 15,000 lb (approx)
Armament: 1×37-mm cannon; 2×23-mm cannon
Speed: 900 mph (approx)

this form. The Delta Dagger was armed with Falcon guided missiles and a battery of air-to-air unguided rockets.

16 December 1953:
Dassault Mystère IVB
Just about two months after its first flight, the Mystère IVB joined the level-flight supersonic club and became the first European fighter to do so. It was one of several progressive developments of the original Mystère prototype, and used after-burning on its jet engine to improve its takeoff, climb and speed performance.

7 February 1954:
Lockheed XF-104 Starfighter
One answer to the unofficial requirements of the Korean war was the Starfighter, designed as an uncomplicated day fighter.

It had searing performance, and held three absolute world records for speed and altitude. Its primary mission was air superiority, but it was to find its greatest employment as a multi-mission aircraft in a developed version sold and produced widely abroad. It was the first fighter armed with the M61A-1 Vulcan 20-mm cannon, a six-barrelled weapon with an awesome rate of fire. It also carried Sidewinder missiles for air-to-air combat.

30 July 1954:
Grumman YF9F-9 Tiger
The area rule that benefited the Convair F-102 had been applied earlier to the Grumman YF9F-9, a major modification of the Panther/Cougar series of Naval fighters. It was later redesignated F11F-1. It preceded the area-ruled YF-102A into the air by several months, and was the first aircraft to fly with this new applied principle of aerodynamics. As one result, it became the Navy's, and the world's, first supersonic carrier-based fighter. But its delivery to the fleet was delayed by engine problems, and it began to arrive at the same time as the

later Crusader, which soon replaced the Tigers. They lasted only about two years in fleet service, and then went ashore to training duties. The Tiger's fame remains, because it was the mount for the US Navy's superb aerobatic team, the Blue Angels, for several seasons.

4 August 1954:
English Electric P 1
The angular shape of the P 1 prototype and the over-and-under arrangement of its twin engines looked like power personified. It was: the P 1 was the basis for development of the outstanding Lightning interceptor, still in active service with the Royal Air Force. It was Britain's first fighter capable of level-flight supersonic speed. Designed for the specific conditions of defence of the British Isles, the Lightning and its later

Lockheed F-104G Super Starfighter
Crew: 1 *Powerplant:* 1 General Electric J79-GE-11A, 10,350 lb thrust *Span:* 21·9 ft *Length:* 54·8 ft *Weight:* 20,900 lb *Armament:* 1 × 20-mm Vulcan cannon; 2 Sidewinder missiles *Speed:* Mach 2·2

A Lockheed F-104G Starfighter during instant takeoff tests for the German air force at Edwards Air Force Base. The solid fuel rocket motor propelled it into the air, and was then jettisoned

Associated Press

35

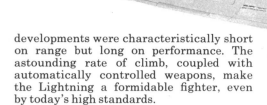

Grumman F11F-1 Tiger
Crew: 1 *Powerplant:* 1 Wright J65-W-18,
7800 lb thrust *Span:* 31·6 ft *Length:* 44·9 ft
Weight: 21,035 lb *Armament:* 4×20-mm cannon;
4 Sidewinders *Speed:* 740 mph at 35,000 ft

developments were characteristically short on range but long on performance. The astounding rate of climb, coupled with automatically controlled weapons, make the Lightning a formidable fighter, even by today's high standards.

29 September 1954:

McDonnell F-101A Voodoo

USAF's Strategic Air Command, drawing on its Korean experience, wanted a long-range fighter capable of escorting bomber fleets to distant targets. The F-101 Voodoo was the result. This twin-jet, two-place fighter was developed from an earlier prototype, the XF-88, designed as a fighter able to strike deeply into enemy territory. SAC cancelled its requirements before the Voodoo flew, but the design was adopted by Tactical Air Command, was developed as a fighter-bomber, and later was further developed into a long-range all-weather interceptor of high performance, and a low-level photo-reconnaissance aircraft. In the latter role, Voodoos furnished many photographs of the missile sites emplaced by the Russians in Cuba in 1961.

1954:

Yakovlev Yak-25

This twin-engined, two-place night- and all-weather fighter was first seen publicly in 1955, and therefore probably flew late in 1954. As the first Russian aircraft of its type, the layout and systems were a bit behind the state of the art, a deficiency that was remedied with surprising speed in later designs from the Yakovlev design bureau. The large nose radome hints at a radar dish dimensioned for long-range detection.

2 March 1955:

Dassault Super Mystère B-2

For a quick and effective survey of the state of the French jet fighter art in the 1950s, look at the Dassault Mystère series. This model, the end of the line, was a major redesign of the basic format, featuring a thinner wing with a higher sweep angle, a redesigned windshield for lower drag, and other refinements. It easily went supersonic in level flight on its first flight.

25 March 1955:

Vought XF8U-1 Crusader

The Navy, drawing on its Korean experience, asked for a supersonic day fighter for fleet defence. The Crusader was the answer. It flew supersonically on its first flight, was the first carrier-based aircraft to exceed 1000 mph in level flight, and crossed the United States at supersonic speed. Its technical innovations included a variable-incidence wing for superb visibility during approaches to carrier landings, and full application of the area rule. Armed with

Flight International

English Electric P1A, prototype Lightning, whose performance has kept it in front line service

Chance Vought F8U-2 Crusader
Crew: 1 *Powerplant:* 1 Pratt & Whitney
J57-P-16, 10,700 lb *Span:* 35·2 ft
Length: 54·5 ft *Weight:* 28,000 lb
Armament: 4×20-mm cannon; 4 Sidewinders
Speed: Mach 1·7

English Electric Lightning F1

Crew: 1 *Powerplant:* 2 Rolls-Royce Avon 200,
11,250 lb thrust each *Span:* 34·9 ft
Length: 50 ft *Weight:* 40,000 lb (approx)
Armament: 2 Aden cannon; 2 Firestreak missiles
Speed: Mach 2·1 at 40,000 ft

cannon and Sidewinder, it packed a powerful punch. At its maximum deployment, it equipped about half of the Navy and Marine fighter squadrons. It was further developed with a boundary-layer control system for the French Navy. Most recently, it fought in the Vietnam war where it acquired a reputation as the 'best gun fighter' in the theatre. It was redesignated as the F-8 Crusader in 1962.

25 June 1955:
Dassault MD 550-01 Mirage I

Like the Trident before it, the Mirage I featured a mixed powerplant. But its paired turbojets were in the fuselage, and the rocket motor was slung in a droppable package under the belly. It was the ancestor of the current Mirage III line, and was developed through a series of engine and wing changes to become France's most successful fighter, one of its best export programmes, and one of the world's best fighters, proven in combat against topnotch Russian-built aircraft in the Middle East wars.

18 July 1955:
Folland Gnat

Even though USAF pilots in Korea argued loud and long for a simple, light fighter, nobody took them seriously. All the fighters inspired by that conflict were heavier and more complex than the Sabres and MiG-15s

except for one: the Gnat. It was a small and light fighter designed to carry the optimum minimum in armament and fuel while still being an effective interceptor. The Gnat was not accepted in Britain until much later, and then only as a trainer. But Finland bought them and India built them, and they fought in the Indo-Pakistan wars, earning the nickname of 'giant-killer'.

25 October 1955:
SAAB 35 Draken

The Draken's unusual double-delta layout was SAAB's answer to a Swedish requirement for a supersonic interceptor with short takeoff and landing performance. The unusual planform was first tested on the SAAB 210, a little aeroplane with similar aerodynamics, and then translated into the full-scale Draken. Armed with cannon and missiles, the Draken has a phenomenal rate of climb and is highly manoeuvrable at low and high altitudes. It has been operated from ordinary stretches of highway, one indicator of its handling qualities and its runway requirements.

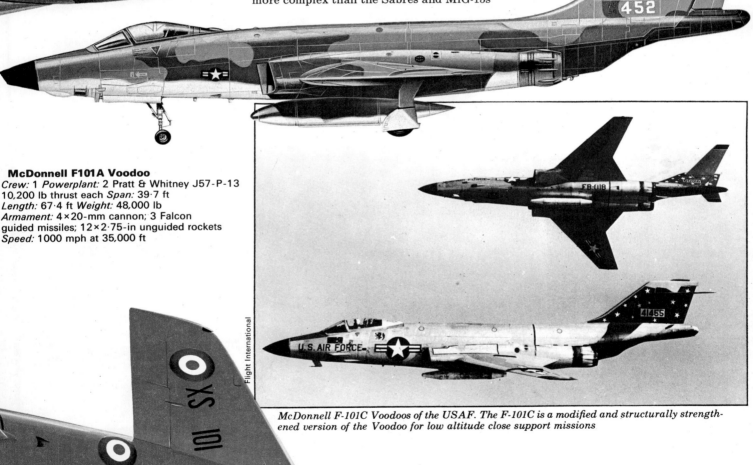

Flight International

McDonnell F101A Voodoo

Crew: 1 *Powerplant:* 2 Pratt & Whitney J57-P-13
10,200 lb thrust each *Span:* 39·7 ft
Length: 67·4 ft *Weight:* 48,000 lb
Armament: 4×20-mm cannon; 3 Falcon
guided missiles; 12×2·75-in unguided rockets
Speed: 1000 mph at 35,000 ft

McDonnell F-101C Voodoos of the USAF. The F-101C is a modified and structurally strengthened version of the Voodoo for low altitude close support missions

Folland Gnat T1

Trainer version of the Gnat, shown here in the colours of the RAF Red Arrows aerobatic team
Crew: 2 *Powerplant:* 1 Bristol Siddeley
Orpheus 107, 4400 lb thrust *Span:* 24 ft
Length: 37·8 ft *Weight:* 8077 lb
Armament (fighter version): 2×30-mm cannon
Speed: Mach 1·15

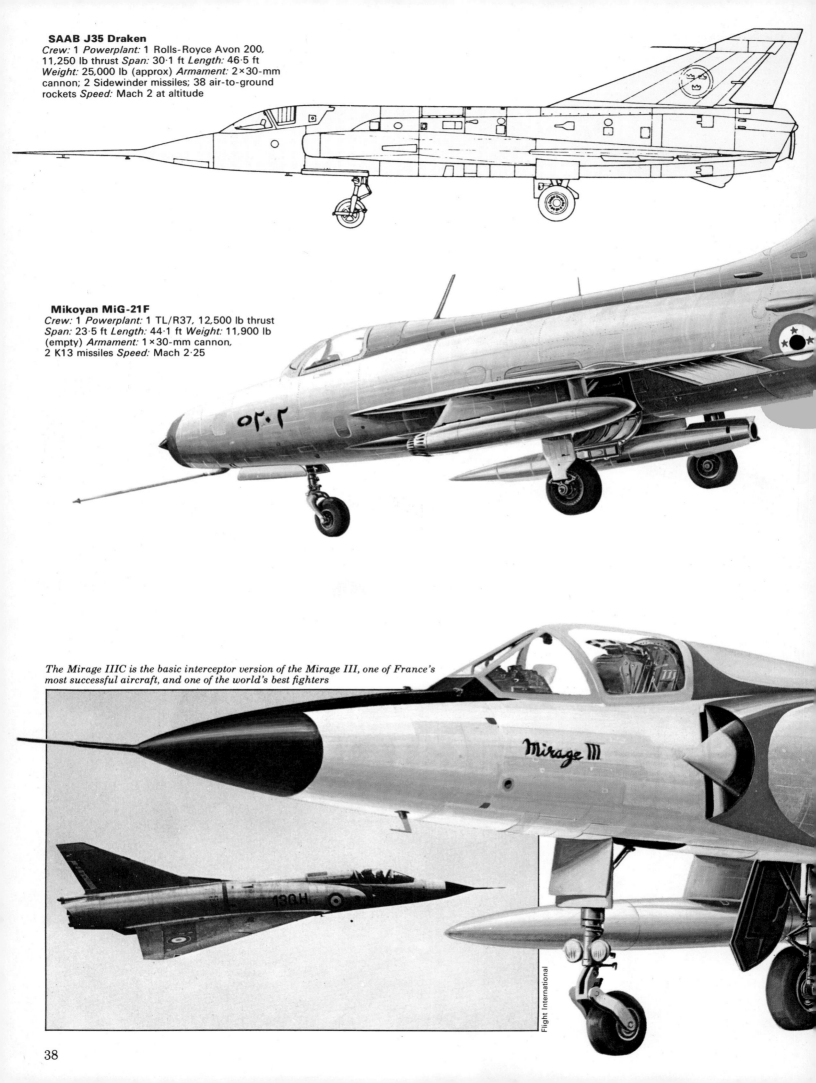

SAAB J35 Draken

Crew: 1 *Powerplant:* 1 Rolls-Royce Avon 200, 11,250 lb thrust *Span:* 30·1 ft *Length:* 46·5 ft *Weight:* 25,000 lb (approx) *Armament:* 2×30-mm cannon; 2 Sidewinder missiles; 38 air-to-ground rockets *Speed:* Mach 2 at altitude

Mikoyan MiG-21F

Crew: 1 *Powerplant:* 1 TL/R37, 12,500 lb thrust *Span:* 23·5 ft *Length:* 44·1 ft *Weight:* 11,900 lb (empty) *Armament:* 1×30-mm cannon, 2 K13 missiles *Speed:* Mach 2·25

The Mirage IIIC is the basic interceptor version of the Mirage III, one of France's most successful aircraft, and one of the world's best fighters

Flight International

38

1955:
Mikoyan MiG-21
First publicly seen in 1956, the MiG-21 must have made its first flight during the previous year. Primarily an all-weather interceptor with secondary ground-attack capability in some models, the MiG-21 has been widely distributed among the allies and friends of the Soviet Union. Its design is based on a thin delta with a swept horizontal tail to improve altitude performance and landing characteristics. The MiG-21 is armed with both cannon and air-to-air missiles. Its defence of North Vietnam in later years was regarded with almost universal admiration and even some envy by its adversaries.
1955:
Sukhoi Su-9
This single-engined all-weather fighter is

also a tailed delta, like its contemporary, the MiG-21. But the Sukhoi design is larger, and its afterburning turbojet has a considerably higher thrust. Armament is based on missiles only, rather than on the com-

bined cannon and air-to-air missile weaponry of the MiG-21.
20 January 1956:
Supermarine Type 544 Scimitar
This single-place sweptwing fighter for the Royal Navy was area-ruled, had power controls and blown flaps, all innovations for a Fleet Air Arm fighter. It was also the FAA's first sweptwing fighter, their first able to top supersonic speed in a shallow dive, and their first equipped to carry nuclear weapons. Its high performance was a great advance over the straight-winged Sea Hawk which it replaced in service.
23 July 1956:
Dassault Etendard
The French went to a smaller and lighter concept for their first carrier-based jet fighter. The Etendard was a loser in a NATO competition for a light fighter, but it became the basis for further development into the only true supersonic carrier-based fighter in European naval service at that time. Its design is aerodynamically similar to that of the long Mystère line, but it features layout modifications that make it more suitable for carrier use.

The Convair F-106 Delta Dart high altitude fighter has been continuously updated, and is expected to continue in front-line service until the late 1970s

Dassault Mirage IIIE
Crew: 1 *Powerplant:* 1 SNECMA Atar 9B, 9370 lb thrust *Span:* 27 ft *Length:* 47 ft
Weight: 32,630 lb *Armament:* 2×30-mm cannon; 1 Nord AS 30 plus 2 Sidewinder missiles
Speed: Mach 2 at 36,000 ft

McDonnell F-4E Phantom
Crew: 2 *Powerplant:* 2 General Electric
J79-GE-10, 11,870 lb thrust each *Span* 38·4 ft
Length: 63 ft *Weight:* 59,000 lb (max)
Armament: 1×20-mm Vulcan cannon
Speed: Mach 2·4 at 40,000 ft

17 November 1956:
Dassault Mirage III
This was a redesigned Mirage I, and more nearly the true prototype of the contemporary line of Mirage III fighters. It used a single turbojet engine, setting the powerplant style that is maintained today in the latest of the Mirage fighters.

26 December 1956:
Convair F-106A Delta Dart
This delta-winged interceptor started life as the F-102B, but incorporated so many changes that it was redesignated with the later number. It is an automatically directed and fired weapon system; the pilot is along mostly to monitor the complex and advanced avionics systems that cram every cubic inch of this all-weather aircraft. By continuing modification programmes, this elderly design has been kept current, electronically speaking, and can handle the contemporary threat of high-altitude jet bombers. Like the F-102, it relies on both unguided and guided missiles for weapons.

16 May 1957:
Saunders-Roe SR 53
It's tempting to dismiss this as another mixed-powerplant interceptor, but its concept was a good one that ignored the ridiculous official requirements in favour of a logical design that would do the job envisioned. Unfortunately, it was caught in Britain's myopic White Paper of the late 1950s, which said that there was no foreseeable need for a manned fighter programme beyond the English Electric P 1. That bureaucratic decision knocked out the Saunders-Roe programme as well as some other innovative British designs of the time, and set the stage for the final decline of British fighter technology.

27 May 1958:

McDonnell XF4H-1 Phantom II

The second Phantom originated as a McDonnell study for a single-seat fighter, was modified to match a later Navy requirement for a long-range attack fighter, and finally emerged in its present configuration as a multi-mission fighter, carrying a crew of two and powered by a pair of afterburning turbojets. In some ways it is a brute-force fighter, using the high thrust of its jets for near-vertical climbs after takeoff. Adopted by all three air arms in the United States, the Phantom II also serves with allies and customers of the US. It was first only missile-armed, but later an internal Vulcan cannon was added. It can carry up to eight tons of bombs, rockets and guided missiles on underwing strong points. Faster than twice the speed of sound at altitude, the Phantom II once held 15 world performance records. It was redesignated as F-4 in 1962.

30 July 1959:

Northrop N-156F Freedom Fighter

Northrop designers had been studying and building mockups of minimum-fighter concepts for several years, finally settling on the basic N-156 design form. First adapted to trainer requirements, and bought by the USAF as the highly successful T-38 Talon series, the N-156F (for fighter) was built in prototype form with USAF funds, and then received further government support to become the standard fighter in the Military Assistance Program. It has since been widely accepted and operated in a multi-mission role.

McDonnell F-4H1 Phantom II
Shown (opposite) in flight, is an RAF Phantom in 1971
Crew: 2 *Powerplant:* 2 General Electric J79-GE-3, 9600 lb thrust each *Span:* 38·4 ft
Length: 58·3 ft *Weight:* 50,000 lb (approx)
Armament: Guided missiles
Speed: Mach 2 at altitude

Northrop F-5 Freedom Fighter
Crew: 1 *Powerplant:* 2 General Electric J85-GE-21, 5000 lb thrust each *Span:* 26·7 ft
Length: 48·3 ft *Weight:* 24,080 lb
Armament: 2×20-mm cannon *Speed:* Mach 1·6

Opposite page, bottom: T-38 Talons (trainer version of the Freedom Fighter) of the USAF Thunderjets during the spectacular 'roll back to arrowhead' manoeuvre. Picture courtesy of Capt Bob Gore, PIO of the USAF Thunderjets

A mid fifties revival of the parasite fighter concept, launched from the belly of an airship, teamed the giant Vultee B-36 strategic bomber with the F-84 fighter. The concept was already obsolete, and surface-to-air missiles and advanced interceptors gave the escort fighter a doubtful utility

DEAD END DEVELOPMENTS

During the 1940s and 1950s, boom years for jet fighter development, many strange ideas were put into practice: on these pages we illustrate some of those that were built

McDonnell XF-85

Parasite fighter of 1948, designed to be carried in the bomb-bay of a B-36 bomber. Powerplant was a Westinghouse J34 of 3400 lb thrust; span was 21 ft and length 15 ft. The unusual tail configuration was adopted for maximum flight stability

Saunders-Roe SRA-1
Saunders-Roe's postwar flying boat
development ranged from the giant Princess to
the diminutive SRA-1 fighter, whose fuselage
incorporated a planing hull
Crew: 1 *Powerplant:* 2 Metro-Vick F2/4A
Beryl MVB1, 3850 lb thrust *Span:* 25·1 ft
Length: 45 ft *Weight:* 16,255 lb
Armament: 4×20-mm cannon *Speed:* 516 mph

*The Convair XF2Y-1 Sea Dart of 1953 was the first and last hydroski jet fighter to be built. Its Westinghouse J46 engine gave it a maximum
speed of 724 mph; armament was a single cannon; dimensions were 33·7 ft span and 52·6 ft length*

LESSONS FROM SMALL WARS

The wars in Vietnam and the Middle East, coupled with rapid advances in missile technology, had a profound effect on jet fighter design. Outside Russia, the emphasis switched away from pure interceptors; guns came back into fashion as armament; and the nature of local wars emphasised the usefulness of vertical takeoff aircraft

By the beginning of the 1960s, the design of jet fighters had begun to turn away from continued emphasis on interception. During the late 1950s, strategic and tactical missiles were being developed and deployed, and the nature of any offensive threat was changing. Instead of relying on a high-altitude bomber force exclusively, major powers were switching to a strike force mix of bombers and missiles. Further, bombers were being modified and crews retrained for low-level missions, to get to their targets under radar coverage and below effective anti-aircraft missile height.

This had a profound effect on fighter development. The interceptor was no longer the ·be-all and end-all of fighter design. There were defence planners who seriously questioned the need for any further development of manned interceptors at all. In the United States, for example, no interceptors have been designed and built since the Convair F-106A, first flown in 1956. Almost 20 years later, that aircraft was still the USAF's only all-weather interceptor.

The Russians, on the other hand, apparently still clung to the belief that the major threat against them would include strikes by manned bombers. They have continued to develop interceptors, and during the 1960s turned out five new types.

But missile strikes by major powers were considered as the ultimate recourse in some future apocalyptic event. Meantime, there were some smaller wars that had happened, that were happening, and that were about to happen. From these, too, came useful lessons for fighter designers.

The Suez crisis in 1956 clearly showed that the primary use for fighters in wars of that kind was in ground attack. They still needed residual ability to fight their way home if they were jumped by an enemy counter-air strike, but the primary job was that of airborne artillery.

Continuing aerial engagements between Israeli aircraft and adversaries from one or another of the several Arab air forces in the area taught other lessons. They re-emphasised the importance of heavy calibre cannon with high rates of fire. They redirected some

of the earlier thinking that had concentrated on missiles as the only air-to-air weapon. It became apparent that mixed armament was better than a single type of weapon, and that the ideal mix for a fighter expecting trouble was cannon and missiles, the latter being able to home on infra-red signatures or radar returns.

The vulnerability of airfields to missile strikes and to bombing – the latter point made brilliantly by the Israelis in the Six-Day War of 1967 – gave emphasis to the concept of the vertical-takeoff and vertical-landing fighter. This novel type would be able to operate from any small cleared area – a pasture, a crossroads, a clearing in a forest – and would not be restricted to the long and very vulnerable concrete runways. It was a prototype of this new class of fighters that first flew during the first year of the time period we are considering here.
21 October 1960:

Hawker Siddeley P 1127
This prototype, built to explore the concept of vertical takeoff and landing for a tactical fighter, was developed into the first, and still the only, such fighter known to be in active service with military forces. The first flight was a captive one, made while the

P 1127 was tethered by cables to the ground. But it was the first time the aircraft left the ground under the power of its vectored-thrust turbofan engine. The P 1127 was developed further into the Kestrel and then the Harrier, a tactical fighter now in service with both the Royal Air Force and the United States Marine Corps. It is one of the truly pioneering designs in the development of fighter aircraft.
1960:

Tupolev Tu-28P
This huge, all-weather interceptor was first shown publicly in 1961, and then was lost to Western view until the 1967 display at Domodedovo, the airport near Moscow chosen for the public display that year of many new and different Russian types. The Tu-28P is a two-place, twin-engined aircraft, weighing an estimated 100,000 lb. It is very obviously capable of supersonic performance, and is armed with four air-to-air missiles externally mounted, and possibly others in an internal bay. The likelihood is that it was designed as a specific counter to high-altitude strikes by the USAF's B-58A supersonic delta-winged bomber, then in very conspicuous service with the Strategic Air Command.

Keystone

Mirage kill. During the 1973 Middle East War an Israeli Mirage III downs an Arab Sukkoi Su-7. Both planes first flew in the late 1950s, proved their worth during the wars of the 1960s, and continued in front line service in many parts of the world during the 1970s

1960:

Yakovlev Yak-28P
This twin-engined, two-place Russian interceptor seems at first glance to be an enlarged Yak-25. But all the indications are that it is basically a new design aerodynamically and internally, with new powerplants. It carries a pair of air-to-air missiles externally, and has trans-sonic performance. It would be capable of intercepting any subsonic bomber force targeted against Russia. The Yak-28P has been fitted with progressively updated avionics and more powerful turbojets since its service introduction.

The Hawker Siddeley Harrier provides a complete contrast to the YF-12 concept. A subsonic V/STOL aircraft, it is designed specifically to meet the conditions encountered in local wars

The Lockheed YF-12A long-range interceptor, capable of sustained flight at Mach 3+ at altitudes of over 80,000 ft, was the peak development of supersonic cruise aircraft in the early 1960s. It was largely redundant as a fighter, however, and became the SR-71 strategic reconnaissance aircraft

26 April 1962:
Lockheed YF-12A

There have been USAF requirements for advanced manned interceptors from time to time, and the development of the YF-12A may have resulted from one of them. Or it might have been simply a cover operation to conceal the development of the SR-71 strategic reconnaissance aircraft. In either case, the dark blue-black YF-12A prototypes were built as potential interceptors, optimised for cruise speeds three times that of sound at altitudes above 80,000 ft. They carried missiles in belly bays. The unusual

layout, with its lifting-body aerodynamics and canted twin tails, represented the peak of the development of supersonic cruise design features at that time. The configuration was later modified slightly to produce the unarmed SR-71, a global reconnaissance aircraft that collects data supplementing that obtained from satellite photography.

21 December 1964:
General Dynamics F-111

Variable-sweep wings had been tried and studied, with varying degrees of success, for nearly twenty years when a technical

innovation developed by the US National Aeronautics and Space Administration offered promise for a practical application. The idea was to pivot the wing sections outboard, rather than on the aircraft centreline. Technically, it worked. Then USAF and Navy fighter requirements and a new Secretary of Defence combined with the NASA innovation to give birth to the TFX, a multi-role combat aircraft that was intended to become the standard tactical fighter with all three US air arms. In the event, only the USAF got the developed TFX, or the F-111, as it was later designated after four design competitions and evaluations, and a controversial production contract. But the performance of the variable-sweep plane has marked it as one of the outstanding fighter designs of any era, and assured it of a place in aeronautical history. Missile-armed and loaded with advanced avionics, the F-111 series serves with Tactical Air Command and the Australian air force. In its FB-111A version, it equips two Strategic Air Command medium-bomber wings.

1964:
Sukhoi Su-11

On display at Domodedovo in 1967, the Su-11 attracted notice as an obvious further development of the same designer's Su-9, then in widespread service as an all-weather fighter with the Red air forces. The Su-11 follows the same formula of the single-engined, single-seat all-weather fighter, but it carries improved missiles under its delta wings, has a longer fuselage nose, and an engine with perhaps a 20% thrust increase. It is supersonic, reaching speeds close to Mach 2 at altitude.

1964:
Sukhoi Su-15

Second of the new Sukhoi designs to be shown in 1967 at the Domodedovo display, the Su-15 all-weather fighter forsakes the single-engine scheme for the power of twin turbojets with afterburning for super performance. Its aerodynamic layout draws heavily on the design bureau's experience with the Su-9 and Su-11, but the basic wing has been modified in one prototype to produce a compound-sweep planform. Another version of the Su-15, modified for short takeoff and landing operations, was also displayed and flown at Domodedovo.

1964:
Mikoyan MiG-23

The Russian application of variable-sweep geometry to a fighter produced the MiG-23, a smaller and lighter aircraft than the F-111 series, although designed for approximately the same missions. It is a single-seat, single-engined tactical fighter and fighter-bomber, armed with a twin-barrelled 23-mm cannon. Performance estimates place it in the Mach 2 class at altitude. Apparently the MiG-23 ran into some development troubles, because it was not until several years after the first public display at Domodedovo in 1967 that it was reported in active service with front-line squadrons. It has since been exported to Russian allies and friends, including those in the Middle East arena.

1964:
Mikoyan MiG-25

An all-weather interceptor with phenomenal performance, the MiG-25 has been the standard of comparison and of the fighter threat in almost any consideration of strategic or tactical aircraft design in the West during the past decade. The speedy

Hawker Siddeley Aviation

Smithsonian Institution Photo No 20560

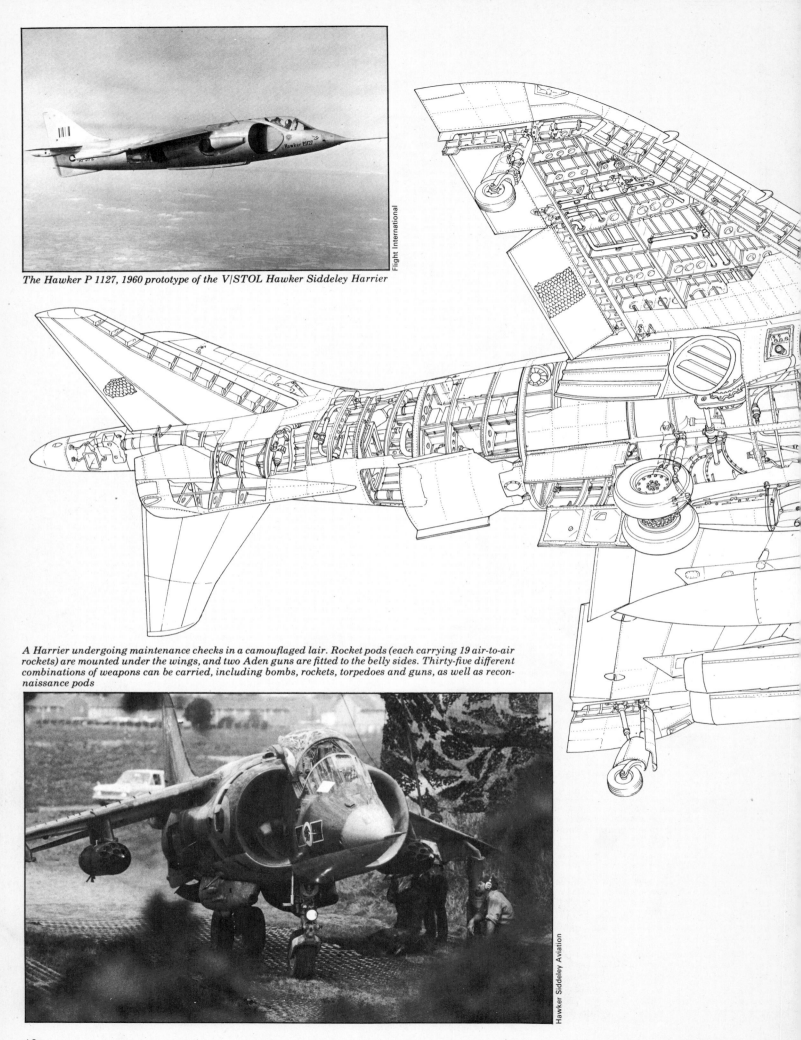

Flight International

The Hawker P 1127, 1960 prototype of the V/STOL Hawker Siddeley Harrier

A Harrier undergoing maintenance checks in a camouflaged lair. Rocket pods (each carrying 19 air-to-air rockets) are mounted under the wings, and two Aden guns are fitted to the belly sides. Thirty-five different combinations of weapons can be carried, including bombs, rockets, torpedoes and guns, as well as reconnaissance pods

Hawker Siddeley Aviation

THE HARRIER

The Hawker Siddeley Harrier V/STOL is unique among serving combat aircraft. The prototype P 1127 first flew in 1960; the Harrier itself in August 1966. At present serving with the RAF and US Marine Corps, the Sea Harrier version will shortly enter service with the Royal Navy.
Crew: 1 *Powerplant:* 1 Rolls-Royce Pegasus 11, 21,500 lb vectored thrust *Span:* 25·3 ft
Length: 45·5 ft *Speed:* 680 mph at sea level

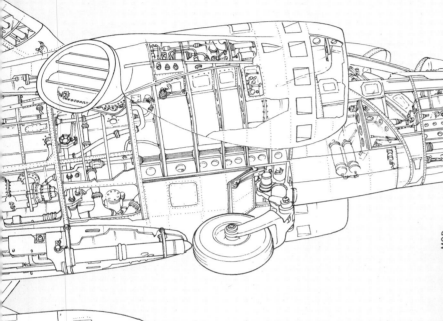

The Harrier can lift one-third of its maximum load in vertical takeoff (below). In a short takeoff run (approximately a quarter of that required by conventional combat aircraft) it can lift a fuel and weapons load of 13,050 lb – greater than its own empty weight of 12,200 lb

MOD

Hawker Siddeley Aviation

Pilot Press

Yakovlev Yak-28P
Crew: 2 *Powerplant:* 2 RD11, 13,100 lb thrust
each *Span:* 42·5 ft *Length:* 71 ft
Weight: 30,000 lb (approx)
Armament: 2 air-to-air missiles
Speed: 730 mph (approx) at altitude

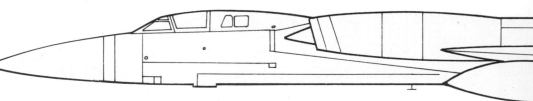

Tupolev Tu-28P
Crew: 1 *Powerplant:* 2 afterburning jets,
27,000 lb thrust each (estimate) *Span:* 65 ft
Length: 85 ft *Weight:* 100,000 lb
Armament: 4 air-to-air guided missiles
Speed: Mach 1·75 at altitude

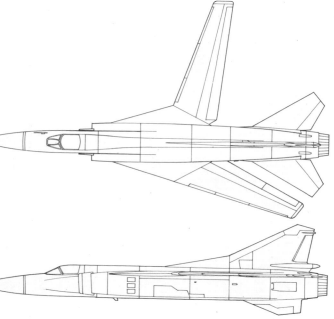

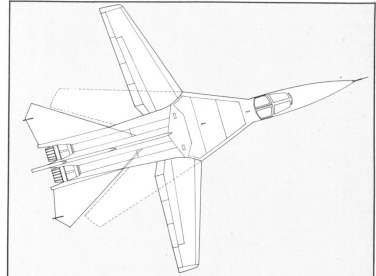

Mikoyan MiG-23
Crew: 1 *Powerplant:* 1 afterburning turbojet,
9300 lb thrust (estimate) *Span:* 46·7 ft
Length: 55·1 ft *Weight:* 12,700 lb
Armament: 2×23-mm cannon
Speed: Mach 2·3 at altitude

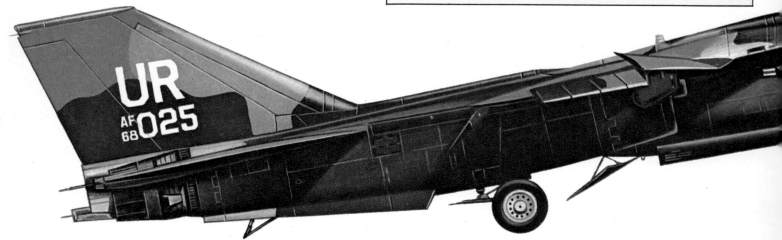

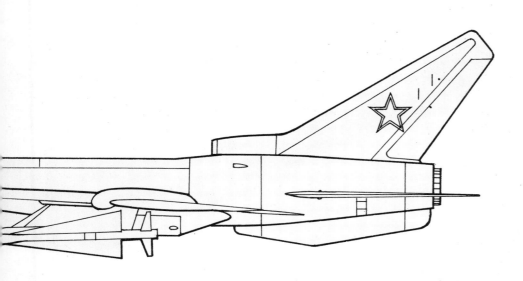

twin-jet design held several absolute world speed and time-to-climb records, and held some of them unbeaten for nearly ten years. (In early 1975, the time-to-climb records, the last of the batch held by the MiG-25, were topped, and substantially, by a USAF McDonnell F-15A Eagle.) It carries four air-to-air missiles of a new type beneath its stubby swept wings, and can do better than Mach 3 at altitude. In a reconnaissance version, the MiG-25 has been observed, but not intercepted, in high-level flights in the Middle East. It is a single-place aircraft.
23 December 1966:

Dassault Mirage F 1

Like so many of the series of advanced Dassault designs, this one grew out of earlier attempts to meet an entirely different requirement. The F 1 was developed into a multi-mission fighter, with its greatest strength in the air-superiority role. Yet its genesis was as a flying test bed aircraft built for development work with a new engine planned for a Dassault VTOL fighter. It is a single-seat fighter, powered by a single SNECMA Atar engine, probably the final development of that long line that traces its ancestry all the way back to the Junkers 004B. The F 1 wing design uses advanced aerodynamic features, tried and tested on other Dassault aircraft and refined for optimum performance in the specific F 1 configuration. Rugged landing gear gives the F 1 the ability to operate out of grass strips, or from unimproved airfields. It carries very heavy armament; as an interceptor, for example, it is armed with a pair of 30-mm cannon, a pair of Matra R 530 radar-homing missiles, and another pair of air-to-air missiles at the wingtips. It has been ordered by the French air force and will undoubtedly be sold abroad as well.
8 February 1967:

SAAB System 37 Viggen

The Viggen is the major component of a complete air defence system, and the product of a most ambitious effort by Sweden that can stand comparison to any such effort by any country. The Viggen aircraft was designed to be a flying platform capable of carrying a variety of sub-systems into the air for a variety of missions. Four major missions were chosen for the development: strike, reconnaissance, interception, and training. These requirements were all built into the airplane as far as possible, so that the final result is a multi-mission aircraft with cross-capabilities. Its unique aerodynamic layout with its main wing and the forward, separate, auxiliary wing produces low approach speeds. With thrust reversers, the Viggen can land in less than 1700 ft of runway. Its low-speed characteristics give it STOL (short takeoff and landing) performance and it can operate from highways. At altitude it can streak along at twice the speed of sound. It carries missiles and advanced avionics for navigation and attack.

The SAAB Viggen, Dassault F 1 and General Dynamics F-111, all multi-mission fighters, are one product of their times. Capable of a wide range of performance, from STOL to supersonic, and able to arm with missiles for dog-fighting or bombs for ground attack, their versatility assures them of continued use in the air arms of their respective countries.

But they begin to show a trend which will be accentuated in the next time period by the Grumman F-14A and the McDonnell F-15A. That trend will force another look at the philosophy of fighter design.

The variable-sweep F-111 was dogged by trouble during its development

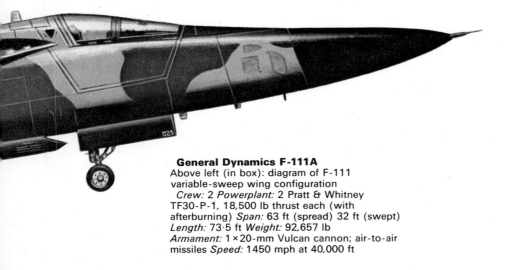

General Dynamics F-111A

Above left (in box): diagram of F-111 variable-sweep wing configuration
Crew: 2 *Powerplant:* 2 Pratt & Whitney TF30-P-1, 18,500 lb thrust each (with afterburning) *Span:* 63 ft (spread) 32 ft (swept) *Length:* 73·5 ft *Weight:* 92,657 lb
Armament: 1 × 20-mm Vulcan cannon; air-to-air missiles *Speed:* 1450 mph at 40,000 ft

The SAAB J37 Viggen, another competitor in the race to replace Europe's combat aircraft

Marcel Dassault, designer and builder of the Mystère/Mirage series, started his career in aviation during the First World War

Dassault Mirage F1, the French candidate to replace the obsolescent NATO Starfighters

Dassault Mirage F1
Crew: 1 *Powerplant:* 1 SNECMA Atar 09K-50,
11,023 lb thrust *Span:* 27·5 ft *Length:* 49·3 ft
Weight: 24,000 lb *Armament:* 2×30-mm cannon;
2 Sidewinders plus other missiles
Speed: Mach 2·2 at altitude

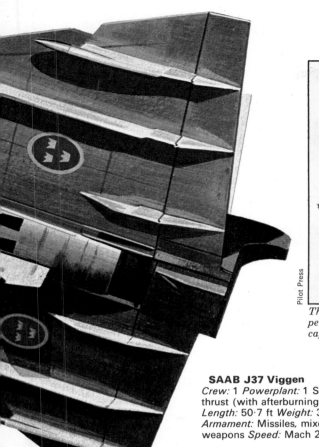

The Mikoyan MiG-25 set the standard of jet fighter performance for a decade, and its phenomenal performance was only recently bettered by the F-15 Eagle. It carries four air-to-air missiles, and is capable of Mach 3·2 at altitude

Pilot Press

SAAB J37 Viggen
Crew: 1 *Powerplant:* 1 Svenska RM8, 26,500 lb thrust (with afterburning) *Span:* 34·8 ft
Length: 50·7 ft *Weight:* 35,000 lb (approx)
Armament: Missiles, mixed external stores and weapons *Speed:* Mach 2 at high altitude

The Dassault Mirage G 8 swing-wing fighter, from which Dassault are developing the Super Mirage fighter

Flight International

SOARING COST AND COMPLEXITY

The escalating costs of fighters like the Grumman Tomcat are causing much heart-searching among aircraft firms and Defence Ministries, and it begins to seem that the General Dynamics YF-16 is the fighter concept of the future

The aerial war in Vietnam continued to teach the same truths about fighter design. Versatility was one such lesson. A fighter-bomber might have to carry bombs on one sortie, rockets on the next, napalm on its third and guns on its fourth. Or it might have to take off with a mixture of all these and, after dumping them, fight its way back home through a curtain of intense flak and enemy missiles.

The concept of a multi-mission fighter was reinforced by Vietnam experience. It also added new emphasis to a lesson from earlier wars: the importance of electronic countermeasures. Electronic warfare had come to the battlefields of Southeast Asia with a vengeance; their environment was criss-crossed with invisible beams of electronic devices for finding, fooling and helping to destroy aircraft.

A major impetus to the growth of electronic warfare was the advance of the guided missile as an anti-aircraft weapon. It could not be shot down; it had to be evaded or avoided or decoyed some way. Evasion techniques had been developed, but – as missile technology improved – the dependence on spotting and manoeuvring grew riskier. The next stop: decoy the missile by giving it a false target to detect, track and intercept. This could be done electronically or physically.

Electronic warfare systems added to fighter capabilities. They could warn a pilot that his plane had been detected; that it was under fire from the rear; and that the missile was beginning its final tracking toward a hit on his plane. These passive indications could be augmented by electronic countermeasures activity. They could, in effect, create a cloud of electronic noise in which the fighter might hide. They could create a completely spurious fighter that would have a stronger attraction for the oncoming missile. They could confuse the missile, decoy it, send it to another quadrant of the sky.

Brains, even electronic ones, are not built cheaply. Further, like human brains, they function best in friendly environments; they tend to be troubled by excessive heat, cold, or physical shocks. Making electronic brains that can withstand those deteriorating factors and still perform involves more complexity, and that equates to more cost.

The US Navy's best and most expensive fighter, the swing-wing Grumman F-14A Tomcat undergoing flight tests over San Clemente Island

And so, as each side added an offensive technique or countered one with a defensive technology, the inevitable happened. Fighters got more complex, and consequently more costly to build.

When the Vietnam aerial action really began in the early 1960s, a North American F-100, then a standard day fighter, could be bought for about $600,000 flyaway factory. If one wanted the greater capability of a McDonnell F-4C, the price was tripled to $1·8 million.

These kinds of cost figures were impressive, especially to those who remembered 1958, when it was possible to get a North American F-86F, then the top-of-the-line day fighter, for $230,000.

But the price of an F-4C was only an indication of the trend. The data were coming in on the then-new General Dynamics F-111 series, with costs – according to testimony in the bitter but fascinating Congressional hearings – of more than $16 million per airplane. Admittedly this was a special case, but it served to send up warning flags. In the depths of the Pentagon in Washington, DC, fighter analysts and planners began to look for alternatives to the high-cost development and production of today's fighters.

Costs and contracts

The final straw, perhaps, was the sobering experience shared by the Navy and Grumman in the development of the variable-sweep F-14A Tomcat series. Cost escalations, caused by inflationary factors and other problems, threatened the continued existence of Grumman as a company. The Navy wanted to hold Grumman to the fixed prices guaranteed in its contract; Grumman said that doing that would bankrupt the company, and claimed that the rules under which the contract had been written had made assumptions that were no longer valid. It was unfair to hold Grumman to those rules, they said.

After some recriminations and refinancings, the programme continued and the Tomcat entered the fleet, where it is serving with great distinction. It is costing the US Navy, and the American taxpayer, about $11 million per airplane, based on a system of accounting which produces agreement between Navy and Air Force cost figures.

The McDonnell-Douglas F-15A Eagle, a fighter, costs about 10% less than the variable-sweep Tomcat.

These amounts of dollars, it might be noted, could have bought a complete Boeing B-52 towards the end of that bomber's production life in 1962, at about the time that the top fighter, the F-4, was purchased for less than $2 million.

It should be realised that costs for aircraft may or may not include all the programme costs amortised out over each airplane. At one end of the cost scale is simply the amount of money the military

pays to the manufacturer for building and assembling the parts that make up one complete airplane. At the other end is the total cost of research, development, tooling, flight test, problem-solving, and all the rest of the programme, including production, for each plane.

The figure of $16·6 million, quoted in Congressional testimony for the F-111, is the total programme cost divided by the number of airplanes produced. In the Grumman F-14A and McDonnell-Douglas F-15A figures cited above, the programme costs are not all included in the airplane's price. To do so might double the figures.

There is black humour used by proponents of low-cost aircraft to make a point. They plot the cost of a fighter (or bomber or whatever) against time, and show how that curve has climbed upward more and more rapidly until, at some date not very far away, the cost of a single fighter exceeds the total US budget. They then speak of the Air Force as flying its fighter, or its bomber, against an enemy strike.

The use of such a simplistic approach dramatises the central fact: fighter costs are escalating out of sight. And a major portion of that cost is chargeable to inflation. By mid-1974, inflation in the price of metals that go into aircraft construction had accounted for more than a 60% rise in materials costs since 1967, or more than 8% annually.

Even stronger was the impact of worldwide inflation during the last few months of 1973. A Department of Defense estimate attributed a 36% cost rise in more than 50 major weapons systems to the financial near-panic of that period.

In some ways, the cost growth of fighter aircraft has been a result of evolution, rather than revolution, in design. It is common to base a new fighter on the latest successful one operational, because the fastest and lowest-cost way has been thought to be by that route. What this meant in practice is that the latest technology, which might have been able to reduce costs if effectively applied, was not used. An existing design was adapted and, although it often brought an apparent low cost with it because of its status as a high-production, amortised programme, it could wind up costing more because of fix after fix necessary to bring the ageing design up to date.

In the early 1970s, the USAF funded a development programme that aimed at reversing the trend to higher costs. The purpose was to evaluate the latest in fighter technology in minimum-sized aircraft, with the primary goal of seeing what could be done with new technology when a preconceived military mission was not a factor in design.

The General Dynamics YF-16 and Northrop YF-17 were the interesting results of that programme. Two different airplanes, they reflect their company's approaches to the design of a lightweight fighter type of aircraft, with carte blanche to use any new idea as long as it appeared promising.

Both these refined designs have won high marks from observers for their adherence to requirements and their low-cost approach.

In early 1975, prices for both were estimated at about $4 million each, should a large-scale production programme follow. This is still an expensive fighter, but it is a remarkable achievement to reach cost figures about one-third those of the immediate predecessors.

Tomcat Variable-sweep Configuration

Grumman F-14A Tomcat
Crew: 2 *Powerplant:* 2 Pratt & Whitney
TF30-P-412, 20,900 lb thrust each
Span: 64·1 ft *Length:* 62 ft *Weight:* 55,000 lb
Armament: 1×20-mm Vulcan cannon; 6 Phoenix
plus 2 Sidewinder missiles
Speed: Mach 2·3 at altitude

McDonnell-Douglas YF-15A Eagle
Crew: 1 *Powerplant:* 2 Pratt & Whitney
F100-P-100 afterburning turbofan, 23,400 lb
thrust each *Span:* 42·8 ft *Length:* 63·8 ft
Weight: 40,000 lb (approx)
Armament: 1×20-mm Vulcan
cannon; 4 Sparrow or
Sidewinder missiles
Speed: Mach 2·5+ at
60,000 ft

The USAF has chosen the YF-16 for further development and the question remaining is whether the price will stand up as the programme moves from its current development state into large-scale fighter production over the next few years.
21 December 1970:
Grumman F-14A Tomcat
Latest and best of the Naval fighters, the Grumman Tomcat is a twin-engined, two-place aircraft with variable-sweep wings automatically programmed to flight requirements. It serves the fleet in a multi-mission role: fighter escort, fleet defence, and ground attack. Designed to cope with any foreseeable enemy threat well into the 1980/90 decade, the F-14A features high supersonic speed and manoeuvrability, especially at high altitude. It has fast acceleration, but a slow approach and landing speed. The bubble canopy, once thought to be detrimental and known to be difficult to achieve on a supersonic aircraft, gives round-the-clock visibility to the two-man crew. It carries a heavy load of mixed armament, including a 20-mm Vulcan M61 six-barrel cannon, and a half-dozen Hughes Phoenix long-range intercept missiles. Additional weapons include Sparrow and Sidewinder air-to-air missiles. The Tomcat became operational with the US Navy in March 1974, serving in 12-plane squadrons on board carriers. The Iranian government has ordered 80 for its air arm.

General Dynamics YF-16

On its first flight, it staggered into the air as the only alternative to possible destruction on the ground. Oscillations had developed during a high-speed taxi run and, after the wingtip scraped, the best thing to do seemed to be to get it into the air. Since then, the General Dynamics YF-16 has been impressing pilots and technicians alike with its advanced features and its consistently good performance. One of the prettiest fighters to come along in years, the Ft Worth fighter design is based on blended wing-body technology to produce an exciting, flowing fuselage shape that combines with a stubby trapezoidal wing to mix body and wing lift in proper proportion. Its single engine is fed from an underslung duct with the inlet almost directly under the cockpit. But the real feature of the YF-16 – and its proto-typed programme partner, the YF-17 – is advanced technology. The YF-16 features leading-edge manoeuvring flaps and fore-body strakes, both to improve performance at the high angles of attack characteristic of high-altitude fighting. It is a fly-by-wire airplane, unstable – or nearly so – on its aerodynamics alone, but kept stable and flyable by an advanced electronic system of sensors and controls. The pilot sits in a reclining position for a higher level of tolerance to accelerations of combat turns, and flies the YF-16, not with a central control stick, but with a side-arm controller mounted at the right of the cockpit. Armed with a single Vulcan cannon and a pair of Sidewinder dog-fighting missiles, the YF-16 also can carry external stores and weapon pods on seven underwing strong points.

9 June 1974:

Northrop YF-17

The other half of the lightweight fighter programme flew about six months later, and revealed a different approach from the one chosen by General Dynamics. The YF-17 designers used a pair of smaller engines, citing the dependability and reliability of a twin-engined installation, verified in practice with their F-5/T-38 line. Aerodynamically, the YF-17 builds on advanced technology, using a refinement of the basic Tiger II wing and a forward modification of that surface. A shoulder-wing design, the Northrop fighter uses twin canted vertical tails. Engine intakes are what have been inelegantly called armpit types, located between wing root and the fuselage side. Armament is identical to that of the YF-16. Northrop designers optimised their aircraft around the turning rate performance, which they had concluded was the single most important factor in aerial combat. The radius of turn, the ability to pull high loads during the turn, and all the other arguments of pilots and technicians were boiled down to a shape and a powerplant that would get the nose of the airplane turned into a fight as rapidly as possible.

27 July 1972:

McDonnell-Douglas F-15A Eagle

For the first time in a quarter of a century, the USAF has a fighter optimised specifically for the air-superiority mission. The single-seat Eagle is built around a stubby sweptwing of low aspect ratio and high area, for extra manoeuvrability at high altitude. It carries mixed armament: a 20-mm Vulcan cannon, and Sidewinder and Sparrow missiles, updated specifically for dogfighting at closer ranges. Early in 1975, the Eagle set eight world time-to-altitude records in flights under the project name of Streak Eagle. In timed climbs from three to 30 kilometres, the Eagle broke mark after mark in a staggering performance with numbers that almost defy the imagination. On the climb to three kilometres, the F-15A lifted off the ground after a roll of 400 ft, about seven lengths of the fuselage. On a single flight which broke three of the existing records, the F-15A accelerated to sonic speed within 19 seconds after takeoff. In the climb to the highest altitude, the pilot accelerated in climb to Mach 2 in less than two minutes from takeoff, and the subsequent energy climb got him to 102,000 ft before the Eagle slacked off. In less than one minute, the Eagle reached 12 kilometres (39,360 ft); its average rate of climb to 30 kilometres (98,400 ft) was better than 144 metres per second, or 28,438 ft per minute.

The rapid increases in cost and complexity are not the only considerations in assessing the future of the jet fighter. Most fighters of the last 20 years have had some capacity as strike/attack/reconnaissance aircraft, while some high performance interceptors such as the YF-12 and F-111 have failed to get into service. History is not encouraging, and the future is far from clear

Are the YF-16 and YF-17 the trend-setters for future fighter design? Or are they slated to be remembered as brilliant design efforts that gradually turned into heavy, complex and costly multi-purpose fighters?

History does not provide much encouragement for answering the first question positively. The one recent example – the Folland Gnat – was a successful approach to the problem, and it offered some unique and innovative solutions, but alone it could not stem the tide.

The avowed purpose of the YF-16/YF-17 programme was to develop a fighter-type aircraft without the need to meet a specific operational requirement for one. For that reason, the design teams at General Dynamics and Northrop were free to apply any late technology, almost without regard for its suitability in a combat aircraft.

But neither company got where it is by

THE FUTURE

WHERE DO WE GO FROM HERE?

being unaware of military requirements. Consequently, both aircraft reflect the extensive experience of their manufacturers in the development of recent high-speed combat aircraft. Further, along the line the Air Force began to have second thoughts about the programme, and let it be known that they might consider developing the better of the two into a combat-ready fighter, and that it might then be purchased in substantial quantity.

That is what happened. There was a competitive fly-off between the two, which gave the nod to the General Dynamics entry. Soon after, the USAF announced plans to purchase up to 650 of the little fighters. They would become part of the hi-lo mix, the compound word referring not to mission profiles, but to cost. Future USAF fighter fleets would be mixed, with a small number of versatile, expensive fighters and a larger number of less versatile, less-expensive fighters.

Current cost estimates for the YF-16 as developed into a production fighter vary between $4 and $5 million, with the majority view clustering around the lower end of

that range. Undoubtedly, escalation, inflation and the other enemies of constant cost will lay heavy influence on the development programme. Further, every fighter that has started out in pristine form has soon had all kinds of external and internal modifications added. Still further, the production cost of a large number of McDonnell-Douglas F-15 Eagles has been estimated as not too far above the $5 million mark, throwing another factor into the YF-16 equation.

But it is natural to expect that the YF-16 and YF-17 will be developed, and that they inexorably will grow heavier and more expensive. But at the same time, the same process will be happening to the F-15, and at some future point it may be possible to see an F-15 costing $20 million and an F-16 costing $8 million. And then, the Air Force will announce a competition for a revolutionary new concept in aircraft development: a fighter-type aircraft to use the very latest technology to achieve optimum performance at minimum cost.

There is no way of knowing certainly what the future will bring in technology,

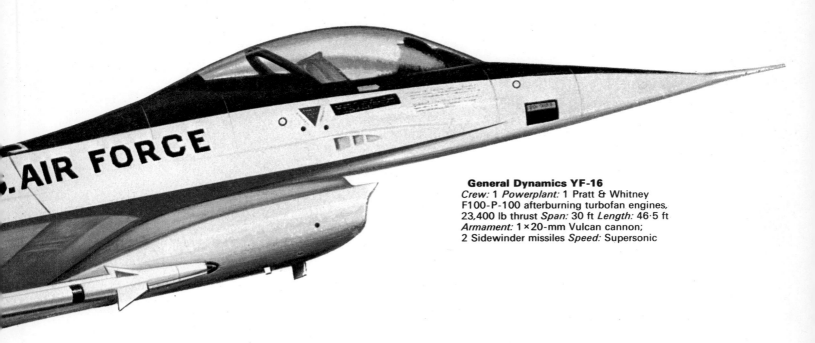

General Dynamics YF-16
Crew: 1 *Powerplant:* 1 Pratt & Whitney
F100-P-100 afterburning turbofan engines,
23,400 lb thrust *Span:* 30 ft *Length:* 46·5 ft
Armament: 1 × 20-mm Vulcan cannon;
2 Sidewinder missiles *Speed:* Supersonic

but it may be instructive to look at the YF-16 and YF-17 to see what the present offers.

General Dynamics wanted to build the smallest and lightest aeroplane possible, using low-risk developments. They emphasised the air-superiority mission almost to the exclusion of any other possibility, and wound up with a single-place, single-engine airplane built primarily of conventional materials.

Northrop, with the experience of a long line of small, light combat aircraft to draw upon, carried that series one step further forward in applying what they had learned in extrapolation of the technology. But they stressed the concept of an operational prototype, one that could make the transition from development to production and service with a minimum of change and difficulty.

The YF-16 is a blended wing-body configuration, in which the contours of wing and fuselage are aerodynamically melded to a smooth and continuous fairing of surfaces. This was done to draw on body lift; the resulting wing size is smaller, and therefore lighter, and therefore cheaper. The wing has leading-edge manoeuvring flaps, which are programmed to function automatically as Mach number and angle of attack change in flight. They increase the camber of the wing and the lift at altitude.

Strakes – long, thin, horizontal fences ahead of the wing leading edge – are placed there to generate vortices. These rotating streams of energised air then move aft, and keep the boundary-layer flow from breaking away in the intersection area between

The YF-17, Northrop's latest idea for a low-cost lightweight fighter, has similar performance and armament to the YF-16, and in spite of its twin-jet configuration the two designs are strikingly similar

wing and fuselage. All these features – the blended wing-body shape, the leading-edge manoeuvring flaps, the strakes – work to improve the lift characteristics of the aircraft, especially at high altitudes and high angles of attack that are typical of dog-fighting. And they save weight also – General Dynamics say that the wing-body blending saved them about 320 lb in the fuselage, and another 250 on the wing. The strakes made a smaller wing possible, saving another 490 lb.

Weight saved means money saved. A pound of aircraft weight represents many dollars in direct labour and material costs, plus indirect research, development, design, engineering, and tooling costs. In aircraft, smaller means lighter means cheaper.

In order to get a very agile fighter, General Dynamics engineers deliberately reduced static stability, because a stable aircraft – while desirable for cruise flight and other portions of a mission – is not the best for manoeuvring. Next, they designed

An interceptor version of the MRCA (Multi-Role Combat Aircraft) is scheduled to replace RAF Phantoms and Lightnings in the air-superiority role for the 1980s. Different versions of the MRCA will be equipped with extremely advanced avionics for a wide range of different combat roles

in a fly-by-wire system, making the YF-16 the first aircraft planned from the start around such a control system. Fly-by-wire uses electronics to transfer the input signal from the pilot's control stick to the moveable surface; it reduces weight and vulnerability of the airplane. But it does more; it can be used to give unusual groupings of control motions, something no conventionally rigged system could do. In a combat situation, a pilot could easily pop up his airplane above the enemy on his tail by using fly-by-wire signals to move all of the horizontal surfaces to generate lift simultaneously. On an enemy's tail, he could aim the fuselage independently of what flight path his plane was following.

Further recognising that the pilot is under maximum physical stress during combat, the YF-16 design team slanted the pilot's seat back to a 30° angle, to increase his tolerance to high-g turns, and to make it easier for him to see and to look around in those situations. They gave him a side-arm controller instead of a central control stick.

By using a simple engine inlet under the belly, General Dynamics engineers saved another major weight increment. The inlet duct is short, and its leading edge is fixed, rather than built with the sharp-edged

variable geometry of most supersonic fighters. In the speed range where the YF-16 will fight, the complexity is unnecessary.

Finally, they built the airplane out of familiar aluminium alloys, with minimum use of steel and titanium. There is some use of graphite epoxy skins on the tails for stiffness with reduced weight, but that is the only area where new and different materials are used.

One novel feature of the overall design is that many of these features can be removed and replaced if they should not prove to be what they were predicted to be. The entire wing is quickly removeable, and can either be replaced, or moved back along the fuselage to restore some of the static stability designed out of the layout. The forward strakes can come off, the inlet can be simply changed, the canopy can be replaced, and even the side-arm controller can be removed and replaced by a central control stick in the conventional manner.

Northrop were faced with the same set of conditions, and it is interesting to note that their solutions differ in detail but not so much in concept. The twin-tailed YF-17

uses a pair of engines, rather than the single jet of the YF-16. Paired engines present unique problems, among which is 'base drag', that portion of the total airplane drag due to the blunt end of the jet exhaust. Northrop has been working on the problem a long time and the YF-17 is claimed to have the lowest base drag of any twin-jet fighter.

The wing is basically the wing of the Tiger II, with extra leading-edge extensions which reach well forward along the fuselage and which serve basically the same purpose as the YF-16's strakes: generation of strong vortex flow to re-energise the wing root boundary layer flow. But rather than relax the stability standards, Northrop chose to handle the vortex flow by using twin tails, canted outboard, and placed far forward on the fuselage. Here they also serve to close an aerodynamic gap between the wing trailing edge and the horizontal tail, and

they do not require a carry-through structure that pierces the rear fuselage. That means a lighter fuselage back there, and also an engine bay free of internal obstructions. The engines can be easily dropped out for maintenance or replacement.

The horizontal tail is larger than usual, and was sized for manoeuvring to give the best turning rate at high speeds. It is set as far back as possible, which means a slightly heavier and longer fuselage, but Northrop think that the manoeuvring advantages outweigh the objections in this case.

The YF-17 also uses fly-by-wire, but on the ailerons only. The control stick is the conventional central one, and the pilot's seat is tilted aft to an 18° angle. Like its competitor, the YF-17 is largely aluminium alloys with some graphite composite skins. One nice detail is the use of fireproofing paint in the engine bay. The paint expands under the heat and creates an air-filled insulating layer which effectively can contain and delay the fire for longer periods of time than usual.

These two aircraft characterise the best aerodynamic features and the best structural techniques available to designers today, given the restraints of the programme.

Heart of the fighter

Powerplants are the heart of the fighter. The technology of today's afterburning turbofans is a far cry from the inventions of von Ohain and Whittle. New metals, much higher temperatures, improved fuels and better internal flow characteristics have all added their incremental improvements to those early engines. The general feeling in the engine industry is that future changes are going to continue to be incremental, as better materials come along to permit higher operating temperatures. There should be no major changes in powerplant design for perhaps another decade.

Weaponry, another major factor in fighter design, is considered in the succeeding chapter.

The Israel Aircraft Industries Kfir, essentially a revamped Mirage III, was revealed in April 1975. Maximum speed is around Mach 2·2; armament is a 30-mm cannon plus missiles and stores of various types

Today, the over-riding considerations of costs are in the minds of every planner and designer of fighter aircraft. It can be expected that there will be at least one round of lightweight and low-cost fighters of the YF-16/YF-17 type. The success of translating those prototypes into operational fighters will determine to a large extent whether there will be a second round.

The future is not clear. It is difficult to see a follow-up as being more complex, more versatile and with higher performance than today's breeds. Besides, the fighter cannot be considered alone, but must be treated as part of an overall strategic battlefield system, working with ground troops and weaponry, airborne command and control systems, and perhaps in the context of long-range missile strikes as well as bomber and fighter-bomber assaults.

Consequently, the future trend of fighter design will be affected primarily by the overall defence programme of any country. It has been decided in the United States, for example, that there will be no more manned interceptors. The British once decided that there would be no more manned fighters at all after the Lightning.

It is possible that the current round of fighters could be the last. The average life of today's types is predicted to be about ten years at the beginning of their programme lives. Yet as the ten-year mark approaches, ways are found to stretch that life. Look at two fighters in large-scale service today. The Russian MiG-21 first flew in 1955; the McDonnell-Douglas F-4 prototype in 1958. Both are still very much the front-line fighters of their respective countries and allies, far from the end of their useful lives.

Applying that kind of a life span to the F-14 through F-17 series gets close to the end of this century. What will be the state of international affairs then? Will multilateral agreements have been worked out that will systematically reduce armaments? Or will an apocalypse of natural forces – lack of pure air and water, a starved earth and stagnant oceans – be controlling our international relations?

It's safer to look at the short-term approach. For the foreseeable future, the YF-16/YF-17 will be the route of future fighter development.

SEPECAT Jaguar S2
The first prototype of this tactical strike fighter flew in 1968. It will equip several RAF and *Armée de l'Air* squadrons
Crew: 2 *Powerplant:* 2 Rolls-Royce Turboméca RT172 Adour 102 turbofans, 4620 lb thrust each
Span: 28·5 ft *Length:* 53·8 ft *Weight:* 23,000 lb
Apartment: 1×30-mm cannon; 10,000 lb ordnance load *Speed:* Mach 1·6 at 33,000 ft

EJECTOR SEATS

John Batchelor

Martin-Baker Mk IV Ejector Seat
A fully automatic ejector seat incorporating a
half second delay and a duplex drogue system.
Ejection with this seat took place at the rate of
80 ft per second; it was the standard British
ejector seat in the mid-1950s. The photo
sequence above shows a pilot ejecting from a
Meteor at ground zero

John Batchelor

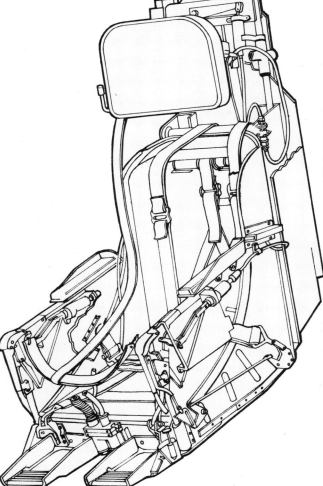

US Ejector Seat

This is the model of ejector seat fitted to the Sabre fighter; ejection was effected by means of a cartridge exploding under the seat to propel it into the air. The photo sequence below shows a Crusader making a bad landing on the deck of an aircraft carrier; as the plane goes overboard into the sea the pilot is shot to safety by his seat

FIGHTER ARMAMENT
CHOOSE YOUR WEAPON

The first jet fighters carried cannon, with some experimental air-to-air rockets on German planes. Since then, cannon, for weight of fire, and machine-guns, for maximum rpm, have vied for popularity, while missiles almost took over

Guns to missiles to guns and missiles is the short history of fighter armament.

At the end of the Second World War, most of the standard fighters on the Allied side were armed with machine-guns, characterised by a high rate of fire. Cannon had been introduced on the German fighters, and on some of the Allied types, and there was some use of unguided air-to-air rockets by the Germans.

This mixed weaponry set a trend that has continued to this day. Since then, fighters have been armed with machine-guns, cannon and unguided rockets, plus a newer development, the guided missile.

Most early jet fighters were armed with cannon. The value of the heavier weapon had been proved during the Second World War. Only in the United States was there a holdout position for the machine-gun, and not until the Korean war did the military finally make an all-out switch away from those weapons.

It would seem obvious that a cannon is better than a machine-gun; it fires a heavier shell, and therefore has greater striking power. It also has a generally higher muzzle velocity and greater range, both desirable attributes. But there is a strong argument for the 'buzz-saw' theory of aircraft armament. A cluster of six or eight heavy calibre machine-guns can bring an effective weight of fire upon an enemy aircraft that is sufficient to cut it to pieces – literally. There is a problem, though; the firing has to be done within effective range, and it must be accurately aimed.

Korean combat of jet against jet introduced a new element. That kind of combat stretched the combat range of the machine-gun to the point where it was no longer effective. The ranges were increased substantially from those the USAF pilots had grown used to in their previous war. And eight machine-guns at those distances were often totally ineffective. Strikes could be seen on the MiGs, but the Russian-built planes absorbed them and continued to fly and fight.

A Lockheed F-94C Starfire fires a salvo of rockets over the California Desert in 1952. Inset: 'Phantom' effect of heat condensation as a Lightning fires its three 30-mm cannon

Keystone

Actually, two things were happening: the range had opened up, and the airplanes had grown more rugged. The speed of jet aircraft dictated thicker skins, approaching the thickness of armour plating in some cases. And, hit at a shallow angle in the classic tail-chase, those surfaces were almost as good as armour in deflecting machine-gun bullets.

Korea, then, spelled the end of the machine-gun as an armament for jet fighters. As cannon batteries took their place, certain national characteristics began to emerge. The United States standardised on the 20-mm cannon; Europe built around the heavier 30-mm weapon. The Russians tried several – they have used 20-mm, 23-mm and 37-mm cannon in their fighters.

Conventional designs of aircraft cannon lacked the really high rate of fire that fighter pilots wanted. A fierce combat gives very little time to a pilot to aim and fire. He wants to be able to fire a maximum weight of slugs in minimum time.

There are two apparent ways to solve this problem, and the United States and Europe took different paths. The European developments generally were based on the revolving chamber concepts that were evolved by Mauser in Germany during the Second World War. The United States reached back into history to the Gatling gun, a 19th Century field weapon with a multiple barrel. The six barrels rotated and fired as they came opposite the breech mechanism. The Gatling patents were a basis for the modern 20-mm Vulcan cannon with an awesome rate of fire which reaches 6000 rpm.

But while these developments were going on, significant changes were being made in overall fighter armament concepts. For one thing, the guided and unguided rockets were beginning to come into their own. By the mid-1950s, just a few short years after the start of the Korean war, the first air-to-air guided missiles began to appear. Early guidance methods were improved, and homing missiles evolved, able to fly unerringly towards an enemy by reading his radar reflection, or his infrared signature, and homing on it.

It was only a matter of time until the nuclear weapons that had once filled bomb bays were reduced in size to fit into the warheads of air-to-air missiles. Unguided, because their lethal radius was so great that guidance would have been gilding the lily, these weapons were carried as standard armament on USAF interceptors for many years. They since have been replaced by a further updating, a smaller nuclear device in a guided weapon.

In fighter-against-bomber combat, the fighter held the speed advantage for many years. The standard way to shoot down a bomber was to approach from the rear in a tail chase, or a curve of pursuit as it was more elegantly called. The fighter pilot kept the nose of his aircraft bearing on the enemy target, and when he was within range of the bomber, the bomber was within range of him, and he was often met with a blast of fire from the enemy.

Obviously the curve of pursuit had drawbacks as a fighter tactic. But to replace it with anything else would seem to call for superhuman skill in piloting, because from any other approach angle, the speed differentials in the approach and the rapidly changing bearing of the target made hitting it more a matter of luck than skill.

The Germans developed a different tactical manoeuvre: they flew their jet interceptors in a line abeam at right angles to the bomber stream, and fired salvos of unguided rockets into the stream. They had to be successful; the densities of the bomber stream and the rocket salvos were so high that missing was impossible.

This technique was refined for single interceptors after the war. Armed with unguided rockets, the interceptor would fly against its target on an intersecting path, called a lead-collision course, heading for the point in the sky where the bomber would be when the interceptor's missiles got there. This called for skill in piloting and firing, and it was inevitable that a simple computing sight would be developed for this particularly difficult situation.

But the unguided rocket was short-lived, and was soon replaced by a guided missile with a brain of its own. It could change course to match any last-second evasion by the bomber, and it was infinitely more accurate than the unguided rockets.

In a sense, then, armament for the fighter-against-bomber combat evolved from an airplane carrying guns to a two-stage missile. The first stage, of course, is the

A US Navy F-14 Tomcat with its load of Phoenix missiles. In 1973 a world record was set when a Phoenix scored a hit on a supersonic jet drone at 126 miles range. They were introduced into service in 1973/74

Republic F-105D Thunderchief
This long-range fighter-bomber typifies the weight of armament carried by modern combat planes
 Crew: 1 *Powerplant:* 1 Pratt & Whitney J75-P-19W, 17,200 lb thrust *Span:* 35 ft
Length: 64·2 ft *Weight:* 38,034 lb
Armament: 1 × 20-mm cannon; 8000 lb internal plus 6000 lb external ordnance load
Speed: Mach 2·1 at 36,000 ft

Supermarine Scimitar
This naval fighter was a victim of the swing towards missiles in the late 1950s, when its original armament of four 30-mm cannon was replaced by four Sidewinder missiles
 Crew: 1 *Powerplant:* 2 Rolls-Royce Avon 202, 11,250 lb thrust each *Span:* 37·1 ft
Length: 55·3 ft *Weight:* 27,000 lb
Armament: 4 × 30-mm cannon
Speed: 710 mph at 10,000 ft

carrying airplane; the second stage is the guided weapon which delivers the warhead.

Fighter-fighter combat was and remains different. No matter how carefully planned are the tactics, and no matter if the first salvos are made on a lead-collision intercept basis, the contact soon swings into a swirling dog-fight, with the simple objective of getting on the enemy's tail. In the Korean war and subsequently, typical fighting ranges were on the order of 500 to 750 yards; beyond those ranges, the chances of kills were greatly reduced.

With guided missiles, that range could be increased greatly; ranges of several thousand yards were thought of as typical for the missiles. And so, fighter designs switched to an armament of all missiles, and the cannon was considered obsolete. Air-to-air missiles, either with radar or infrared homing, were further developed and became the standard weapons to the exclusion of anything else.

And then there was another war, in Southeast Asia, and there it became obvious that a gun was an absolute necessity for air-to-air combat. Missiles did not do so well at short ranges. And there were times when the enemy fighters did not stay off at long ranges, as they so often had in Korea – this time, the enemy fighters were eager to

Most modern jet fighters have some strike capability: here a Phantom drops napalm over Vietnam

close for combat. In such situations a fighter pilot calls for guns – and fast. The answer was supplied in the form of external podded guns that could be hung below the wings of fighters for either air-to-air combat or strafing ground positions.

Those external stores, of course, slow the fighter, and may even reduce its manoeuvrability considerably, so they were not the ideal solution. Further, the guns were distant from the pilot, robbing him of that aiming feeling that he normally has with guns on the fuselage centreline. Finally, unless the pods were unusually rigid, and rigidly mounted, they might deflect enough under the loads of firing to increase the scatter and degrade the accuracy of the burst. At best the pods were a temporary solution for fighter-fighter combat.

As one result of the Vietnam action, guns have been reintroduced into USAF fighters where they had been lacking. (The Navy had never given them up.) Nor did most designers succumb to the siren call of the missiles. Very few European and Russian fighters have been built during the last 30 years around a missile battery only.

As the weapons progressed from form to form, so did the rest of the armament system. Gunsights, which were simple optical types with a lead-angle computer in early jet fighters, soon added more and more semi-automatic features. Today, firing controls range from the nearly automatic to the automatic. In a modern interceptor, it is possible for the pilot to find, fix and destroy his target without ever seeing it, or initiat-

ing any action except arming the system and the weapons. The automatic systems on board have searched for the target, found it, locked on to it, computed its position, corrected the aircraft course, moved into firing position, released the weapon, and confirmed the destruction of the enemy target, and all without the touch of the pilot's hands.

For interception missions, this is the future, as well as the present, until the unmanned guided missiles take over completely. For air-to-air combat between fighters, the trend is back to the automatic cannon with a high rate of fire, like the Vulcan. For fighter against bomber, the future is the same as that of the interceptor.

For the common foray against ground targets, there are whole packages of weapons that can be loaded under the wings.

Future fighters will continue to be armed as in the past. They will carry a single cannon battery with a high rate of fire, and probably a pair of long-range dog-fight missiles. They will have strong points under the wing and fuselage for a variety of external weapons. The fire-control systems will be advanced and semi-automatic, with an automatic mode for intercept or all-weather missions. Sighting data will be shown on the windshield in a head-up display.

The second half of this book traces the development of the manned jet bomber from its early beginnings in the last days of the Third Reich up to the present day. The order is chronological, with the reference date being either the first flight of the bomber prototype, or the development aircraft that immediately preceded it.

With few exceptions, the aircraft here described were designed from the start as bombers. And with two exceptions, all of them were originally designed around gas turbines for jet propulsion.

Powering a fighter with jet engines is one thing: thrusting a bomber through the air with them is quite another. The useful load for a fighter is small, or it was then: some guns and ammunition, and fuel enough to enable it to defend a small area near its home base. A bomber, on the other hand, had to carry a load of bombs, equipment to drop them, large quantities of fuel to reach enemy targets behind their front lines and guns to defend itself . This added up to thousands of pounds, instead of the few-hundred-pound load of the fighter.

To carry several thousand pounds of load required an aeroplane at least three times as heavy when empty. The Avro Lancaster, for example, normally carried an 8000-lb bombload on long missions. Empty, it weighed about 37,000 lb. The Boeing B-29 carried 10,000 lb on its long-range raids, and weighed 70,000 lb empty.

These were piston engined bombers, the best of their day, and as efficient a pair of load carriers as could have been built in their time. They were powered by four of the most powerful piston engines available. So a jet bomber would need multiple engines and – since jet engines burned at least twice as much fuel per thrust horsepower as did a piston engine – they would also need at least double the fuel load. The sums worked against early development of jet bombers with load or range comparable to those of piston-engined equivalents.

That's one reason the jet bomber was slow in arriving on the scene, and why its development had to wait for several new concepts in technology to be discovered.

JET BOMBERS
THE STARTING PLACE

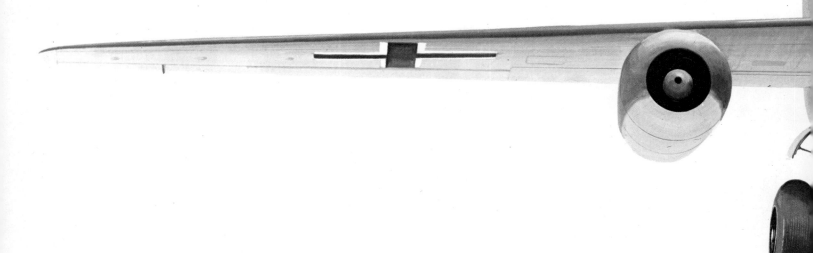

The advanced German aeronautical technology that spawned the jet engine and the fighter also gave birth to the jet bomber. But in contrast to the relatively major success enjoyed by the fighter programme, the jet bombers made little or no contribution to the long-range development of jet aircraft, or to the advancement of aeronautical technology.

This probably was due to Germany's wartime aeronautical policy, primarily one of whims, favouritism and offhand decisions. It is remarkable how much was accomplished, given the atmosphere of the times, the dreams and eccentricities of Hitler and the sycophantic officials around him.

The jet bomber programme did not produce a major striking force capable of inflicting telling damage on Allied targets. As an operational achievement, then, it was a complete failure. But as a technical achievement, it had some bright spots of interest to the historian of things aeronautical. One of these was the Arado 234, the world's first jet bomber.

16 June 1943:

Arado Ar 234 V-1

The surprise German offensive through the Ardennes in December 1944 – the Battle of the Bulge – was the last major strike by combined forces of the Third Reich. Backing up the infantry and armoured units was every available aircraft the Germans could get into the air. Fighters and fighter-bombers flew ground-support missions as often as possible in the foul weather that dogged that offensive. They tangled with Mustangs and Tempests, Thunderbolts and Spitfires, in swirling dogfights or high-speed passes at low levels.

But there was a new sound in the skies over the Ardennes, and it came from jet engines. The Germans had committed their new jet fighter-bombers to that action, and among them were the aircraft of *Kampf-geschwader* 76.

KG 76 recently had completed training on the Arado 234B, a sleek twin-jet bomber, and they were taking the aircraft into operation for the first time. Streaking down in a gentle dive from the leaden skies, the Arados dropped their bombs against targets in the Allied lines.

Who dropped the first bomb from that first jet bomber may never be known. But that action, around the Ardennes, was the first in which jet bombers, designed as such, were committed to action against an enemy force.

The results were inconclusive. The maximum bomb load that could be carried by the Arado was about 2000 lb, essentially the same as the bomb load of the USAAF's Thunderbolts. The Arado's asset was its speed, which made for more difficulties on the bomb drop but which gave definite advantages in getting away from encounters with Allied fighters.

The first interceptions ended when the Arados accelerated away from their pursuers while taking an abnormal amount of hits from Allied machine-guns and cannon. This may have been due to the slightly heavier construction of jet aircraft, but it may have been because the bullets were striking at very shallow angles in the tail chase, and glancing off without doing much damage.

The war ended before the Arados really could show their abilities. More than 200 were built and there were plans to build them by the hundreds. But those plans were ended by the final destruction of Germany, and the bomber version must be judged as unsuccessful in terms of what it accomplished for the expended effort.

It was a fine design, using conventional aerodynamics and a pair of jet engines in clean underwing nacelles to achieve its performance. The original intention was to produce a high-altitude reconnaissance aircraft, and it was in that role that the Arado 234 Blitz (Lightning) was best employed. It flew an experimental series of high-altitude photographic missions over the beaches during and after the invasion of Normandy, and made other runs over Allied installations at its operating altitudes above 30,000 ft. But the reconnaissance role is outside the scope of this history.

The designers tried to strip all useless weight from the airframe to give the Blitz maximum performance. One of the useless things, they decided, was the landing gear. They planned to have the aircraft mounted on a takeoff trolley, jettisoned after the takeoff. Landing would be done on a skid gear mounted to the belly. Weight and drag savings had been calculated to be considerable. But using the belly in this way meant that no bomb could be carried underneath, and Hitler wanted every new aircraft to be a bomber or a fighter-bomber. So the prototype 234 was redesigned as a high-level bomber, with retractable landing gear and a bomb snuggled up against its belly in a recess that partially submerged the weapon.

It was a single-place bomber, with a unique control system for the bomb run. A standard level-flight bombsight was mounted in the nose of the aircraft behind an optically flat glazed panel. Further back was the cockpit. Before the bomb run the pilot trimmed the aircraft for steady flight, swung his control stick to one side and moved forward into the bombardier position, to lie face down and fly the airplane through the automatic pilot circuits of the bombsight.

A variety of bombs could be carried under the belly, from a single 2200-pounder to a cluster of incendiaries or fragmentation bombs. Auxiliary fuel tanks could be mounted under the engines; but if they were not used, 1100-lb bombs could be carried, one under each nacelle. The alternative method of bomb-dropping was in a shallow dive, typical of the standard fighter-bomber attack. Rocket packs were developed to assist the takeoff of the heavily loaded Blitz, and were used whenever the maximum bomb and fuel load were carried.

Developments of the Arado as long-range bomber, reconnaissance aircraft and night-fighter, with two or four engines and various special equipments, were planned, and were in various stages of development when Germany's surrender brought them to a halt.

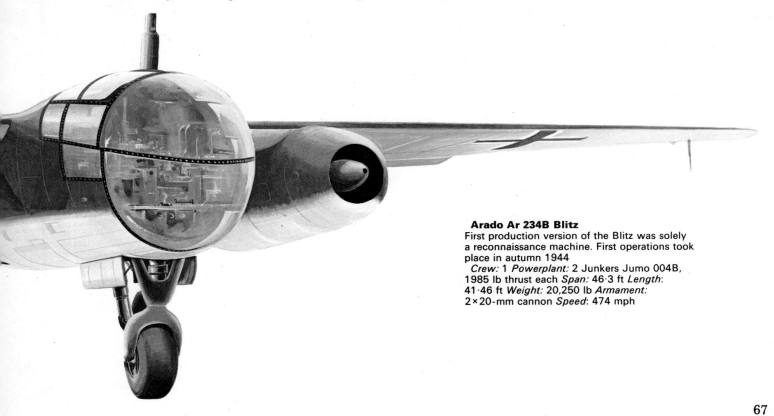

Arado Ar 234B Blitz
First production version of the Blitz was solely a reconnaissance machine. First operations took place in autumn 1944
Crew: 1 *Powerplant:* 2 Junkers Jumo 004B, 1985 lb thrust each *Span:* 46·3 ft *Length:* 41·46 ft *Weight:* 20,250 lb *Armament:* 2×20-mm cannon *Speed:* 474 mph

Junkers Ju 287V-1
Crew: 2 *Powerplant:* 4 Junkers Jumo 004B,
1985 lb thrust each *Span:* 66·9 ft *Length:*
60·02 ft *Weight:* 44,100 lb *Armament:* 2×13-mm
mg *Speed:* 346 mph

Horten Ho IXV-2
Crew: 1 *Powerplant:* 2 Junkers Jumo 004B,
1985 lb thrust each *Span:* 54·97 ft *Length:*
24·48 ft *Weight:* 18,742 lb *Estimated speed:*
540 mph (Data for Gotha Go 229 are similar)

16 August 1944:
Junkers Ju 287 V-1

This flying test bed was the result of a 1943 study project by Junkers, intended to produce a heavy bomber with performance that would enable it to outrun any known or expected Allied fighter.

Swept wings were then coming into fashion in Germany as a result of theoretical studies and wind-tunnel tests at research institutes, and the first Junkers idea was to sweep the wings back in what would become the standard fashion. But the Junkers team finally elected to sweep the wings forward. They had their reasons.

Sweptback wings have poor low-speed characteristics, which is why they now are adorned with so many aerodynamic tricks. A plain swept wing will have very poor aileron control at low speed because the airflow tends to slide spanwise along the wing. By the time it gets to the tip, the combination of lateral flow and tip stall has just about wiped out that portion of the wing as a lifting and control surface.

By sweeping the wing forward, the Junkers team felt they could overcome this

dead weight would resist the aerodynamic twisting, and would – it was hoped – prevent disaster.

Understandably, nobody wanted to start an aircraft programme without testing this idea. So the Junkers team received an order to build a test vehicle employing the principle and to get it flying as soon as possible.

To do so, they put together a fuselage from the Heinkel He 177 heavy bomber, and the tail assembly from a Junkers Ju 388. The main landing gear was built from Ju 352 components and the nosewheels were salvaged from captured USAAF B-24 bombers. The wing of course was completely new, fabricated by Junkers to their own design.

Since the wing was to be typical of the final bomber proposal, it only carried two engines. But the huge test aircraft needed more power to get off the ground, and another pair of engines was mounted, one on each side of the forward fuselage. Still more thrust for takeoff came from podded rocket powerplants attached beneath each wing nacelle and jettisoned after takeoff.

abbreviation for *Versuchsmaschine*, or research machine. V-1 therefore would be the first research aircraft, or prototype, V-5 the fifth, and so on.) This aircraft was to be built and tested as a glider, which was the primary field of Horten expertise.

It flew during 1944, and work continued on a second prototype to be powered by a pair of Junkers 004B turbojets. It was built of wood except for a welded steel-tubing structure at the centre section and the engine bay area. It was covered with plywood, except for the surfaces around the engine, which were protected with the standard firewall steel panels used in German aircraft.

It was decided that the Hortens needed industrial assistance with their project, and so development of the Ho IX was handed over to Gothaer Waggonfabrik, designers and producers of the famous Gotha bombers during the First World War. Gotha had been active in aviation since then as a developer of troop-carrying gliders and as a sub-contractor for the German aircraft industry.

The Gotha team made some changes,

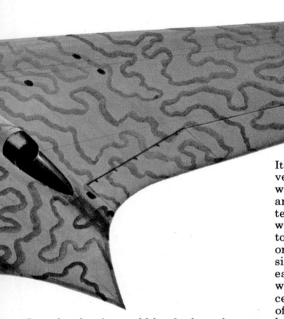

obstacle; the tip would be the last place to stall, and the lateral control should stay available. True – but there was a disadvantage.

Consider what happens when the wing starts to bend upward under gust loads. A swept-back wing tends to flex so that its trailing edge, near the tip, bends up more than the leading edge. In other words, the wing twists when it bends. In swept-back wings, that twist-when-bent is kept from being disastrous because the airflow tries to blow the trailing edge down again.

In a swept-forward wing, things are reversed. The leading edge of the wing tends to bend up higher than the trailing edge, and the airflow wants to get underneath the leading edge and increase the wing twist. When that happens, the wing twists more and more and is literally ripped off the fuselage.

But there are ways to prevent this. One of the most useful is to hang weights on the wings in key locations to resist the twist. Jet engine nacelles are such weights, and so the Ju 287 was designed with single nacelles, well out along the span. Their

Surprisingly, the test vehicle flew well. It was intended only for low-speed investigations, and whatever other flights were necessary to measure wing performance within the limited speed range of the test aircraft. Meanwhile, a second prototype was being developed for high-speed tests, to be powered by six jets instead of the four or less envisioned for the final design. The six were clustered in two nacelles of three each, with a triangular cross-section, and were mounted with their weight concentrated well ahead of the torsional axis of the wing. The Junkers designers had learned where to put the weight to counter the wing twist.

Construction had begun on a third prototype, and plans were at hand for the start of a pre-production run when advancing Russian troops arrived in the area and seized the aircraft and the designers. Both prototypes were taken to Russia and – so the story goes – were flown there in a test programme. But there is no further evidence of any Russian interest in the Ju 287's peculiar swept-forward wing geometry.

Late January 1945:
Horten Ho IX V-2

The most daring of all the German jet bomber designs was a flying wing, developed by the Horten brothers who had achieved fame as designers of elegant flying-wing sailplanes.

Like most devotees of drag reduction, the Hortens thought in terms of speed, and fighters. So the first approach to their ninth design was to consider it as a jet-propelled fighter. They drew plans for a first prototype, the Ho IX V-1. (German identification of prototypes used the V-number designation; V in this case was the

converting the Ho IX to a fighter-bomber. On that basis, the new aircraft – redesignated Gotha 229 – is included in this history.

Gotha began a prototype line, which included an all-weather fighter and a trainer version as well as the fighter-bomber, and the Horten brothers continued to work to complete their powered prototype. That aircraft, the Horten IX V-2, flew a very conservative flight research programme, gradually working up from the low-speed end of the spectrum to higher speeds. By the spring of 1945 it was ready for high-speed tests, and did achieve one run at close to 500 mph. But in the approach to the field after that test, one engine flamed out, and the aircraft slammed into the ground in a ball of flame.

The programme never progressed further. The Gotha prototypes were not completed in time to fly before the end of the war, although one of them was almost ready when the factory was reached by Allied troops advancing into Germany.

Had the war lasted longer, there might have been other designs to describe. The combination of jet propulsion, new radar, sweepback and other technological advances had spurred German designers to a wide variety of proposed aircraft. And given Hitler's desire to see bombs strapped under the wings of everything that could fly, one must assume that bomber and fighter-bomber designs would have proliferated.

But they didn't, and that is perhaps the fortunate aspect of the German jet bomber programme. It only produced a limited number of operational bombers of one model, plus two flying prototypes of two others. In no sense did it make a major contribution to aeronautical progress.

THE CLASS OF '47

Streams of piston engined bombers being attacked by jet-powered fighters was a prospect too unpleasant to contemplate, and in mid-1944 the USAAF gave the go-ahead for a development programme that was to produce the first crop of postwar jet bombers – the 'Class of '47'

There was no doubt that the jet age had arrived. The ingenious, last-ditch German designs for bombers, night-fighters and interceptors had clinched the argument. The day of the reciprocating engine was well and truly over.

But the war wasn't, and there was an obvious need for the performance of those last products of Third Reich science to be matched, not only by counter-air fighters but also by their primary targets, the bombers.

The thought of a slow-moving bomber stream, harassed by darting fighters, was most unpleasant to strategic planners. Not all of them believed that the war would be brought to an abrupt and chilling conclusion by nuclear weapons, and few suspected the extent of the internal disintegration of Germany. So the word went out to get going fast on jet engine development, and on fighter and bomber designs using the new type of engines. Fighters were the first to benefit, with early engine design, development and production earmarked almost exclusively for them.

A few months after the initial successes of the jet fighter programme in the United States, its military and industry turned their attention to jet bomber development.

Not much could be done to modify existing types; replacing piston engines with jets on a Boeing B-29 just would not pay off in performance.

There was one possible design conversion from piston power to jet thrust: the Douglas XB-42 pusher bomber. But what really gave jet bomber design its initial impetus was an Air Materiel Command (USAAF) competition in mid-1944. It called for a jet bomber to carry a mixed bomb load, up to a single 22,000-lb 'county buster' bomb, and with the ability to drop it from a height of 40,000 ft.

Four competitors were chosen to design, build, and fly experimental prototypes: Boeing, Convair, Martin and North American. All their aircraft first flew during 1947, consequently becoming known to aviation history as the 'Class of 1947'.

In any typical American graduating class, one graduate was most likely to succeed – the star in this case being the radical Boeing B-47, last of the four to fly and really in a class by itself. (It will be described in the next chapter.) Then, late in the war, the Air Materiel Command gave the nod to Northrop for conversion of two piston-engined YB-35 flying wing bombers to jet power. That programme produced the YB-49 and the YRB-49A, both technical achievements, both operational duds.

This is the story of the Class of 1947.

17 May 1946:
Douglas XB-43
First jet bomber to fly in the United States, the Douglas XB-43 was a development of a piston-engined pusher predecessor, the Douglas XB-42. That aircraft, nicknamed the 'Mixmaster' because of its rear-mounted counter-rotating propellers, was the culmination of a major engineering effort. The goal was to develop a smaller, lighter and cheaper bomber capable of doing the job of

heavyweights like the Boeing B-29, which was just entering service.

Early studies convinced Douglas that only a radical approach to aerodynamic layout would meet this goal. They settled on the pusher propeller scheme to leave the laminar-flow wing clean and free of any flow distributors such as portly engine nacelles. They picked a fairly high aspect ratio to reduce one component of drag, and they worked on the wing to make it a high-lift section and to perform at the low-speed end of the scale as well as at the high.

The first figures were exciting. Compared to the B-29 the Douglas design would carry a 2000-lb bomb load for more than 5000 miles, and burn only about 30% of the fuel needed by the bigger bomber. Further, the little bomber would be handled by a much smaller flight and ground crew and would cost less to buy and maintain.

A pair of prototypes were built and flown. They proved most of the basic points of the design, but failed to meet all requirements: the bomb load was much less because the airframe was overweight.

But time was running out for the reciprocating engine and the Douglas XB-42 was transformed into a hybrid aircraft with both piston and jet engines. The jets were little Westinghouse engines slung out board, one under each wing, and – as is obvious with hindsight – the airplane was a dog. The performance was not much better with the jets. But this is getting ahead of the story, because the hybrid XB-42A did not fly until much later than the XB-43. It is included here to show the continuity of the programme.

In October 1943 the Air Materiel Command met with Douglas and worked out an agreement for an all-jet version of the XB-42. Douglas first had to choose between two engines, both originally developed by

Douglas XB-43
Crew: 3 *Powerplant:* 2 General Electric J35-GE-3, 4000 lb thrust each *Span:* 71·17 ft
Length: 51·42 ft *Weight:* 40,000 lb
Bombload: 8000 lb *Speed:* 515 mph

General Electric: the I-40, a 4000-lb thrust centrifugal-flow unit that owed many of its features to the early British Whittle engines, and the TG-180, an axial-flow engine also rated at 4000 lb of thrust.

Douglas preferred the slimmer TG-180 and revised the XB-42 airframe to take the jet engine. The new aircraft was designated XB-43 and the resemblance between it and its predecessor was remarkable. To all intents and purposes, the piston engines of the XB-42 had been replaced by the jets of the XB-43.

On 17 May 1946, after two taxi runs with short hops on each, the XB-43 first flew. By the time it had logged just under 13 flight hours it had been flown faster than 500 mph, the 'magic' speed for those days.

But engine delays plagued the programme, slowing the delivery of the second prototype, and the XB-43 never reached its planned production status. The second prototype flew almost one year after the first and it served for a variety of test purposes at Muroc Army Air Base (later Edwards AFB).

17 March 1947:
North American XB-45 'Tornado'
Overshadowed by the faster and more numerous Boeing B-47, the North American B-45 has never received the full credit for its contributions to the development of jet bombardment in the USAF. But during its relatively short service life, it established a number of significant firsts that pioneered the strategic and tactical bombardment techniques of the jet age.

It was the first operational jet bomber in the United States Air Force. In March 1949 the first B-45A aircraft were accepted by the 84th and 85th Bombardment Squadrons of the 47th Bombardment Wing, and they served with those units for at least eight years.

It was the first jet aircraft to be refuelled in the air. During a test flight, the second RB-45C joined with a Boeing KB-29B 'flying boom' tanker to take on fuel in the first demonstration of this particular type of air-to-air refuelling.

It was the first jet bomber to drop a nuclear device.

And it served in a limited role as a jet reconnaissance aircraft in combat. During 1951, a pair of RB-45C aircraft were sent on detached duty to Korea to gain combat experience for the type. MiGs were faster and more manoeuvrable, and they shot up the slower and clumsier RB-45Cs. That first combat experience led to a restriction to flights with fighter escort only. The prohibition was later extended to forbid any daylight reconnaissance runs into north-western Korea's infamous 'MiG Alley'.

North American's 130th design was entered in the mid-1944 competition, and was planned around the axial-flow TG-180 jet. This engine had a smaller diameter than the I-40 of the same thrust rating. Obviously, a multiple engine installation would be necessary to get the required performance.

North American stayed with the kind of design it knew well: unswept, tapered laminar-flow wings, and structure built in the conventional manner. Its simple appearance belied its performance requirements. That smallish airframe was to carry a 22,000-lb 'county-buster' bomb, or the new nuclear weapons in unspecified number and weight, or large numbers of 500-lb bombs. It was required to drop these weapons accurately, by radar or visual means, from a bombing altitude of 40,000 ft. Its limit speed was expressed in terms of Mach number, the ratio of that speed to the speed of sound. The B-45 was one of the first aircraft to have its limit speed so defined, and it was set at Mach 0·76, or 76% of the speed of sound.

The first XB-45 – three had been ordered, two for flight and the third for static tests on the airframe – first flew on St Patrick's Day 1947. It was the first of the Class of '47 to take to the air.

The Air Force liked the results of that first flight and subsequent testing, even though the XB-45 and its crew were lost in a tragic accident early in the test programme. A production run was ordered, and the first model B-45A was built in two slightly different versions. The first production block of B-45A-1 aircraft was powered by Allison-built J35-A-9 and -11 turbojets. The second block of B-45A-5 aircraft was powered by General Electric J47-GE-7 and -9 engines. The total order for the A model was 74, and all these early aircraft went to Air Training Command and Tactical Air Command.

The C models were equipped with in-flight refuelling plus other changes, but their basic performance was unchanged. After the first ten C models had been produced, the Air Force told North American to finish the production run by modifying the remaining C models to a reconnaissance configuration. As RB-45C-1, the last 33 to be built were extensively changed internally. They were almost totally rebuilt for camera installations, including some that used new and different techniques for low-level high-speed photography.

The B-45s served well and long, and generally in a minor role. But for several years they were the only jet strategic deterrent force on station in Europe with the NATO forces, and they played that vital part well. But by 1958 they were being replaced in service, and the first were finding their way to the scrap heap.

2 April 1947:
Convair XB-46
This was a lovely aircraft, with sleek, extended lines in its fuselage, and a long wing with a high aspect ratio. Inside its cylindrical belly was space for a 22,000-lb county-buster, or a mix of nuclear and non-nuclear weapons. A tail turret, mounting a pair of ·50-cal machine-guns remotely fired by radar control, was the only defensive armament to protect its three-man crew.

But its beauty was only skin deep. The Convair design was slow, or slower than other aircraft in that 1944 competition, and so it never reached production. Only a single prototype was built, and the money for the second and third prototypes was shunted into another unbuilt Convair design, the XB-53, a proposed jet bomber with swept-forward wings like those of the wartime German Ju 287.

With the same powerplants as the North American XB-45, the Convair entry was some five tons heavier. That reduced its performance below that of the XB-45, and the latter aircraft was chosen in preference.

22 June 1947:
Martin XB-48
The third straight-winged member of the Class of '47 was the Martin XB-48. Its high-mounted, thin wing featured a high aspect ratio, although not quite so high as that of the Convair XB-46. Six jet engines were tucked under the wing, three to a side, in what looked like individual nacelles but which were actually integrated installations with contoured cooling passages between the engines.

This thin wing left no room for biging solution to a tough problem, and was probably worth the cost of the entire programme.

21 October 1947:
Northrop YB-49

Although chronologically the Northrop flying wing YB-49 fits into the Class of '47, it was a very different aircraft, and was not an entry in the 1944 competition. It was basically a jet version of two of the 15 YB-35 piston-engined flying wing bombers developed by Northrop under contract to the Army. Further, the YB-49 was about twice the weight of its smaller contemporaries and was designed for much greater load capacity, range and crew requirements.

The fundamental premise was that a flying wing was all load-carrying ability with minimum drag. In the centre was the accommodation for the crew, with full stations for pilot, co-pilot, flight engineer, navigator, radio-operator, bombardier and gunner. Off-duty rest space was provided in the 'fuselage', a fairing behind the crew area. On either side of the crew compartment were three bomb bays, separated two and one by a bay for the landing gear. Fuel tanks filled the wings.

The obvious difference between the YB-35 and YB-49 designs was the replacement of the counter-rotating propellers and piston engines of the former with the eight Allison jets of the latter. But the pusher propellers had also functioned aerodynamically as

Prototype of the USAF's first operational jet bomber, the North American XB-45

wheeled landing gear, and so the ingenious Martin engineers designed a tandem, dual-wheeled landing gear and installed it, bicycle fashion, in the fuselage. Wing outriggers were used to handle the low-speed and turning situations. The gear was tested earlier by Martin on a converted B-26H piston-engined bomber, nicknamed the 'Middle River Stump Jumper'. (Middle River was the location of the Martin plant near Baltimore, Maryland.)

Whether it was the tandem gear or the bomb load of 22,000 lb, or both, the fuselage of the XB-48 was bulky and ungraceful.

Like the others in its class, the XB-48 was to be flown by a three-man crew, and defended by a pair of remote-controlled ·50-cal machine-guns in the tail. Two prototypes were funded, but there is no record whether or not both were flown; only the first is documented to any extent.

The XB-48 eventually was chalked up as another learning experience. It scored a modest first by being the first six-jet aircraft to be built and flown. It is probably fair to credit its tandem landing gear layout with setting a fashion that the Boeing XB-47 was to use also. That was an ingenious engineer-

The XB-45 is given a thorough polish in front of Dakotas, a Beech transport and a row of light planes

Tornado in flight. B-45s served as tactical and strategic bombers and as reconnaissance aircraft with the USAF

vertical stabilising area. On the YB-49 the loss of their effect was compensated for by the addition of four vertical flow separators – anyone else would have called them fins – to increase the directional stability.

But apparently these fins were not successful in curing the permanent affliction of the YB-49: dynamic instability. Unofficial reports on the flight tests of the two prototypes indicated that they were continually hunting around one or more axes, seeking but never finding a single stabilised attitude. This ruined the chances of dropping a bomb with any accuracy.

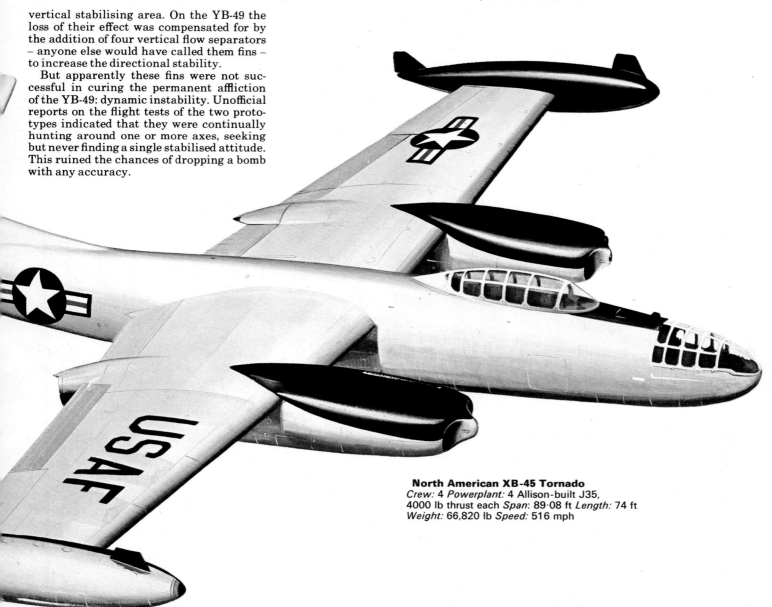

North American XB-45 Tornado
Crew: 4 *Powerplant:* 4 Allison-built J35,
4000 lb thrust each *Span:* 89·08 ft *Length:* 74 ft
Weight: 66,820 lb *Speed:* 516 mph

Smithsonian Institution

Although sleek and graceful, the performance of the Convair XB-46 was not up to standard, and only a single prototype was built

So Northrop proposed to make the YB-49 a reconnaissance bomber, taking advantage of its long range – because of its low drag and, not incidentally, its huge fuel capacity. The Army approved the development of the YRB-49A. That version used four Allison jets mounted internally in the wing, and two hung below the wing in nacelles.

The sole YRB-49A took to the air on 4 May 1950, and it was the last hurrah for

Convair XB-46
Crew: 3 *Powerplant:* 4 Chevrolet-built J35-C-3, 4000 lb thrust each *Span:* 113 ft *Length:* 105·75 ft *Weight:* 91,000 lb *Bombload:* 22,000 lb *Armament:* 2 × ·5-in mg *Speed:* 491 mph

the flying wing. Development was halted after both YB-49 prototypes were lost in crashes, with their crews.

One major point about the flying wing designs was their low wing loading, of the order of 20 lb per square foot. By contrast, other members of the Class of '47 had wing loadings of between 62 and 72 lb per square foot. This made a considerable difference, in take-off and climb performance for

example. The Northrop wings were able to fly from the mile-long runway of Northrop Field, at Inglewood, California, but the other bombers had to operate from the dry lake bed at Muroc Army Air Base because of their 7000–8000 ft take-off distance.

The wings had an interesting and unusual control system, featuring elevons which combined the functions of elevators and ailerons. There were no conventional

rudders; split wingtip horizontal surfaces opened to cause drag at one wingtip or the other, producing the yawing motion typical of rudder application.

They were interesting aircraft, technically speaking, with some unusual design and engineering features. So history records the Northrop flying wing programme as exciting and advanced in the technological sense, but as an operational failure.

The Martin XB-48 is hauled out on its tandem landing gear and wing outriggers at the Martin plant at Middle River, Baltimore

Martin XB-48
Crew: 3 *Powerplant:* 6 Allison-built J35-A-7,
4000 lb thrust each *Span:* 108·33 ft *Length:*
85·75 ft *Weight:* 102,600 lb *Bombload:* 22,000 lb
Armament: 2 × ·5-in mg *Speed:* 516 mph

The first six-jet aircraft to fly, the XB-48 gave the Martin engineers useful experience of jet bomber design

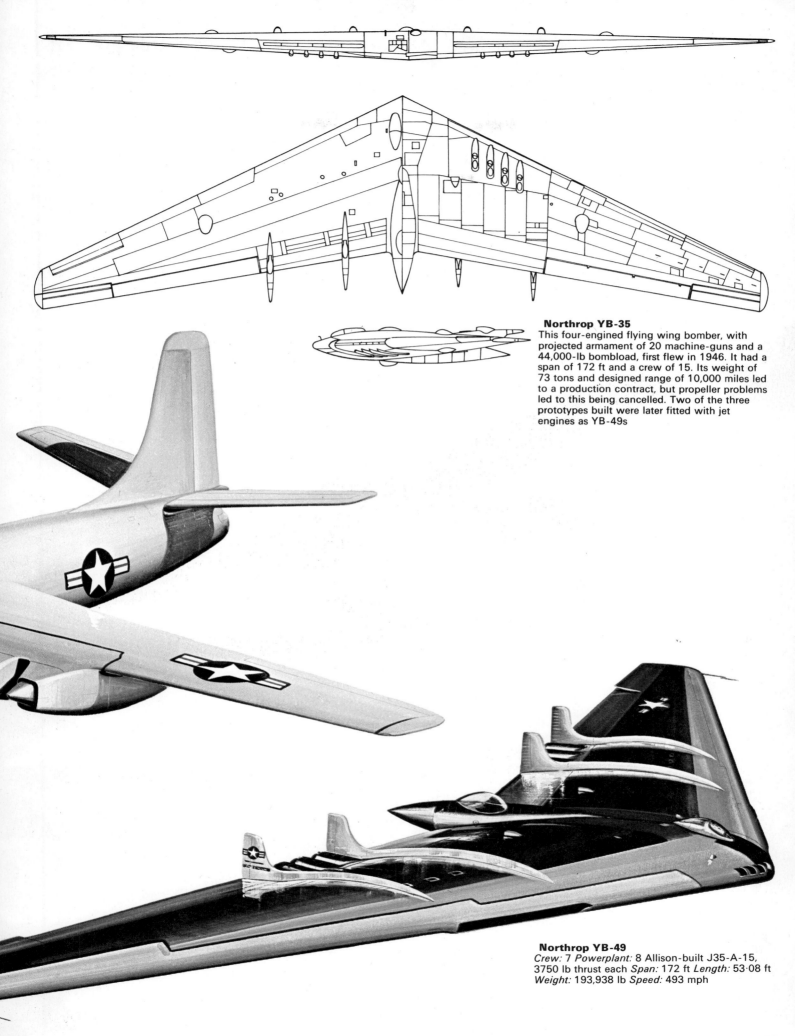

Northrop YB-35
This four-engined flying wing bomber, with projected armament of 20 machine-guns and a 44,000-lb bombload, first flew in 1946. It had a span of 172 ft and a crew of 15. Its weight of 73 tons and designed range of 10,000 miles led to a production contract, but propeller problems led to this being cancelled. Two of the three prototypes built were later fitted with jet engines as YB-49s

Northrop YB-49
Crew: 7 *Powerplant:* 8 Allison-built J35-A-15, 3750 lb thrust each *Span:* 172 ft *Length:* 53·08 ft *Weight:* 193,938 lb *Speed:* 493 mph

IN A CLASS BY ITSELF

Although the Boeing XB-47 Stratojet was, chronologically, a member of the 'Class of '47', it was such a daring exploitation of technology that it deserves to be classed by itself as a milestone in aircraft design

It is probably true to say that the Boeing XB-47 was the first American aircraft to benefit from the wartime studies done in German research institutes on wing sweepback. Although it was beaten into the air by the first flight of the North American XP-86 Sabre, which was both the first US sweptwing fighter and sweptwing aircraft, the difference in time required for the development of a fighter and a bomber almost guaranteed that the smaller Sabre would fly first.

The Sabre lifted off in October 1947; the Boeing XB-47 had been rolled out of the factory the previous month and readied for its first takeoff.

17 December 1947:
Boeing XB-47 Stratojet
The choice of the day was appropriate, though there are those at Boeing who will argue to this day that it was entirely accidental that the XB-47 first flew on the 44th anniversary of the Wright brothers' first flight at Kitty Hawk.

But few would argue the importance of the event, not only to Boeing, but to the USAF and the industry that was then trying to recover from its postwar doldrums. The sleek, sweptback shape – a revolutionary look in aircraft design – was as different from its predecessors as any aircraft had been since that December day in 1903.

It had started as a perfectly conventional design, following the practices that had built the Boeing company. The mid-1944 competition had been preceded by a request from the Army Air Corps during 1943, asking industry to look at designs of jet-propelled aircraft for reconnaissance or bombing. Boeing's first step was the obvious one; they tried to modify the B-29 layout by scaling it down and replacing its piston engines with jets. But this was no good, as they discovered almost immediately.

Subsequent studies resulted in a design with the engines buried in the body. This was as good an arrangement as any, and the Army awarded a first-phase contract to Boeing to work on refining the design. The same kind of contract went to Convair, Martin and North American. Their results are described in the previous chapter.

In the midst of the development programme on the newer Boeing straight-winged configurations, the war in Europe

Boeing B-47E Stratojet
Crew: 3 *Powerplant:* 6 General Electric J47-GE-25, 5970 lb thrust each *Span:* 116 ft *Length:* 107·08 ft *Weight:* 175,000 lb *Bombload:* 18,875 lb *Armament:* 2 × 20-mm cannon *Speed:* 650 mph

began to wind down. The US military then organised systematic searches of German research, development, and production facilities, and took on civilian scientists and engineers as well as military personnel to make these searches and report on what was found.

One of the teams scanning the ruins of Germany's aeronautical research effort included George Schairer, a Boeing engineer whose grasp of new ideas was to be the key to the XB-47 development and to whole generations of aircraft that followed. Schairer saw some of the test data on wing sweepback, studied some of the reports, looked at the wind-tunnel models and put it all together in his mind. The result was a cablegram to Boeing, in effect telling them to drop everything and switch the XB-47 design to a swept-back wing layout.

Sweepback was not a new idea then – it had been openly discussed at technical conferences as far back as 1935. But German scientists had recognised earlier than others that there were advantages in sweepback and that its use could produce a wing design which delayed the onslaught of compressibility. By sweeping the wings back, oncoming air was eased over the wing surfaces much more gently than across a straight wing, and compressibility bubbles did not form until a much higher speed had been reached.

In effect, sweepback fooled the air into thinking it was passing over a much thinner wing. Thick wings are the enemy of air; they cause drag and as the speed increases they force a flow breakdown that causes the phenomenon described as compressibility. Shock waves form, the drag suddenly rises, and there is no way to go any faster.

Thin airfoils have much less drag and disturb the air so much less that they can be used to reach much higher speeds. But thin wings then were difficult to build, and difficult to make strong enough to respond to high flight loads and gusts without failure of the structure.

Boeing knew all this intuitively, and yet they had hesitated to make the big step until prodded by Schairer and the results of the German research. Then their engineers laid out a new design around a swept, graceful wing angled back at 35°, measured at the quarter-chord line, the correct way to define the amount of sweep. Wind-tunnel models were built, using the new wing but retaining the buried engines of the earlier design.

But the military had objections to the buried engines, and there was only one other logical place to put them. So Boeing laid out wing nacelles, paired engines inboard and single engines outboard in the six-jet installation.

Understand the magnitude of the problem. The XB-47 swept wing was as thin as Boeing's knowledgeable manufacturing personnel could guarantee it, but as thick as the stress engineers wanted it for reasons of strength. Nicely balanced between too thick and too thin, the wing was suddenly called upon to handle the installation of six hot, thrusting jet engines with their own and some new aerodynamic loads. It might have defeated the whole concept.

But some unsung hero, or heroes, at Boeing solved the problem by thinking of the engines as damping weights. If they were properly positioned, they could reduce, rather than increase, the tendency of the thin wing to flutter and fail. By locating the engines properly, their dead weight could be used to relieve the bending movements in the wing due to upward air loads. Further, they could increase the torsional stiffness of the wing and minimise the chances of torsional flutter. And that is what happened. Instead of being a liability, the engines served as stress relievers on the wings.

The different wing demanded a different control system. (Spoilers were the primary lateral control surfaces on the B-47 series.) And because the wing was thin, there was no room for the main landing gear. Tandem bicycle gear was chosen, and outrigger wheels were installed for retracting into the inboard engine nacelles.

The early generation of jet engines had really bad characteristics at low airspeeds. They did not accelerate well, and it took a long time to get full power after the throttle was opened all the way. So the takeoff was comparatively long and hazardous. Consequently, additional take-off thrust was built into the XB-47 in the form of 18,000 lb of thrust from 18 auxiliary solid-propellant rocket units.

But that only solved half the slow-speed problem. The other half was that the early jets had no thrust reversers, as they do today. An aborted takeoff almost certainly meant an accident as the aircraft rapidly ran out of runway. Drag on demand was the need, and it was met by another wartime German innovation, the brake parachute. Streamed from the tail of the B-47, the high-speed ribbon chute was the equivalent of lots of thrust reversal and braking power, and it dragged the B-47s to a halt. The addition reduced the accident potential considerably.

The fuel tanks were in the fuselage – if there was no room for landing gear in the wings, there was less for fuel. Late models of the B-47 did have some wing fuel in self-sealing tanks, but the bulk of the fuel was carried in the fuselage, augmented by drop tanks, also carefully located on the wings to minimise their effects on drag, and on spanwise bending and torsional stiffness.

These were the basic design concepts that went into the XB-47: thin, swept wings; nacelles used productively to relieve normal and gusting wing loads; extra installed thrust from rockets, and installed drag from a brake parachute; tandem landing gear and fuel in the fuselage.

The weapons, meanwhile, had not been ignored. There was room in the fuselage for the early hulking nuclear weapons, their steel casings swollen by the moderating materials used to control the rate of the chain reaction.

The two experimental XB-47s went through their test programme; the Air Force liked what it saw and ordered the airplane into production. The first batch was of a service test version, ten B-47A models to be built at Boeing's Wichita, Kansas, plant, and to include a few changes, the most important being more powerful engines.

The first flight of the first B-47A took place almost unnoticed on 25 June 1950. Screaming headlines announced other news: that day the North Koreans had slashed across the border into South Korea and that unhappy conflict was launched.

A combination of events during the

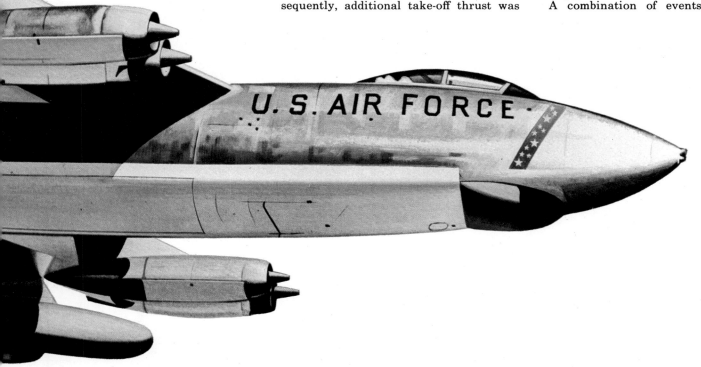

Korean war moved B-47 production to a level of highest national priority. SAC's war-weary B-29 bombers were doing yeoman work in the Korean theatre, but they were far outclassed by the Russian-built MiGs. Only continuing development of tactics and the use of escorts and electronic warfare allowed the B-29s to survive in the hostile skies over Korea.

Jet speed and altitude were essential, and the B-47 programme swung into high gear. Following the pattern of the Boeing B-17 programme, Douglas and Lockheed helped build the newer B-47. Douglas built their versions at Tulsa, Oklahoma and Lockheed operated the huge wartime B-29 bomber plant at Marietta, Georgia. Boeing continued to turn out the B-47 at its Wichita plant, and sent components and personnel out to Douglas and Lockheed in the initial transition stages of their production of the new bomber.

With the A models delivered, the B-47B entered production, and nearly 400 were built before the next major model change was made. Again there was an increase in engine thrust, and in the aircraft weight and performance. The first few models produced by Douglas and Lockheed were B-47B types; the real effort was to come with the next production bomber model.

The B-47E was the high point of the entire series, and more than 1570 were built. Still more powerful engines were featured, and in-flight refuelling ability was included, so that the range of the B-47 was now limited only by the endurance of its three-man crew. That was dramatically demonstrated in November 1954, about three years after the bombers had made their debut with USAF's Strategic Air Command.

On 17 November that year, Col David A Burchinal, then commanding the 43rd Bombardment Wing, took off from the long runway at Sidi Slimane, French Morocco, and headed back to Fairford RAF Station in England, where the 43rd was in the midst of a 90-day rotational tour outside the United States. By the time he was near the RAF base, the local weather had become so bad that Burchinal decided to head back to Sidi Slimane. That also had soaked in while he was airborne.

So Burchinal called for a tanker rendezvous, and decided to wait out the weather. He refuelled nine times in the air before the weather had cleared enough at Fairford to permit final approach and landing. The wheels of the B-47 touched down 47 hours and 35 minutes after they had lifted off the runway in Morocco. During the two-day flight, the B-47 had logged a distance of

Boeing B-47E Stratojet
John Batchelor and the Editor would like to thank the Boeing Company for their help in the preparation of this cutaway illustration

21,163 miles, nearly once around the world at the equator.

Few B-47 flights demanded as much as that one. Most of the time the training missions were accomplished with one refuelling on the outbound leg and one on the inbound.

Just a few months before the first B-47s had entered service with SAC, another Boeing product, the KC-97 tanker, had joined the Command. This combination made SAC a truly global and jet-propelled force. Earlier bombers had the range, but not the speed; the Boeing B-47 had the speed, but not the range. But combined with the KC-97s, stationed around the world at key locations for aerial refuelling, the range of the SAC bomber force was no longer limited.

The Korean truce had been established, but other crises were popping up. In June 1953, East Berlin erupted in a general strike by the workers. It was put down with Russian tanks and troops.

During those eventful weeks, SAC moved its first B-47 wing out of the United States to England on a standard 90-day overseas rotational mission. At the end of the tour, the wing was replaced by a second wing of B-47s, and a third followed that one, establishing a practice that continued until 1958. For five years there was always a combat-ready B-47 wing based in England.

The B-47E was the last 'pure' bomber version of the series to serve with SAC. Later models were primarily reconnaissance aircraft, built for intelligence gathering by photographic and electronic means. They retained a bomber capability, however, and

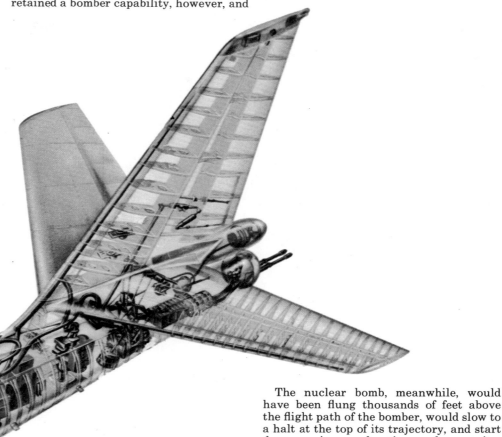

could have been used in that role. But the story of the reconnaissance B-47s, although equally fascinating, is not part of a history of jet bombers.

The original mission of the B-47 was to carry thermonuclear weapons to distant targets and drop them from high altitudes. When tactical considerations and enemy strengths in air defence made a second look at this approach necessary, a new tactic was evolved. The idea was a novel one. The bomber would come streaking in at probably less than 500 ft altitude, heading straight for the target. It would pull up in the start of a loop, and release its nuclear weapon on the upward zoom, in effect tossing it high into the air ahead of the bomber. The bomber would then continue through half of the loop and roll out at the top, breaking for low level again and a speedy departure from the scene.

The nuclear bomb, meanwhile, would have been flung thousands of feet above the flight path of the bomber, would slow to a halt at the top of its trajectory, and start down again, accelerating under gravity. By the time it was at the target, the bomber would be far away, safe from the searing blast of radiation that accompanied the bomb's detonation.

High-altitude and low-altitude flying demand different kinds of design, and the high-altitude B-47 had to be extensively modified to strengthen key structure to take the aerobatic manoeuvre.

The final total of B-47s of all types built exceeded 2000. They served for many years as the United States' credible strategic deterrent. By moving rapidly from the US to foreign bases on redeployment, they could emphasise the presence of SAC and the United States. It was battleship diplomacy brought into the jet age.

The first B-47s were delivered to SAC in October 1951. Only ten were delivered to the Command that year, but by 1958 SAC had equipped 29 full bombardment wings with a total of 1367 B-47 aircraft. They were replaced gradually by the newer and bigger Boeing B-52. But they soldiered on in the reconnaissance role, still able to double as a bomber, until the very last one was flown away to storage on 29 December 1967.

LIGHT TWINS AND LOSERS

Ilyushin Il-28 (Beagle)
Crew: 3 *Powerplant:* 2 Klimov VK-1, 5954 lb thrust each *Span:* 70·36 ft *Length:* 57·89 ft *Weight:* 40,572 lb *Bombload:* 2205 lb *Armament:* 4×23-mm cannon *Speed:* 559 mph

Where the United States was first, Britain, France and Russia were soon to follow: the late 1940s saw the first jet bomber designs in each of those countries – all of them twin-engined, two of them successful and the remaining three doomed to be classed as unfortunate failures

In the early years after the Second World War, Britain, France and Russia also began development of jet bombers for their specific strategic and tactical needs.

In the United States the pace was faster, following a speedier start. But Britain, France and Russia had been hard hit by the war, in complete contrast to the United States, and there were tasks of higher priority than the development of new jet aircraft; people had to be housed and fed, and countrysides and cities had to be rebuilt or repaired. But even in the tightest times there has always been money, some-

where, for armament, and these years were no exceptions.

Five light bombers are described here. One of them, the English Electric Canberra, is deservedly a classic. A second, the Ilyushin 28, is an example of how mediocrity can be utilised, and how a lot of second-class bombers are a greater threat than a few first-class ones. The other three aircraft were, unfortunately perhaps, losers. This chapter tells their stories.

8 August 1948:

Ilyushin Il-28

This long-lived light tactical bomber was Russia's first. It served in both the Soviet air force and navy, and with the military arms of satellite and Russian-influenced countries such as Poland, Czechoslovakia, the German Democratic Republic and China. More recently, it has turned up in the air arms of some African countries.

It has operated in every kind of environment from tropical jungle to Arctic wastes, and has been flown and maintained by pilots and ground crews of every level from intellectual to functional illiterate. It is a basic, simple design built around the conventional structural and aerodynamic practices of the late 1940s.

Design work on the aircraft that was to lead to the 28th Ilyushin design probably

began late in the Second World War, or soon after, when the Russians acquired a large number of German turbojets, technicians, reports and factories as a result of their systematic exploitation of their zones of occupation.

The Russians did not make much progress on the German foundation. But their salvation was at hand in the form of British permission to import a batch of Rolls-Royce Derwent and Nene turbojets. Although these were not the very latest British gas turbine designs, they were current enough

to show a major advance over any of the German-produced engines in the Russians' possession. The deal was welcomed, and it is cursed to this day by some knowledgeable observers for having given the Russians a healthy boost upward in their aeronautical development.

Russian designers welcomed the new powerplants and immediately set to sketching layouts around them. Sergei Ilyushin's design bureau competed with the offices of Andrei Tupolev in trying to meet the requirements of the Soviet air arm for a light tactical bomber powered by a pair of jets. Both bureaus developed their designs and produced prototypes which were evaluated by experienced flight crews who flew both types. The nod went to the Ilyushin aircraft, and it was placed in production.

But first the factory had to meet Stalin's order for 25 of the bombers to parade in the May Day fly-past in 1950 – just about a year away from the date Ilyushin was told his bomber had won the competition. Hammering out 25 new and untried jet bombers, a first in the country, getting them airworthy and training enough flight and ground crews to fly and maintain them for a huge public spectacle was a major accomplishment. Ilyushin's people delivered on time. The bombers might have been nearly empty shells, lacking operational equipment, and they may have been totally unfit for operational duties. But they were in the parade, and they were noticed by Western observers, which is what Stalin might have had in mind.

But it was to be 12 more years before they were really noticed in the West, except by interested military intelligence and technical personnel. The later event occurred during the 1962 Cuban confrontation. The Russians had begun to move missiles into Cuba and to site them in positions where they were obviously a threat to the United States. As if this wasn't bad enough, they

also began shipping in crated Ilyushin bombers, which were uncrated and started through an assembly process at a Cuban airfield. There, photographed by high-flying reconnaissance aircraft from the United States, rows of Il-28 fuselages, crated wings, tails and powerplants told their story. It was a shocking one: a tactical nuclear bombing force was being based 90 miles off the shores of the United States.

The dénouement of that crisis is well-known. The Russians backed down, the Ilyushins were put back in their crates, and left Cuba as deck cargo, photographed again in low-level passes by USN and USAF aircraft checking the contents of freighters leaving Cuban waters for Russian ports.

The Il-28 was a Russian technical success, enabling the rapid build-up and deployment of a strong tactical bombardment force that could have delivered nuclear weapons against any target in the NATO alliance. They were a formidable threat, and they forced some uncomfortable defensive postures and programmes on the West.
1948:

Tupolev Tu-14

The Russians being the way they are, there is little hard data on this contemporary of the Ilyushin 28. Aleksandr Yakovlev's authorised – if not necessarily authoritative – book *Fifty Years of Soviet Aircraft Construction*, makes only a single reference to the '. . . three-engined bomber Tu-14 . . .' Yet pictures of the Tupolev design, which did see limited service with the Russian naval air arm, show it clearly to be similar to the Il-28, with an unswept wing, swept

Tupolev Tu-14 (Bosun)
Crew: 3 *Powerplant:* 2 Klimov VK-1, 5954 lb thrust each *Span:* 70 ft approx *Length:* 65 ft approx *Weight:* 46,297 lb *Bombload:* 6614 lb max *Armament:* 4×23-mm cannon *Speed:* 525 mph

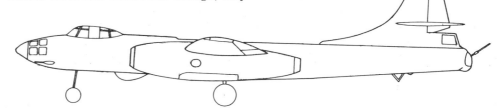

A flight of Ilyushin Il-28 light tactical bombers, still in service with several air forces

tail, and definitely only two powerplants, housed in individual nacelles which are very similar to those of the Il-28.

It is known that the Tu-14, if that is even its correct designation, lost the competition to the Il-28. But a limited quantity was produced anyway, and they went to the Russian navy for torpedo dropping and similar activity.

The torpedo bomber was a casualty of the Second World War. When the war ended, so did the useful life of the type. They were just too vulnerable. So relegating the Tu-14 to this assignment, postwar and in the jet age, was some kind of an admission that it wasn't much of an airplane.

It must have been heavier than the Il-28, and it certainly had inferior performance, otherwise it might have been produced instead of the Il-28. With the same powerplants, and basically the same aerodynamic layout, one expects comparable performance.

Apparently the first deliveries were made to squadrons in 1949. There are a few pictures of the type that have been published, some heavily retouched, others pristine. What the true story is may never be known; for the purposes of this history, let us record that there was once a light bomber design from the Tupolev design bureau. It served with Russian naval units and it faded into history unhonoured and almost unsung.

13 May 1949:

English Electric Canberra

This elegant light jet bomber is the closest approximation to an immortal in its field. Conceived before the end of the Second World War, the Canberra was not to be blooded in combat until the Suez crisis of 1956. Today, it still serves actively in military air units, including those of Great Britain and the United States.

In the years that have passed since its first flight, the Canberra has been used in a number of roles other than the one for which it was originally designed. In them, as in its light bomber task, it has shown outstanding performance.

It started as a replacement for the piston-engined Avro Lincoln heavy bomber, itself a development of the famed Lancaster which was in turn an extrapolation of the ill-fated Manchester bomber. The original requirement was for a high-altitude, high-speed bomber, and it was apparent to the design staff at English Electric, working under the brilliant W E W Petter, that only the then-new jet engine could produce the performance.

But Petter's ideas moved at a faster pace than did the development of the jet engine,

and a continuing iteration process was necessary during the design. The Air Ministry had written Specification B 3/45 to spell out the desired characteristics. It seemed as if a single huge turbojet would do the job. But Rolls-Royce design teams were working at top speed to develop a really new and different jet engine, and it was around the first development of the line that Petter finally froze the basic Canberra.

The Rolls-Royce engines, then designated AJ 65 (referring, no doubt, to an axial-flow jet with a design thrust of 6500 lb), were slim and light, and two of them could be used in partially submerged nacelles out along the wingspan. Petter had selected a large wing area for altitude performance and manoeuvrability, coupled with a low aspect ratio to keep the rolling performance high. The Canberra is one of the most manoeuvrable of aircraft as a result of those basic design choices.

The design was submitted to the Ministry in mid-1945; the Ministry looked, discussed and finally got around to awarding a contract for four prototypes in January 1946. There was still some scepticism in high quarters about the ability of Rolls-Royce to deliver their advanced engines on time, so one of the prototypes was earmarked for the installation of Rolls-Royce Nenes as an alternate powerplant.

The original intention had been to use radar bombing only in the Canberra. But the development of the radar lagged behind that of the aircraft. Consequently, when the Air Ministry awarded a contract for the first bomber version in March 1949, it was for the Canberra B 2, a visual-systems bomber to Specification B 5/47.

The Korean war moved the Canberra high on the list of British priority programmes, along with its Rolls-Royce engine, now named the Avon. Both powerplant and airframe were sub-contracted extensively throughout the British industry.

Early in 1951, the Canberra was chosen to be the standard tactical bomber of the USAF, and negotiations were begun for its manufacture in the United States.

The Royal Air Force received its first jet bombers on 25 May 1951, with deliveries to 101 Squadron to replace its Avro Lincolns. At the peak of its deployment with the RAF, Canberras equipped at least 34 squadrons, including nine that were specifically established to use the type.

Canberras were called to the Middle East in 1956. The seizure of the Suez Canal rang the alarm, and Canberras were deployed from their British bases to stations on Cyprus and Malta. On 31 October the Canberras of No 10 Squadron dropped their first bombs in combat on Egyptian targets in the brief but intense action that marked the Suez war.

Canberras saw combat with the Australian forces in Southeast Asia, flying

Martin XB-51

Crew: 2 *Powerplant:* 3 General Electric J47-GE-13, 5200 lb thrust each *Span:* 53·08 ft *Length:* 85·08 ft *Weight:* 55,923 lb *Bombload:* 10,400 lb *Projected armament:* 8×20-mm cannon *Speed:* 645 mph

sorties against North Vietnamese targets in that air war. They also fought on both sides during the combat between India and Pakistan in 1965, because both countries operated the type.

28 October 1949:

Martin XB-51

The Martin XB-51 was most unconventional. It was loaded with advanced technical features, and that might have been the major reason it never got beyond the prototype stage. Only two were built and both were lost in crashes. Its planned place in production was taken by the Canberra.

The design had begun under an attack designation as one of a group of heavy attack aircraft planned toward the end of the war years. Its intended mission was ground support, the destruction of surface targets by bombs, gunfire, or both. Consequently, the XB-51 was designed with a battery of eight 20-mm cannon in its nose, and a bomb load of 10,400 lb.

Its swept wings had variable incidence, so that the wing could be set for the optimum angle of attack for takeoff, flight and landing. Because of the high wing loading, the layout included large-span flaps. Top-wing spoilers were used for lateral control instead of ailerons, but small ailerons were fitted to give some force feedback into the control system.

The empennage featured one of the first of the high Tee-tail layouts; Martin engineers located the horizontal stabiliser there to keep it out of the wake of the swept wing.

Two XB-51 prototypes were built, flown and in time crashed. That was the end of the programme. Viewed in retrospect, it may have been a case of engineers amusing themselves with an elegant design of little practical value; but that seems to be given the lie by the knowledge that spoiler controls, variable-incidence wings and Tee-tails have since been used on successful aircraft and have proved their value.

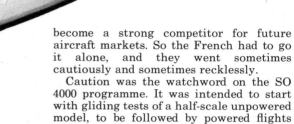

To help the XB-51 get off the ground, four solid-propellant rockets were used to augment the thrust of the three jet engines. And a brake parachute was fitted for reducing speed on landing.

The interesting touch was the bomb bay design. High speeds and flows around open bomb bays had been giving trouble in other aircraft. The bombs literally would not drop out of the bay, but would float there, to the great distraction of the crew. Two Martin engineers invented and patented the rotary bomb-bay door, a structure mounted on a fore-and-aft axis. Before the drop, it was rotated so that its bombs, which were mounted on the inner surface of the structure, were exposed to the air. No hinged doors and no open cavity were there to produce ejection or drop problems. It was a unique approach to a difficult problem, and one which was later to see service on the redesigned Canberras built in the United States as the Martin B-57.

15 March 1951:
SNCASO SO 4000
The postwar French aircraft industry reminded some observers of the excited cavalryman who leaped on his horse and galloped off in all directions. The pent-up dreams of French designers showed in a stream of aircraft, most of which never got beyond the prototype stage.

The SO 4000 was one of a pair of jet bombers that had been chosen, out of the welter of designs available, to be developed for the French Armée de l'Air. Its only competitor was dropped before it reached the prototype stage.

At this point the French industry was making a comeback from the devastation of the war; experimental facilities were lacking, and neither the British nor the Americans were about to help France become a strong competitor for future aircraft markets. So the French had to go it alone, and they went sometimes cautiously and sometimes recklessly.

Caution was the watchword on the SO 4000 programme. It was intended to start with gliding tests of a half-scale unpowered model, to be followed by powered flights with a second half-scale model. This was the only way the French then had of getting aerodynamic data without a huge wind tunnel, which they did not have.

The glider was beaten into the air by the powered model, which first flew in April 1949. In September the glider was launched on its test programme.

The following March the SO 4000 was rolled out and began its ground runs and taxi tests. It was a slick looking aircraft, with its two turbojets mounted side-by-side in its wide-oval fuselage. There didn't seem to be straight lines anywhere on the fuselage, from its forward tandem cockpit for the crew to the flattened elliptical shape that faired around the two engine tailpipes.

The wing was huge, by comparison, and with moderate sweep. Its strange-looking landing gear consisted of four independent main wheels and struts retracting into the wing root, and a high nosewheel gear. During taxi tests, the gear failed; the bomber settled ignominiously to the runway in a shower of sparks and with great grinding sounds. It took the better part of a year to repair the plane.

Daniel Rastel, who had flown the very first French jet aircraft, was the pilot for the first flight, and it turned out to be the only flight of the plane. The flight was successful, and Rastel landed safely. But irreparable harm had been done to the French aircraft development programme by budget cuts as the government found it was living beyond its means. Besides, better and newer ideas were coming along for bomber design.

So the SO 4000 programme was stopped cold. The prototype was wheeled off the ramp and into a corner of the hangar, eventually to be scrapped.

English Electric Canberra B Mk 2
Crew: 3 *Powerplant:* 2 Rolls-Royce Avon 101, 6500 lb thrust each *Span:* 63·96 ft *Length:* 65·5 ft *Weight:* 46,000 lb *Bombload:* 6000 lb *Speed:* 570 mph

NEW PROGRAMMES
TWO NEW
TWO FOR INSURANCE

As the builders of jet bombers gained experience in the years around 1950, significant advances were made in the art of their design. But governments were still wary. Back-up programmes were called for: the Short Sperrin flew in the same summer as the Vickers Valiant, and the Convair YB-60 took to the air within days of the first XB-52

In the late 1940s and early 1950s, three major bomber programmes began to take shape. In Britain, the first specifications leading to the V-bomber programme were drawn up and issued. In the United States, the heavy follow-up to the Boeing B-47 was in design and development. In Russia, the first-generation medium bomber was being designed around native powerplants that were to startle observers in the West.

Two of the bombers to be described in this chapter were new designs, built to specific needs that advanced the art of large jet aircraft: the Vickers-Armstrong Valiant, and the Tupolev 16. And two of them were back-up programmes, insurance against delays or failures in other advanced designs: the Short Sperrin and the Convair YB-60.

The same period saw the high point of heavy jet bomber design, the Boeing XB-52. Because that bomber, like its predecessor, the Boeing XB-47, was – and remains – in a class by itself, it is considered separately.

18 May 1951:
Vickers-Armstrong Type 660 Valiant
The Valiant was developed as an interim bomber to fill the time gap between the RAF's piston-engined bombers and a new generation of jet-propelled, high-altitude V-bombers. The interim stretched to a service life of about ten years, during which Valiants dropped Britain's first nuclear and thermonuclear devices and saw combat in the Suez crisis. They might still be in service if the right model had been produced, or if they had continued to be used in the manner for which they were designed.

The Valiant grew out of a 1946 specification for a high-altitude, high-speed bomber capable of carrying nuclear weapons at speeds approaching that of sound. The major British companies responded with a large collection of designs. Two were chosen for development. A third had been placed under contract to an earlier specification in case the fancier

Vickers Valiant B Mk 1
Crew: 5 *Powerplant:* 4 Rolls-Royce Avon,
10,000 lb thrust each *Span:* 114·33 ft *Length:*
108·25 ft *Weight:* 138,000 lb *Bombload:*
21,000 lb *Speed:* 567 mph

designs did not pan out. The Vickers design was rejected, but management would not accept the refusal, and continued to argue the merits of the Type 660 design.

Yes, it was fairly conventional. But it was powered by the same four Rolls-Royce Avons that were being considered for the advanced bombers. And it had essentially the same speed over the target, the same bomb load, the same available volume for advanced electronic systems for bombing and navigation. All it lacked was the desired unrefuelled range. The arguments were persuasive, finally. A new specification was written around the Type 660 and Vickers went into production.

Two prototypes were built. The first was lost about eight months into its flight test programme, but by then the performance had impressed officialdom and the second prototype was nearing its flight date. The programme was continued, aiming at early service of the B Mk 1 version.

A second type was ordered later, which was intended as a low-level pathfinder bomber. It was the subject of a major re-design to add necessary structure to take the high air loads that result from going fast at low altitudes. It was painted black all over and had a distinctive shape because its wheels rotated to retract into trailing-edge pods. It was a fine performer at low levels, and the B Mk 2, as events proved, was the bomber that should have been ordered into production.

Valiants began to equip RAF units late in 1955, and the force began transition to its first jet bomber capable of serving as a strategic deterrent force. Hardly a year had passed before the Valiants were in action, striking with conventional weapons against Egyptian targets during the Suez campaign. They were the first British bombers to see combat in that brief action.

Meanwhile, a Valiant squadron (No 49) had been involved in the dropping and monitoring of Britain's first atomic bomb at Maralinga, Australia. That drop and the first strike by Valiants at Suez took place on the same day, 11 October 1956. On 15 May of the following year a Valiant from No 49 Squadron dropped the first British thermonuclear device against a target array on Malden Island. Two later drops of the British H-bomb were made, also by Valiants of 49 Squadron.

One measure of the Valiant's capabilities was its placing near the top of the list in the USAF Strategic Air Command's bombing, navigation and reconnaissance competitions. These events, staged on an annual basis by SAC to improve its own capabilities, were opened to British crews by invitation. The Valiant teams did well in their first competition and better in their second.

Early in 1964, the Royal Air Force switched its bombing attack from high- to low-altitude. The change signified that the effective ground-to-air missile had arrived. The change in tactics was evolved to avoid long-range anti-aircraft missiles, and to come in under enemy radar coverage so that there would be no warning time in which to ready the short-range AA defences.

The whole V-bomber force (by then including Vulcans and Victors as well as Valiants) began to operate near the ground at high speed. Any aircraft designed for

Only prototype of the Valiant B Mk 2, designed for low-level pathfinding missions, which first flew on 4 September 1953. Structural strengthening needed for the low-level role involved using underslung pods for the backward-retracting bogie undercarriage

Vickers Ltd

Short SA 4 Sperrin
Crew: 5 *Powerplant:* 4 Rolls-Royce RA 3 Avon, 6500 lb thrust each *Span:* 114·33 ft *Length:* 102·2 ft *Weight:* 115,000 lb *Speed:* 564 mph

high-altitude flight will suffer if it is flown low and fast, and the Valiants were no exception. They had not been designed for this kind of attack; only the single B Mk 2 prototype had been developed for low-level bombing runs – and it had not been ordered.

Predictably, the wing spars began to crack. There was a choice: fix the damage through extensive rebuilding, or scrap the force. The latter decision was made. The entire Valiant force was first grounded and then, in official parlance, 'reduced to produce', which is a nice way of saying that they were sold for junk. They deserved better than that.

10 August 1951:
Short SA 4 Sperrin
This conventional straight-winged jet bomber with an unconventional engine installation was Britain's insurance policy against the failure of its advanced V-bomber programme. Like many insurance policies, it was never needed and the premiums paid were wasted, though fortunately small.

In these days of multi-billion dollar (or pound or franc or rouble) costs for aircraft development, it is interesting to look back at the Sperrin and see that the whole programme cost 3·5 million pounds sterling. That included the design, development, tooling, construction and flight testing of two prototypes. Today, that kind of money will hardly buy a major piece of the Rockwell International B-1.

The Sperrin was designed around a specification dated 1946, but issued in 1948. By that time, the Boeing XB-47 had flown and was in volume production. But the British, showing their first signs of jet lag, opted for low-risk projects at a time when just one daring leap forward might have made all the difference to the state of their aircraft industry today.

Hindsight, however, is a commodity very useful to commentators on history, but unavailable to the planner whose neck is out with every decision.

The Sperrin could have been a piston-engined bomber just as well, with its shoulder-height straight wing, its huge

fuselage, its conventional tail and high ground clearance. But it used four of the newly available Rolls-Royce Avon jets, stacked in an over-and-under installation in two nacelles which were split by the wing.

By the time the Sperrin flew, almost three months after the Valiant, it was already a loser: a loser in terms of production contracts, but definitely not in terms of how smoothly the flight test programme went. The Sperrin had no real troubles; it handled nicely at altitude, showed a fair turn of speed for its size, power and layout and had a substantial range with the equivalent of its intended nuclear weapon.

The second prototype was flown a year later, and both then went into general

flight research, testing new bombing systems and dropping models of proposed bomber missiles. The second prototype was cannibalised in 1956 to repair the first, and a year later the first prototype was grounded, never to fly again, when the experimental engine it was flying on tests was dropped from the list of approved projects.

18 April 1952:
Convair YB-60
Like any other aircraft company, Convair tried to stretch the life of its product line as far as possible. They proposed the B-36G as a sweptwing, jet-propelled version of the gigantic B-36 piston-engined, jet-boosted bomber. It would use almost three-quarters of the parts of a standard production B-36. That would make it a relatively economical project, and the jet engines would give it a major increment of performance. The Air Force approved the idea, and ordered a pair of prototypes in March 1951, giving them the new designation of YB-60.

Convair redesigned the big wing of the B-36, maintaining most of its lines but sweeping it back to the standard 35° mark. They designed a new vertical and horizontal tail, slung eight Pratt & Whitney J57 engines in four nacelles under the wings, and they had a new bomber. Unfortunately,

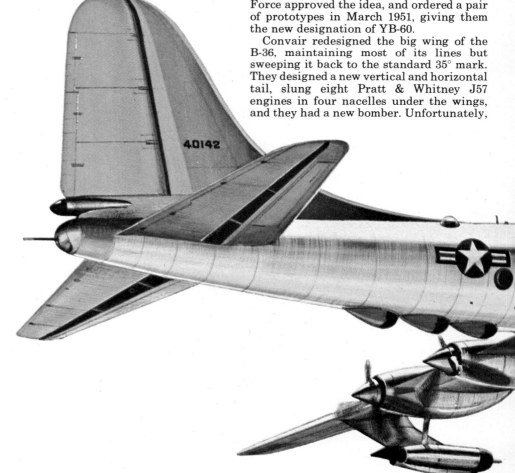

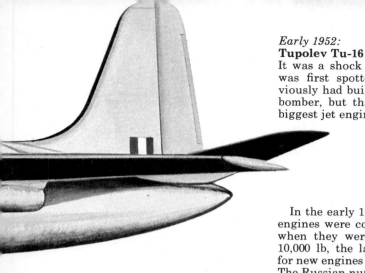

Early 1952:
Tupolev Tu-16

It was a shock to realise, when the Tu-16 was first spotted, that the Russians obviously had built not only a fairly good jet bomber, but that they had developed the biggest jet engines in the world.

they had the fuselage of the old one, and that was a big fuselage. And they may not have spent enough time thinking through the wing design, because they ended up with an aircraft that was almost 100 mph slower than the Boeing XB-52. Both aircraft had about the same empty weight, both had the same engines. But the best performance for the YB-60 was just a shade over 500 mph, while the XB-52 could go close to 600 mph at the same altitude. That was too big a difference to be ignored in favour of economy in production.

Convair engineers had put together, creditably, a multi-jet bomber that would carry up to the 72,000-lb bomb load of its piston-engined parent. It would have been flown by a crew of ten. Its defensive armament was a quintet of remote-controlled turrets, each with a pair of 20-mm cannon and 360 rounds per gun.

Axiom: it's very difficult to adapt an airplane to do something that it was not originally intended to do. High-altitude bombers do not work well in low-level dashes; interceptors do not make good ground-support aircraft; and piston-engined planes create whole new sets of problems when they are converted to jet power.

The Convair YB-60 proved that axiom all over again.

In the early 1950s, British and American engines were considered high thrust units when they were rated between 8000 and 10,000 lb, the latter figure being reserved for new engines just off the production line. The Russian numbers were about the same, but their thrusts were measured in kilograms, and the big new Mikulin powerplants that thrust the Tu-16 through the air were rated somewhere between 19,000 and 21,000 lb thrust.

That was the real significance of the Tu-16. It had been a foregone conclusion that the Russians would develop a jet bomber. But most observers expected that it would have four or more powerplants.

Today, the Tu-16 looks back on a service life of more than 20 years, during which time it has served with Russian air force and naval units. Some were exported to Iraq, Indonesia and Egypt, and the Egyptians used them, with air-to-surface missiles, in the 1973 war between Israel and the allied Arabian states.

Hard data on the Tu-16 is difficult to come by. Aleksandr Yakovlev, in *Fifty Years of Aircraft Construction*, has this to say:

'A N Tupolev's Tu-16 was powered by two AM-3 engines, each with a thrust of 8750 kg, mounted laterally where the wings were joined to the fuselage. With a weight of 72 tons, the Tu-16 could carry a bomb load of 3 tons, having a range of 5760 km. Its maximum speed was almost 1000 kmph. The six-man crew had powerful defensive armament, seven 23-mm cannon. Later the Tu-16 became a terrifying rocket carrier able to destroy ground targets without entering the enemy's air defence zone.'

Several versions of the Tu-16 have been noted by Western observers and, like other Russian aircraft, have been given NATO code names in a sort of spoken or written shorthand. The Tu-16 basic name is Badger. Badger-A was the first bomber version observed, with a standard bombardier's compartment in the nose. Badger-E, -F and -G are similar but contain special installations: E has bomb-bay cameras, F carries electronic intelligence gathering pods, and G has rocket-powered air-to-surface missiles. Badger-C is an anti-shipping version which carries another kind of air-to-surface missile beneath its wings, and Badger-D is similar, but is used for maritime reconnaissance. Some of these versions may be really only one basic model with hard points

Convair B-36D
Basis for the giant Convair YB-60 eight-engined jet bomber *Crew:* 15 *Powerplant:* 6 Pratt & Whitney R-4360, 3500 lb thrust each; 4 General Electric J47, 5600 lb thrust each *Weight:* 370,000 lb *Bombload:* 72,000 lb *Armament:* 16×20-mm cannon *Speed:* 406 mph

Top: A Badger-D electronic surveillance version of the Tu-16 flies over HMS Royal Oak. Above left: Badger-F, a maritime reconnaissance type with underwing electronic pods. Above right: Soviet airmen parade in front of their Badger-B anti-shipping missile carriers

under the wings for alternate mission loadings of missiles and electronic pods.

These aircraft have been well documented photographically by British and American pilots who have flown formation with them as the Russians scouted NATO fleet manoeuvres or patrols. Badgers have been photographed from the decks of US carriers, escorted by close formations of F-4 or F-8 fighters. So it is likely that there is much detailed knowledge about the weapons and electronics installations on board these bombers, and considerable other knowledge that can be gleaned from the external appearance.

The Badger is becoming obsolete, but it continues to form part of Russia's medium-bomber strength. One current estimate suggests that 500 are so employed, out of about 2000 believed to have been built.

Tupolev Tu-16 (Badger A)
Initial production version of the Soviet medium-range strategic bomber, shown here in Egyptian markings Crew: 6/7 Powerplant: 2 Mikulin AM-3M, 19, 290 lb thrust each Span: 109·88 ft Length: 120·93 ft Weight: 170,000 lb Bombload: 19,800 lb max Armament: 7×23-mm cannon Speed: 586 mph

Badger-E maritime reconnaissance aircraft, with camera equipment in their weapon bays, demonstrate their wingtip-to-wingtip refuelling

HEAVYWEIGHT WARRIOR

All-time classic among heavy jet bombers, the Boeing B-52 Stratofortress has served the US Air Force's Strategic Air Command for more than two decades – and its days are not yet numbered

It is *the* heavy bomber. There has been no other aircraft like it in the world and there is not likely to be.

Its preliminary design was done in a Dayton, Ohio, hotel over a long weekend in October 1948. Since then, it has been continually refined so that more than 25 years after its first flight and more than 20 years after its introduction into opera-

tional service, the Boeing B-52 remains a modern aircraft.

It has set world records, officially and unofficially, for speed and distance in its class. It has carried rocket-powered research aircraft aloft to probe the near reaches of space. And recent modification programmes have reworked and rebuilt some of the B-52 fleet to extend their useful operational life into the 1980s.

This is part of the story of the USAF's heavyweight warrior.
15 April 1952
Boeing YB-52 Stratofortress
For more than 20 years this huge bomber has been the mainstay of Strategic Air Command, USAF. Its swept wings and long fuselage have become the symbol of strategic deterrence. Designed to carry nuclear weapons, particularly the big thermonuclear weapons just entering develop-

ment in the early 1950s, the B-52 had to be modified to carry enough 'iron' bombs to make the game worth the candle in Southeast Asia.

Its record is a proud one. In their most effective aerial battle, against military targets in North Vietnam at the end of 1972, B-52s struck and destroyed with great precision. The number of civilian deaths was minimal according to official North Vietnamese casualty figures. In fact, so low were these figures that no attempt was made to propagandise against the United States by using them.

In the mid-1970s there were B-52s of the Strategic Air Command flying practice missions, honing the skills of the highly trained crews in continuing exercises and simulated runs on scattered targets. And modification programmes will guarantee the life of the B-52 well into the 1980s, giving the bomber a useful operational life of 30 years or more.

Boeing B-52D Stratofortress
Crew: 6 *Powerplant:* 8 Pratt & Whitney
J57-P-29W, 10,900 lb thrust each *Span:* 185 ft
Length: 157·58 ft *Weight:* 450,000 lb
Bombload: 70,000 lb *Armament:* 2×20-mm
cannon *Speed:* 612 mph

To put that on another time scale, it is as if the British and Americans had entered the Second World War still using de Havilland DH 4s as their primary heavy bomber, and continued to use them until the end of the war and beyond.

The Boeing design started as an attempt to meet an Air Materiel Command requirement of 1945 for a second-generation long-range bomber. The first-generation contract had just been awarded to Convair for what was to become the B-36. Convair and Boeing competed to meet the new requirement, and Boeing won with a conservative approach. They substituted turboprop engines for the piston engines of the B-50, itself only a more powerful B-29. It was a case of trying to stretch the stretched, and it was destined to fail. But before it did, Boeing got a contract to develop the model, by then designated the XB-52.

Beginning in April 1946, Boeing designers laid out a new airframe around four giant Wright turboprop engines, and began to detail the major components. By then it was becoming apparent that the straight wing and the propeller were approaching obsolescence faster than they could be improved. Swept wings and jet engines were the answer, and the turboprop XB-52 was doomed before it ever got off the drawing board. Besides, Wright was beginning to slip into its slough of mediocrity, and the Boeing team, ever alert to the possibility of being let down by somebody outside of Seattle, began to look for alternatives.

They found a new Pratt & Whitney jet engine which combined the thrust they would need with a promise of fuel economies on a scale then unheard of.

Boeing began a parallel study of the bomber requirement with company funds, designing a sweptwing aircraft with the new P & W jets. They continued work on the turboprop version as well. When the Air Force experts began to consider that turboprop bomber in more detail, they grew less satisfied. The performance increment wasn't enough of a jump over a re-engined B-36.

So the Air Force wrote a new require-ment during mid-1948, handed it to the Boeing team that was visiting Air Materiel Command in October that year and sat back to see what would happen.

In one of the classic stories of the aircraft industry, the Boeing team headed for their Dayton hotel to study the requirement. The next day – a Friday – they telephoned to tell the AMC they would submit their official proposal on the following Monday.

The first three-view drawings were completed on Saturday, and a balsa model was made with materials purchased from a Dayton hobby shop that day. The proposal was typed, the model was completed, and a red-eyed Boeing team confronted the USAF planners on Monday morning with their answer to the requirement.

Now this is not to imply that the XB-52 was 'designed' in four days, any more than one is expected to believe the stories about fighters that were designed on the backs of convenient envelopes. But the team that represented Boeing to the Air Force had been so immersed in heavy bomber requirements and possibilities that among them they knew all the basic answers. They could, and did, do a fairly complete preliminary design of the XB-52, choosing its basic layout, dimensions and powerplants, and estimating its weights and performance. And they could do that in a matter of days, because of the close professional relations that existed among the team. It was a remarkable technical and engineering feat.

Boeing already had contracts for two prototype bombers to the original requirement and design, and it did not take much to shuffle paperwork around various desks to make those same contracts cover the new XB-52.

Less than four years after that concentrated weekend in Dayton, the YB-52 was rolled out, taxied and flown for the first time. It preceded the XB-52 into the air in a reverse of the usual procedure. The XB-52 was known to need some improvements that had been planned for, and built into, the YB version from the start. Even so, the XB-52 made its first flight on 2 October 1952, still under four years from that famous weekend.

There were similarities between the new bomber and the B-47 series. They shared swept wings, podded powerplants, and bicycle landing gear in the fuselage. Everything was, of course, bigger and more developed than it had been on the B-47. The two prototypes featured a bubble canopy for the pilot and co-pilot, similar to the cockpit layout of the B-47. This was one of the first things to be changed in subsequent models.

Boeing had received a contract for a block of 13 service test aircraft, designated B-52A. The first three were actually used by Boeing as developmental aircraft, and they pioneered the new flight deck layout, with its blunted multi-paned nose and the pilot and co-pilot seated side-by-side instead of in tandem. The first of the B-52A models flew on 5 August 1954.

The remaining ten of the original B-52A contract were redesignated B-52B and incorporated further improvements. These were the first aircraft to go to the USAF. The 12th B-52B, by then including provisions for reconnaissance and officially designated RN-52B (Serial No 52-8711) was the first Stratofortress delivered to the Strategic Air Command. It stands today in the museum that borders on Offutt AFB, near Omaha, Nebraska, headquarters of SAC.

On 25 June 1975 General Russell E Dougherty, SAC commander, was joined in front of that bomber by retired Major General William E Eubank Jr. Eubank had made the flyaway delivery of the plane exactly 20 years earlier while commander of the wing at Castle AFB, California.

Boeing B-52G Stratofortress
Crew: 6 *Powerplant:* 8 Pratt & Whitney J57-P-43W, 11,200 lb (13,750 lb with water injection) thrust each *Span:* 185 ft *Length:* 157·67 ft *Weight:* 480,000 lb *Bombload:* 60,000 lb plus 2 Hound Dog stand-off ASMs *Armament:* 4 × ·5-in mg *Speed:* 665 mph

General Dougherty commented, 'The aircraft that General Bill Eubank delivered to the 93rd Bomb Wing 20 years ago is a far different aircraft from the one he arrived in today . . . The one Bill used to fly, like aircraft 711 [the USAF call sign for RB-52B 52-8711], was designed to operate in the stratosphere at altitudes around 40,000 ft, and deliver weapons from that high altitude.

'He came up here this morning in the later G-model, from Barksdale AFB, Louisiana. And a portion of that flight was flown at 400 ft, the stratum in which we plan to operate today if we must.'

There is no better simplified account of the change in the B-52 over the years than Dougherty's comments. Designed to fly and operate at 40,000 ft, the B-52 now is a ground-hugger flown in low-level penetrations of target areas, under the far-seeing eyes of radar. It still retains the ability to fly and fight at high altitudes, but to this it has added the capability to fly near the ground, guided by a wide variety of new electronic and infrared systems and by the skills and high competence of its crew.

As mentioned earlier in this history, flying at low level is a sure way to place high stresses on an airframe, and particularly one that was never designed to fly that kind of mission. The B-52 was planned for manoeuvres at high altitude, where the dynamic pressure and the air loads are comparatively low. There have been major modification programmes on the entire SAC fleet of B-52s to make them capable of coping with these new and higher stresses.

Currently, 80 of the B-52D models are being cycled through a 200-million-dollar effort to replace primary wing and fuselage structures, and to make other additions and changes in systems and structures to enable the D models to handle low-level missions.

One earlier modification programme arose out of the needs of the Southeast Asia theatre, where military requirements called for saturation bombing of fairly large areas. The B-52s, designed for a pair of thermonuclear weapons, were hastily adapted to the 'iron' bomb, but their capacity was limited. A major modification, called 'Big Belly', was carried out on the B-52D fleet. Before this rework, the standard internal iron-bomb load of a B-52 was 27 of the 750-lb bombs, for a nominal bomb load of 20,000 lb. 'Big Belly' increased that number to 66 of the 750-pounders, and an additional 24 slung on pylon racks under the wings. The total iron-bomb load then was 90, or a nominal weight of 67,500 lb, more than triple the original design bomb load.

'Big Belly' also provided for an alternative loading of 84 × 500-lb bombs on internal racks, plus 24 × 750-lb bombs externally, for a total of just under 61,000 lb.

SAC is now equipped with B-52D and B-52G models which are powered by versions of the original Pratt & Whitney J57 engines that sparked off the design, and the B-52H,

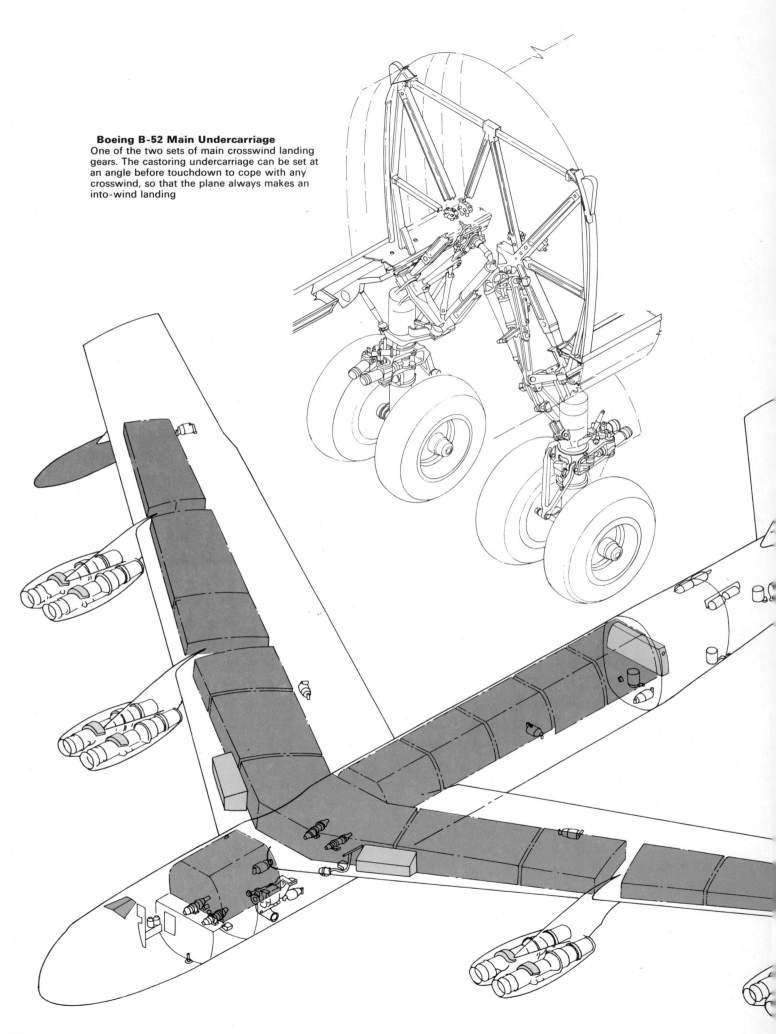

Boeing B-52 Main Undercarriage
One of the two sets of main crosswind landing gears. The castoring undercarriage can be set at an angle before touchdown to cope with any crosswind, so that the plane always makes an into-wind landing

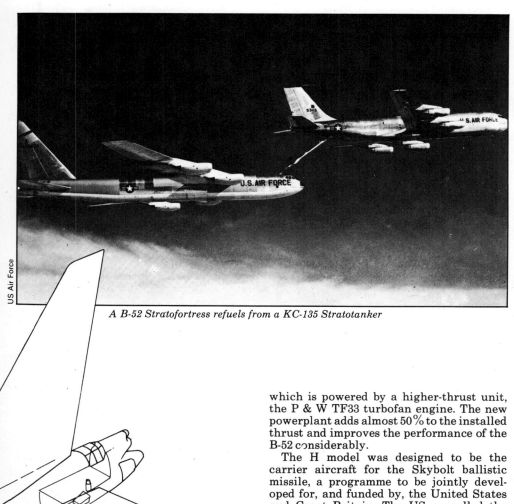

A B-52 Stratofortress refuels from a KC-135 Stratotanker

To board a B-52H, you enter just behind the nose radome through a belly hatch, climb to the first level, turn right and climb to the flight deck. Racks of equipment are on your right as you move forward, a bunk for crew rest is at your left, then comes a check-pilot's seat and then the two ejection seats for pilot and co-pilot.

Between them, the eight throttles are mounted on a console, and they are ingeniously placed so that each engine can be handled individually, or as one of a group of up to all eight engines at once. The co-pilot and pilot have the usual primary display instruments; the co-pilot has more engine instrumentation because he does a lot of the tasks that would be done by a flight engineer on a transport. He also has the separate console for starting and launching the Hound Dog missiles.

Each flight panel mounts a 6-in terrain-avoidance scope in its centre which gives a presentation of the terrain at three different slant ranges ahead of the flight, and also shows the profile at right angles to the flight path. The B-52H is flown manually using indications from these scopes for terrain avoidance.

All B-52s have crosswind landing gear. The crab angle of the gear can be set before touchdown to cope with whatever crosswinds there are. If the nose is angled to the left the co-pilot makes the touchdown; to the right it is the pilot's job.

At the rear of the flight deck are side-by-side positions for the electronics warfare officer (starboard) and the tail gunner (port side). Earlier models of the B-52 had manned turrets; the H model has a remote-controlled one.

In a compartment one level below the flight deck sit the navigator and the radar-operator, who is actually the bombardier. It is a comment on modern technology and the complexity of the mechanics of the bomb that it is still not possible to drop weapons accurately without preceding the drop with a long, stabilised, constant-speed, constant-altitude run into the target area.

Behind the entrance hatch are the two bomb bays. Racks for the nuclear weapons are stowed flat against the roof of the bay itself. Iron bombs are slung on vertical racks at three or more stations in each of the bays. Other kinds of stores can be carried and dropped or launched from these cavernous bomb bays, such as decoy missiles like the Quail. SRAM missiles are mounted on a single rotary launcher in the bomb bay, holding eight missiles. Twelve more can be carried, six to a side, on underwing pylon racks.

The B-52Ds, with their 'Big Belly' modifications, are even more versatile. Their official mission includes ocean surveillance and other naval support, so it is likely they can carry a variety of mines and other anti-shipping arms.

Both the B-52G and H aircraft will get new detection and bombing systems for the low-level, all-weather penetration attack. An electro-optical system is now being delivered, using infrared and low-level-light television to present a picture of the area ahead of the bomber. A further advance in electronic countermeasures has been planned, and will be installed.

SAC's fleet now consists of about 300 of the late model G and H aircraft, plus the 80 D bombers. They will remain operational, according to plans current in the mid-1970s, until the 1980s.

Boeing B-52 Fuel Distribution
Designed as a long-range strategic bomber, the B-52's massive fuel load gives it an official unrefuelled range of over 9000 nautical miles — and one B-52H made a record unrefuelled flight of 12,532 nautical miles

Fuel tanks

Water injection tanks

Engine oil tanks

Air refuelling point

which is powered by a higher-thrust unit, the P & W TF33 turbofan engine. The new powerplant adds almost 50% to the installed thrust and improves the performance of the B-52 considerably.

The H model was designed to be the carrier aircraft for the Skybolt ballistic missile, a programme to be jointly developed for, and funded by, the United States and Great Britain. The US cancelled the programme unilaterally, amid much feeling of annoyance by the British and the RAF. They had spent much effort and many pounds as their share of the programme, and were at best vexed when Skybolt was dropped.

The B-52H now carries a pair of Hound Dog missiles which resemble small fighter aircraft, but are loaded with nuclear warheads. More recently, SRAMs (Short-Range Attack Missiles) are replacing Hound Dogs.

The strong point of the B-52H is high-altitude range. They are all equipped for in-flight refuelling, as is standard these days; but the official unrefuelled range figure is in excess of 9000 nautical miles. The validity of that figure can be understood in the frame of reference of a record-setting flight by an unrefuelled B-52H, which logged a point-to-point flight of 12,532 nautical miles.

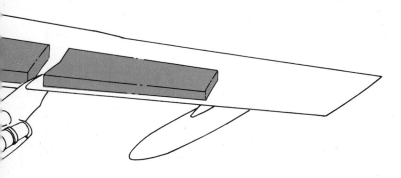

THE LAST OF THE SUBSONIC BOMBERS

Hawker Siddeley Vulcan B Mk 2
Crew: 5 *Powerplant:* 4 Rolls-Royce Bristol Olympus 301, 20,000 lb thrust each *Span:* 111 ft *Length:* 99·92 ft *Weight:* 190,000 lb (estimated max) *Bombload:* 21 × 1000-lb or 1 Blue Steel stand-off bomb (shown) *Speed:* 645 mph at 40,000 ft

The ultimate challenge for bomber designers was the other side of the sound barrier, but in the meantime the technology of the 1940s and 1950s was taken to full stretch by the last crop of subsonic bombers – each of them marking the end of its own particular line of development

There was to be one last fling for the subsonic bomber as designers in the United States, Britain and Russia took one more swing at the basic idea. There was good reason: it was still a workable concept, and the supersonic bomber – the logical next step – could not be achieved with the technology then available.

But there were improved jet engines, and some new aerodynamic tricks. So, during the 1950s a handful of heavy and light bombers exploited that technology and achieved a significant advance in performance in the subsonic regime.

Here are the stories of six such bombers, using widely different design approaches to refine their performance. But each one was the end of the line, each was the last of its type and each marked, in its own way, the end of the subsonic bomber era.

30 August 1952:

Avro Type 698 Vulcan

The flying displays of the Society of British Aircraft Constructors were high points in the aeronautical years of the early 1950s. One of the most thrilling years was 1952. Off the black-topped runway at RAE Farnborough roared a new shape, a large, white triangular aircraft, looking sometimes like a manta ray, sometimes like a racing yacht as

it banked over the field in an amazing low-level demonstration of manoeuvrability.

It was the Avro Vulcan, a four-jet bomber, then one of two new and heavy V-bombers for the Royal Air Force.

The Vulcan grew out of the 1946 specification that also produced the Handley Page Victor, about which more later. The delta-winged geometry – so called because the basic wing shape is a triangle and so is the Greek letter *delta* – evolved from the classical sweptwing formula. It started as a sweptwing aircraft with long and tapered wings and a swept tail, looking remarkably like the Boeing B-47, at least in the general aerodynamic conception.

But structually it would have to be different. American factories had the machine tools necessary to build strength into that kind of aircraft, but the British didn't. Their tooling was almost completely

limited to that used during the Second World War. It was fine for making airplanes out of bits and pieces of thin-gauge alloys, but it could not handle the heavier stuff.

So the bomber designers at Avro began by reducing the span so that they might be able to build a lighter structure. But that didn't work out either, even when the span was reduced to a point where the range began to fall off dramatically. They compromised on a very short-span swept wing and then filled in the area behind it to complete the triangular surface. With some aerodynamic tricks of their own, and their existing tooling, they were able to produce a radical aircraft with conventional structure.

A Blue Steel-armed Vulcan strategic bomber. By 1974 most remaining Vulcans had been switched to the overland strike role

Douglas A-3B Skywarrior
Crew: 3 *Powerplant:* 2 Pratt & Whitney J57-P-10, 10,500 lb thrust each *Span:* 72·5 ft *Length:* 76·33 ft *Weight:* 84,000 lb *Bombload:* 12,000 lb *Armament:* 2×20-mm cannon *Speed:* 610 mph

They received an order to proceed, but the engines they had counted on – Bristol Olympus powerplants with close to 10,000 lb of thrust each – were not available in time, and the prototypes were powered by four Rolls-Royce Avons rated at 6500 lb each. Only a few days after the first prototype had made its first flight, it had qualified to fly at Farnborough in the display. (The rule was that a type needed ten hours of flight time to be allowed to take part in the programme.)

Parallel to the bomber programme, Avro had designed, built and flown a number of small delta-winged aircraft, with the intent of learning about this new shape, particularly its handling qualities. The value of those small deltas would seem now to have been small. Too much time was spent in learning things about them that were never going to be used on the full-scale aircraft, and they were not true scaled models anyway.

But the brightly coloured shapes, escorting the white prototype in flight at Farnborough – remember the 'delta of deltas'? – were a visual delight and may have paid their way in advertising alone.

A Hawker Siddeley Vulcan B Mk 2 flies over the Fylingdales early warning establishment

Handley Page Victor B Mk 2
Crew: 5 *Powerplant:* 4 Bristol Siddeley Sapphire
202, 11,000 lb thrust each *Span:* 110 ft *Length:*
114·92 ft *Weight:* 180,000 lb *Bombload:*
35×1000-lb *Speed:* 630 mph

One of the things learned soon enough on the big aircraft was that the straight leading edge was not a very good answer to the problems of flight. So the leading edge was cranked part-way along the span, and then cranked again, by adding a new section that projected ahead of the straight leading edge. It added more area, it moved the aerodynamic centre of forces and it added camber to the airfoil section. The wing shape was further refined in the Mk 2 version of the Vulcan to show gracefully curved wingtips. By that time there was hardly a straight line on the wing for a distance greater than a few feet; the leading edge was kinked, curved and twisted and the tips were no longer the truncated triangle they had been. The Vulcan grew into an effective high-altitude bomber, and held its own nicely in competition with Strategic Air Command's bombers in the annual USAF bombing, navigation and reconnaissance competitions of those years.

Vulcans began to enter service early in 1957 with operational conversion units, and went to regular squadrons in the RAF, where they still serve today.

28 October 1952:

Douglas XA3D-1 Skywarrior

This was the US Navy's first strategic bomber, masquerading under the attack designation to preserve the official stipulation that strategic bombing was the exclusive province of the United States Air Force. But nobody was fooled by a Navy requirement for a carrier-based bomber that could carry nuclear weapons for long distances. That requirement began to take form in 1947, when the Navy and Douglas began talking together about how to design such an aircraft.

Some preliminary thinking by the Navy had resulted in weights that were astro-nomical for any operations from any carrier then in existence or projected. Successive rethinking of the problem had enabled the Navy to get estimated gross weights down near 100,000 lb, and if they got the big carrier they were working towards that weight would be acceptable.

But Douglas designers were realists. They figured it would be better to design an airplane that could be used on existing carriers than to go all out on a design for use on a carrier that might never be launched. They were right. The super-carrier never was launched, and Douglas were well ahead in their design for the smaller aircraft.

The goal was to save weight everywhere. Every pared pound actually saved more than its own weight by permitting a reduction in the weight of structure needed to support it, the weight of the fuel needed to carry it around and the weight of the wing needed to lift it. In fact, for the design that Douglas finally settled on, one pound saved was worth more than six pounds overall. This was the first real recognition of the 'growth factor', and it was a major contribution to the designer's art.

Dozens of 'paper' airplanes were developed to the stage where they could be either rejected or saved for a further study. Finally, the team reached its last evolutionary shape. It was a sweptwing aircraft, powered by a pair of turbojets slung underneath the wings. It was a very clean aircraft; much attention was devoted to keeping the drag low, and the overall aerodynamic efficiency high.

The pilot and co-pilot sat side-by-side in a large cockpit, and their navigator-gunner sat behind the pilot, facing aft. They did not have ejection seats; a slide led out of the fuselage belly behind an escape door, rammed open by cartridge-actuated systems.

The bomb bay was designed for the huge weapons then being turned out by the nuclear explosive people. Because nuclear weapon design was changing continually then, the general procedure was to design a big bomb bay that would be able to hold the Hiroshima or Nagasaki bombs – the theory being that those two were probably the biggest and heaviest that were ever going to be developed.

But Douglas added an idea to make the bomb bay more versatile. About halfway up its height they installed a removable platform. Above it they made a place for an auxiliary fuel tank; below it they hung bombs on ejector racks, one bomb per rack. Ahead of the bomb bay they attached a retractable, perforated flap; before the bomb bay was opened, the flap was extended so that the buffeting of the air into the bomb bay would be reduced. The ejector racks were for positive separation of the bomb from the rack and out of the open bomb bay.

The total bomb load was 12,000 lb. In later years, the bomb load was a versatile mix of depth charges, mines, bombs and any other kind of weapon that could be adapted to the cavernous bomb bay of the Skywarrior.

They served with heavy attack squadrons of the US Navy, and they were the basis for a conversion to a model for the USAF, which will be discussed later in this chapter.

US military aircraft were redesignated in 1962, following a system established by the Department of Defense. The A3D-1 Skywarrior became the A-3A; the standard bomber version, the A3D-2, became the A-3B. There were other models developed for photographic and electronic reconnaissance; they retained some attack capability, but every cubic inch of available

A Victor K Mk 2 tanker refuels a Hawker Siddeley Buccaneer. Inset: The refuelling probe of a Phantom FGR 2 in a Victor tanker's drogue

MOD

Myasischev M-4 (Bison-C)
Crew: 5/6 *Powerplant:* 4 Soloviev D-15,
28,660 lb thrust each *Span:* 170 ft *Length:* 162 ft
Weight: 363,760 lb max *Bombload:* NA
Armament: 6×23-mm cannon *Speed:* 625 mph

Inboard, the wing was highly swept; partway outboard, the sweep angle decreased; near the tips, the sweep angle was low. The critical Mach number – that high speed at which shock waves begin to form, with resulting sudden high drag – was kept constant over the entire wing. In contrast, earlier sweptwing shapes would have, typically, a small section of the span where the Mach number would go critical early and trigger turbulence over a much greater area. Once the critical Mach number is exceeded drag increases enormously, and no amount of power will produce much more speed.

reached its operational units. It served in two basic bomber versions, Mk 1 and Mk 2. The Mk 2 was somewhat larger of fuselage, and carried more things to confuse and annoy the enemy.

As a bomber, the Victor could carry the same nuclear weapons as the Vulcan, and the same Blue Steel stand-off missile. But its capacious bomb bay could carry more of the conventional weapons: 35 of the 1000-lb bombs compared to 21 × 1000-lb in the Vulcan.

Victors have gone through a number of modification programmes and now serve as strategic-reconnaissance bombers and as tankers with the RAF.

1953:
Myasishchev M-4
This four-jet Russian strategic bomber, their first big jet bomber, was a contemporary of the Boeing B-52. They entered design at about the same time, must have flown at about the same time and have been in service with their countries' air forces since their first deliveries.

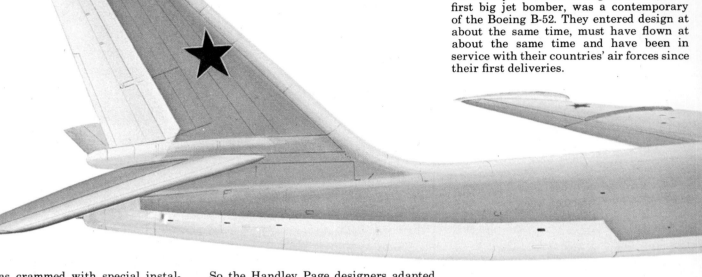

volume was crammed with special installations for the reconnaissance role.

The Douglas Skywarrior bombers served well with the Navy, and the Douglas team contributed greatly to the art of aircraft design when they recognised and applied the growth factor concept.

24 December 1952:
Handley Page HP 80 Victor
The Handley Page Victor, an unconventional design, is one of the best examples of subsonic bomber design technology in the world, and one of the least appreciated.

In its heyday as a strategic bomber, official RAF figures stated that the Victor cruised at Mach 0·94 at 55,000 ft, an astounding performance for an aircraft designed to meet a 1946 specification. It also is capable of low-level flight in a terrain-following mode; can carry and launch the Blue Steel stand-off missile from either low or high altitude; can fly strategic reconnaissance missions; and can refuel Britain's bombers and fighters.

This versatility grew out of necessity, and out of a programme that was the classic example of 'penny-wise and pound-foolish' funding that characterised many of Britain's potentially great aircraft.

It began, as did the other British heavies, with the 1946 specification for a strategic bomber. Handley Page's designers had discovered some exciting aerodynamic ideas during their trips to Germany immediately after hostilities ceased, and among them was the concept of what was to become known as the crescent wing. It was shaped, one fancied, rather like a crescent, and that was an easier term of definition than to call it correctly a constant critical Mach number wing.

So the Handley Page designers adapted this wing, calculating the shape to meet their specific requirements. Remember that this was before the automatic computer, and that all calculations were done with slide rules, logarithm tables and desk calculators of the mechanical type.

The British aerodynamicists of that era were superb at this kind of work. Handley Page and Royal Aircraft Establishment engineers worked out the wing shape, the fuselage contours to go with such an optimised wing, and the characteristic tail that topped off the shape. Even by today's standards the Victor continues to look strange. Yet its basic geometry has not changed since the design was frozen for production, and every line has a specific reason for being that way.

Confronted with two strange shapes, the Victor's 'crescent' wing and the Avro

Vulcan's delta, British officialdom hesitated. Unable to choose between the two designs, they bought both. But like Orwell's equal animals, the Vulcan turned out to be 'more equal' than the Victor. Handley Page had to struggle along under a series of annoying small contracts, buying a few of these and a few of those, instead of being able to place large orders well in advance of the needs of the ongoing production line.

Finally, later than the Vulcan, the Victor

The M-4 was not built in the quantities of the B-52, however, and it definitely is not today the first-line bomber with the Russian forces. It has been relegated to the maritime reconnaissance role, and is generally seen being escorted by British or US interceptors as they fly over NATO fleet units on manoeuvres.

The M-4, or Bison, to give it the NATO code name, was built around four of the big Mikulin engines that powered the earlier

Bison-C, above, is the definitive production version of the M-4, with a redesigned nose and Soloviev D-15 turbofans. Bison-B, below, is the maritime reconnaissance version, with nose radome and a bulged weapons bay to accommodate in-flight refuelling equipment

NIGHT INTRUDER

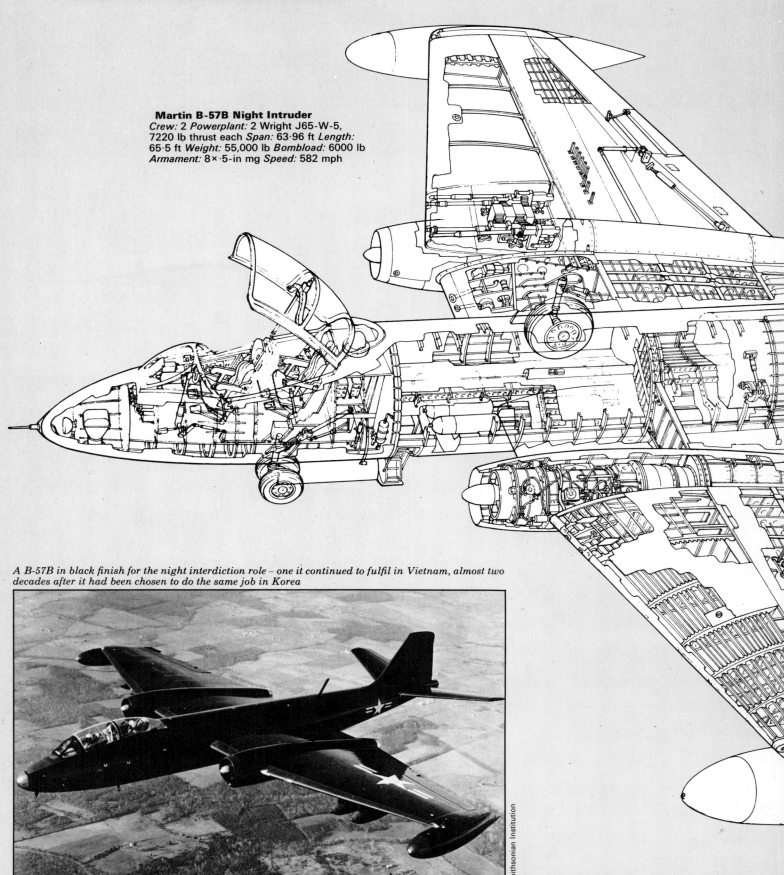

Martin B-57B Night Intruder
Crew: 2 *Powerplant:* 2 Wright J65-W-5,
7220 lb thrust each *Span:* 63·96 ft *Length:*
65·5 ft *Weight:* 55,000 lb *Bombload:* 6000 lb
Armament: 8×·5-in mg *Speed:* 582 mph

A B-57B in black finish for the night interdiction role – one it continued to fulfil in Vietnam, almost two decades after it had been chosen to do the same job in Korea

Smithsonian Institution

Air brakes out and undercarriage down, a B-57E comes in to land. Target-towing apparatus was the main distinguishing feature of this mark

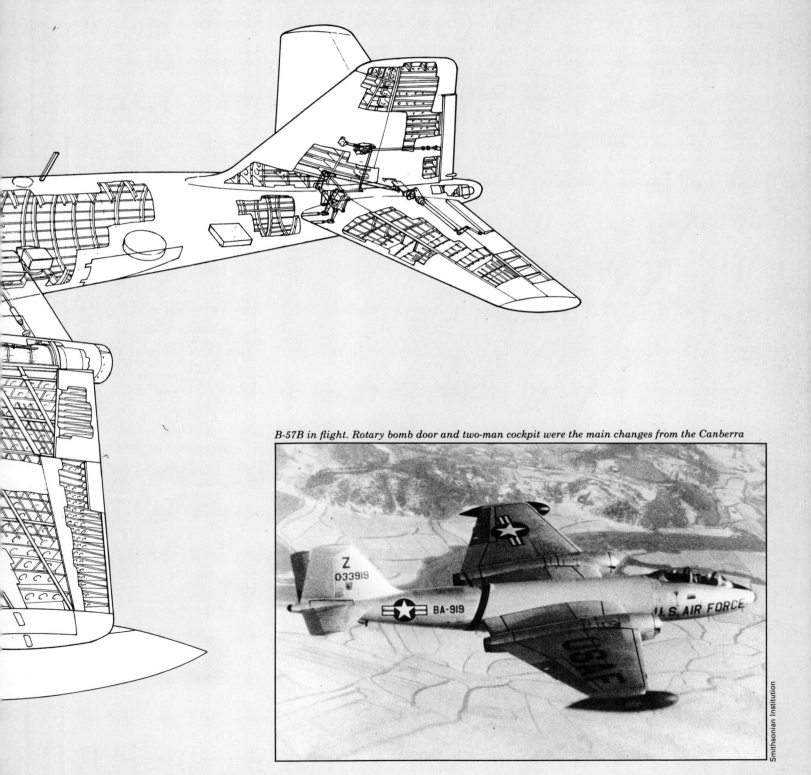

B-57B in flight. Rotary bomb door and two-man cockpit were the main changes from the Canberra

Badger. The layout is rather conventional, and really should not have caused the furore it did when it was first seen publicly over Moscow in the May Day parade of 1954. The real worry was, of course, that the Russians had a strategic jet bomber and that it probably had range enough to carry nuclear weapons to targets in the United States.

Three different versions of the M-4 have been observed. Bison-A is the standard strategic bomber, armed with nuclear or conventional bombs. Bison-B is a maritime reconnaissance version, in which the bombardier's nose position, multi-paned and equipped with an optically flat visual bomb-aiming window, has been replaced with a solid nose. An in-flight refuelling probe has been added above the nose. New bulges on the fuselage are fairings over electronic reconnaissance equipment, mounted inside and in the bomb bay.

Bison-C has a larger nose radar than Bison-B, for increased range in its maritime search mission. Other modifications include a standard in-flight refuelling installation which can be carried as an alternative bomb bay load. The probe-and-drogue system is used to refuel other strategic bombers of the Russian air force.

There is a wide variation in the estimates for sizes, weights and performances of the Bison, as there is for other Russian military aircraft. Those cited in this book have been taken from (one hopes) reliable sources.

One interesting point: Yakovlev's book makes no mention at all of Myasishchev, the M-4, or the designer's later work. Non-mention in official Soviet histories often indicates that the person not mentioned has become a non-person.

20 July 1953:
Martin B-57A Night Intruder
Does it look familiar? It should, because its outlines mark it as a near-twin to the English Electric Canberra. It started as the Canberra, bought from Great Britain by the United States to serve as a tactical bomber. It was redesigned to suit American tooling and production methods, and was operated primarily by USAF's Tactical Air Command. It served in combat in Southeast Asia as a day tactical bomber and later as a night intruder.

The requirement originated during the Korean war, when light tactical bombing was being done by the ageing Douglas B-26 (redesigned from A-26, and not to be confused with the Martin B-26 Marauder of the Second World War). There was only one trained squadron operating B-26s on night interdiction missions; daylight operations were suicidal for one thing, because of the intense anti-aircraft fire, and futile for another, because so much of the logistics supply for the North Korean armies moved at night by road and trail.

A number of aircraft were evaluated, and only the British Canberra met the primary requirement: lots of internal volume for the

special equipment needed for the night and bad-weather interdiction missions. Those systems didn't exist then in much more than paper form, but the decision was made to get an airplane big enough to handle them when they did become available, and not to have to try to compromise the electronics by fitting them into inadequate space later.

Despite the geometric similarity, the missions and details of design were quite different. The B-57 was designed for low-level missions against moving targets at night, which called for low-altitude manoeuvrability, ability to loiter in the target areas and range to reach out to the enemy's supply lines, well behind his front-line structure.

The USAF flew the airplane with two men, instead of the RAF's three-man crew, and added machine-guns to the unarmed Canberra for forward fire. The cockpit was completely redone, powerplants were changed – to another British-designed engine, the licence-built Armstrong-Sideley Sapphire – and a rotary bomb door was installed.

It was to be some years before the B-57 actually was used in the night-interdiction role for which it was designed, although some were used in daylight tactical bombing in Vietnam. A small group – 16 identified aircraft – were modified to include the latest technology for night attack, including forward-looking infrared sensors, laser rangefinding, low-light-level television, and

Douglas B-66B Destroyer
Crew: 3 *Powerplant:* 2 Allison J71-A-13, 10,200 lb thrust each *Span:* 72·5 ft *Length:* 75·17 ft *Weight:* 83,000 lb *Bombload:* 10,000 lb *Armament:* 2 × 20-mm cannon *Speed:* 631 mph

a rapid-firing belly gun target. Designated B-57G, 11 of these aircraft were deployed to Vietnam in September 1970 to work out against targets on the Ho Chi Minh trail at night. But time had caught up with the B-57; USAF reports said it was under-powered for the mission, and its last combat record was not impressive.

28 June 1954:
Douglas RB-66A Destroyer
This was one of those cases where the Air Force decided to buy a Naval aircraft because only minimal changes would be required to meet USAF specifications.

But the changes were not minimal. New engines, new wings, reworked fuselage and dozens of detail changes added up to an aircraft that cost more to buy and modify than it might have cost to design, develop and produce from a clean sheet of paper.

It was to be the USAF's version of the A3D Skywarrior, but most of the 294 Destroyers bought were assigned to the mixed mission of reconnaissance and bombing, and they were issued primarily to Tactical Air Command Reconnaissance squadrons. Only 72 of the type were completed for the bomber mission alone, and most of these were either converted or eased out of service after a short life.

The reconnaissance version stayed in service, and did yeoman work during the Vietnam war, loaded with advanced electronic systems to navigate flights of fighters and to raise an electronic shield of confusion around them to improve their chances of surviving the trip. That is another story.

One example should serve to illustrate the point about the Air Force's minor changes. The empty weight of the Navy's A3D-2 bomber was about 37,000 lb. The empty weight of the Air Force version was about 42,500 lb, nearly three tons heavier.

The B-66 was designed around a variety of internally carried weapons from nuclear to conventional, and could carry up to 15,000 lb of them in the bomb bay. Official Air Force data claims a better performance for the B-66 than Navy figures claim for the A3D, and that is strange. The Air Force version was not only heavier; it had engines that delivered considerably less thrust and at a lower altitude. Official figures have been used for performance of the A3D/B-66 series in the specifications, there being no other choice without an aerodynamic staff and accurate thrust and drag data.

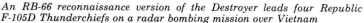
An RB-66 reconnaissance version of the Destroyer leads four Republic F-105D Thunderchiefs on a radar bombing mission over Vietnam

US Air Force

THE SUPERSONIC GENERATION

Tactical and strategic considerations – not to mention the improving efficiency of anti-aircraft missiles – have forced bombers from the stratosphere down to tree-top level, while still demanding ever higher performance. So far, the only solution has been the variable-sweep wing configuration

Over the last 20 years, new aerodynamic tricks have been learned, new structural approaches and new materials have been discovered, and new powerplants have been developed.

Concurrently, new airborne electronic systems have taken over many of the multi-faceted tasks of flying an aircraft.

Automatic flight is a reality in some modes, and automation is proving a great aid in others where the pilot still retains control of the overall flight system.

During these years, bomber design philosophy has changed from requiring supersonic speeds at high altitude to demanding high subsonic or low supersonic speeds just above the contours of the terrain. This change in basic requirements has forced a major change in the design of aircraft because, increasingly, the variable-geometry design appears to offer the only feasible answer. It was pioneered with the General Dynamics F-III series, and currently graces the lithe forms of the two major advanced bombers in the United States and Russia.

Will the next generation of bombers keep that kind of polymorphous shape, or will some entirely new kind of aerodynamic layout appear? That's a difficult question

to answer. But there is an even more difficult question: will there be a next generation of bombers?

11 November 1956:

General Dynamics/Convair B-58A Hustler

This delta-winged jet was the world's first supersonic bomber to enter service. During a ten-year lifetime with the Strategic Air Command, the Hustler set 19 world records. It received five major aviation trophies for outstanding flights: the Bendix, Blériot, Harmon, Mackay and Thompson.

The Hustler was a unique airplane. It carried its weapons outside its fuselage, slung underneath in pods. Reconnaissance systems and fuel were the two most common loads after strategic weapons.

It was designed to perform a high-altitude, high-speed delivery, dashing at Mach 2 into enemy territory, launching or dropping the pod and banking away in a

General Dynamics/Fort Worth B-58A Hustler

Crew: 3 *Powerplant:* 4 General Electric J79-GE-5B, 16,000 lb thrust each with afterburning *Span:* 56·83 ft *Length:* 96·75 ft *Weight:* 163,000 lb *Bombload:* Multi-systems under-fuselage pod *Armament:* 1×20-mm Vulcan cannon *Speed:* Mach 2

A prototype B-58 Hustler in flight

blaze of power and speed to avoid the radiation blast damage.

But when the time came to go in on the deck below the watchful eyes of radar, the B-58 turned to that mission as if it had been designed for it. It could speed along just under the velocity of sound when it was making those low-altitude bombing runs, and no bomber since then has had such performance.

It could also toss-bomb, using the half-loop, half-roll technique described earlier. Its pods included both free-fall and rocket-powered types, so that various options were available to SAC crews for weapons delivery.

The external pods made for a small bomber; its wing span was just under 57 ft. But it stood on towering landing gear to clear the pods, and you always had to look up to look at the B-58.

Under its wings were snuggled a quartet of General Electric J79 powerplants. These engines were cleared for two hours of operation at maximum thrust, compared to the much briefer ratings of most earlier engines. This made it possible for the Hustler to get its dash performance over more than 1500 miles instead of the more normal few hundred.

After a long and noisy takeoff, it could head for altitude faster than many contemporary fighters, with an initial rate of climb, fully loaded, of 17,000 ft per minute. It could nearly triple this figure when lightly loaded.

The list of pioneering achievements of the

B-58 programme is lengthy. For one, it was the first weapon system contract, that term designating the practice of naming a contractor and giving him complete responsibility for every part of the programme through design, development and early flight test. In this case, General Dynamics/Convair made sure that the aircraft, pods, ground support equipment and spare parts were completely integrated into a single weapon system.

The B-58 originated in 1949 as a parasite bomber, to be carried by another bomber to some location within target range, dropped, and then recovered after the attack if all went well. It was small, with a two-man crew, an external weapons pod and just enough fuel to complete the mission. But it grew after the concept changed to a self-launched bomber: the Hustler was built around a three-man crew, lots of fuel, and in-flight refuelling.

Considering that the original ideas began to take form in 1949, one can appreciate what an advanced design the B-58 was. Only 15 months or so earlier, the Bell X-I had first flown in supersonic flight, a shade above Mach 1; already Convair were proposing that a delta-winged bomber be built to fly at twice the speed of sound. Nobody had flown at that speed before; there was no experience in flight research, and there was not that much confidence in the findings of wind-tunnel tests.

But by 1952 General Dynamics had worked out a winner, and were awarded the development contract. Two years and two months

after the day the first drawings were released to the shop, the first B-58 flew. It was a remarkable achievement.

The delta-wing design looked deceptively simple. It had a straight-edged wing, but close examination revealed that its leading edge curved downward, increasingly toward the wingtip, so that the cambered surface resembled a section of a long and finely tapered cone. This gave the Hustler the aerodynamic qualities it needed at both the low- and high-speed ends of the flight regime.

The Hustler had no other high-lift devices. The trailing-edge surfaces were elevons, combining the functions of ailerons and elevators, because the B-58 had no horizontal tail surface.

Aerodynamic refinement was everywhere. The fuselage was area-ruled to minimise drag in the critical trans-sonic flow region, and to reduce the power and time needed to accelerate from subsonic to supersonic speed.

One problem with the B-58 may have been that its dash range was considered inadequate compared with the penetration range of the B-52. Although the B-58 could fly a lot faster than the B-52 in low-level missions speed is not the primary criterion; range is. And, since effective mission range begins from the point at which the last pre-strike refuelling ends, the B-58 could not strike as deeply as could the B-52.

Still, their blistering speed and unique capabilities made the Hustlers a valuable part of the strategic deterrent force. Further, they had a unique reconnaissance role. The pod could carry complex, major electronic and photographic reconnaissance systems. The Hustler could slash through the upper atmosphere, at speeds of Mach 2, on a high-altitude reconnaissance mission in many ways comparable to that of the Lockheed SR-71 that arrived on the scene much later.

Remember the B-58, then, as a first-class weapon system that pioneered much advanced technology, served as the prototype for a new contracting approach, and was the world's first supersonic bomber. It was a pace-setter and a record-breaker, and much of its performance envelope still remains unchallenged by later and newer aircraft designs.

31 August 1958:

North American A3J-1 Vigilante

The Navy's first Mach 2 strategic bomber – although never officially called that – originated as a company-funded proposal during 1954. North American suggested that the Navy consider an aircraft to deliver weapons in low-level attacks at high subsonic speeds.

Fine, said the Navy about a year later, but also let's go for Mach 2 at altitude, and let's be able to launch when there is no wind over the deck of our carriers.

Adding two requirements like that changed the design considerably, and it emerged later as the A3J-1, with a wing that was really too big for the high-speed role and too small for the high-lift requirement of the zero-wind launch. But the wing was a fine compromise, and only one of the many advanced technical features of the A3J design.

High speed at low level is best handled with a small and thin wing; the ride is more comfortable, the drag is lower. On the other hand, a zero-wind launch of a heavy airplane needs high lift, and that means a large and thick wing, speaking aerodynamically. The North American compromise design resulted in a thin wing, with a system of blown flaps at the trailing edge. Blown flaps are rather conventional flaps that

A-5A Vigilantes on the flight deck of USS Enterprise, *the biggest warship ever built*

have their effectiveness increased by blasting air at high pressure around their leading edges. The source of that air is the jet engines, which are bled of a small percentage of their high-pressure air which is then ducted to the flaps.

Additionally, drooped leading edges on the wings could be deflected downward about 30° for takeoff and landing, or only a few degrees for an improvement in the cruise flight regime.

Roll control was handled by spoilers. The horizontal tail was divided into a left and right slab surface; they were deflected together for pitch control, and differentially to trim any rolling tendency of the aircraft. The vertical tail was a one-piece surface.

All of these complex controls, plus navigation, weapons delivery and reconnaissance data, were tied together in a single system designed by North American's Autonetics division. The system featured inertial navigation for one of the first times in an airborne application, and a miniaturised digital computer to tie it all together.

The fuselage was different. The weapons

North American Rockwell A-5A Vigilante
Crew: 2 *Powerplant:* 2 General Electric J79-GE-4, 16,150 lb thrust each with afterburning *Span:* 53 ft *Length:* 73 ft *Weight:* 49,500 lb *Bombload:* Internal nuclear or conventional weapons *Speed:* Mach 2·1

are ejected through a tunnel that leads out the tail of the plane, between the engines. So the fuselage is simply an enclosure for three large, cylindrical spaces. The outboard ones are the engine bays, and the inner one is the weapons bay. The nuclear weapon was attached to two auxiliary fuel tanks; when they were emptied, they were retained to be dropped as part of the weapon.

The Vigilante was developed under the weapon system management concept, with North American responsible for everything except the government-furnished engines. It was redesignated as the A-5 series in 1962.

About then, because of continual arguments in high places about whether or not the Navy had a strategic bombing mission, the Vigilante was converted to a reconnaissance aircraft. Its capacious bomb bay was filled with electronics; its flat-topped fuselage was curved to cover additional fuel volume, and the latest and most advanced reconnaissance systems – photographic and electronic – were installed. That's where our story of the Vigilante ends, because that is where its deployment as a jet bomber ended.

1958(?):

Tupolev Tu-22

This was Russia's first supersonic bomber, and its elegant shape told a story of sophisticated design techniques. It was area-ruled, long and sleek, and from every angle it looked like a beauty.

And Beauty it was called, for a short while, very unofficially; NATO later chose the code name of Blinder. It was first flown publicly at the 1961 Tushino air display.

At that show, two different models of Blinder appeared. One was a conventional bomber; the other was carrying an air-to-surface missile, partially submerged in its belly, and was equipped with a refuelling probe. Its nose radome was considerably larger than that of the other bomber, hinting at the search and guidance role for the airborne missile.

When the Blinder was first analysed from photos and other intelligence data, it appeared that it would have a top speed of about Mach 2. But later data show that the top speed is a more modest Mach 1·4, and that it is most likely a dash speed, not a sustained cruise at altitude.

Other notes about the bomber say that the range is deficient, and for that reason the Blinder has been relegated to the maritime reconnaissance role, where it can remain on station over those waters reachable by a combination of internal fuel and in-flight refuelling.

There are reports that some Blinders have been seen with extensive electronic intelligence installations, and that there is also a training version, with a second cockpit mounted in a stepped configuration aft of the standard tandem three-place cockpit.

The biggest batch of Blinders was seen at the 1967 air display at Domodedovo, an airport near Moscow, on the occasion of a

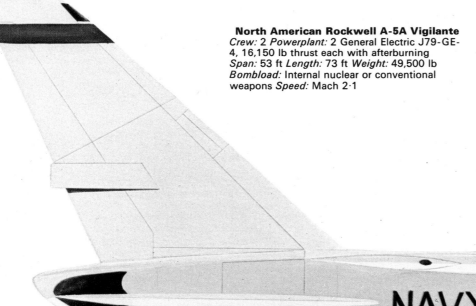

An early model A3J-1 Vigilante comes in to land. All USAF and Navy aircraft were redesignated on 18 September 1962 – the A3J-1 becoming the A-5A

Soviet show of strength. Formations of the bombers flew past, totalling 22 aircraft, and observers noted that most of them were the missile-carrier variety.

Less than 200 of the bombers are believed to have been built, and about one third of them went to the Russian naval forces for maritime reconnaissance.

Blinders may have suffered from some of the same ailments that limited the B-58: deficient unrefuelled range at low level, and limited payload under those conditions. Whatever the reason, Blinder should not now be taken too seriously as a threat, or as a major part of Russian strategic forces in being.

17 June 1959:

Dassault Mirage IV-01

If there is a more efficient group of aircraft

designers anywhere than in Marcel Dassault's employ, they must be well hidden. Time after time, his teams of brilliant designers and engineers have come up with new answers to a wide variety of requirements.

One of their brightest efforts was the first French strategic jet bomber, the Mirage IVA. It started simply enough, with a 1956 requirement for an aircraft that could carry a bomb, weighing about 7000 lb and some 16 ft long, for a distance of about 1200 miles without refuelling. And, added the specification, it ought to do this at supersonic speed.

The last part was the tough one. But Dassault and two competitors produced preliminary designs, and Dassault's was chosen. They began detail design in April

1957; two years and two months later the first prototype flew.

Dassault had basic experience with the thin delta wing in the Mirage III fighter as a foundation. The company always has made its best progress by doing the most with the current state of the art in technology. They made some changes to the basic shape of the delta wing, enlarged the dimensions by about half, powered it with a pair of engines instead of one, and produced the first prototype.

But meantime, the programme itself had changed. French officials wanted a bigger and better bomber, and an enlarged and developed Mirage IVB was to be the answer. Dassault and SNECMA, the engine suppliers, went through a whole routine with the new design and arranged licence rights

to a new Pratt & Whitney engine, and then the project was dropped by the government. It was back to the Mirage IVA as before, with some minor changes.

Three pre-production prototypes were built and tested, the first of these flying for the first time on 12 October 1961, two years and a month after the contract date for the three planes.

Now, the Mirage IVA operates as an air-refuelled bomber, drawing its sustenance from one of 14 Boeing KC-135 tankers the French bought from the United States. Additional fuel can be taken on board via a buddy system from another Mirage IVA.

Tactically, the bombers operate as a pair, one with a bomb and one with only auxiliary fuel tanks and the buddy system. They take off, and top up from a tanker. They then fly together to a pre-plotted mission point and the bomber refuels from the other Mirage IV, leaving it enough fuel to get home or, in the event of war, draining its tanks completely. That way the Mirages can guarantee at least a one-way trip deep into Russia, the theoretical enemy postulated in all their studies.

Like all jet bombers of 15 years or so ago, the Mirage was designed for high-speed, high-altitude strikes, and in the case of the Mirage IV, high speed meant Mach 2. But when an examination of the real effectiveness of anti-aircraft missiles forced the conclusion that attacks would have to be mounted at low level, the Mirages required only minor changes.

The production run was not a large one; Dassault built 62 production Mirage IVA bombers, plus the three pre-production

his design of the M-4 Bison, his name no longer figures in the current pantheon of aircraft designers.

Bounder achieved notoriety when it first showed over Tushino airport in the 1961 air show. It roared over the field, propelled by four powerful turbojets, and then it faded into history.

In retrospect, Myasishchev did almost everything wrong. We can't tell what requirement he was trying to meet, so it is possible that some anonymous Comrade Planner is the real person to blame. What it seems is that he set out to build a long-range jet bomber that could carry the Russian thermonuclear weapons and other stores, and that would have a supersonic dash performance over the target.

Assuming that requirement, the first thing he did wrong was to choose a poor wing shape. That truncated delta with high taper is no good for high-speed design. The next thing he did wrong was to design that hulk of a fuselage, and to ignore the whole concept of the area rule, which by then was known to everybody in the world who studied aeronautics.

Dassault Mirage IV-A
Crew: 2 *Powerplant:* 2 SNECMA Atar 9K, 15,435 lb thrust each with afterburning *Span:* 28·88 ft *Length:* 77·08 ft *Weight:* 73,800 lb *Bombload:* 1 × 70-kiloton nuclear device or 16 × 1000-lb *Speed:* Mach 2

aircraft and the single Mirage IV-01 prototype, a smaller but geometrically similar aircraft. They now form a major component of France's strategic deterrent force.
1960(?):
Myasishchev M-50
If there is a single reason why Vladimir Myasishchev is not currently listed among the heroes of Soviet aviation, this bomber is it. NATO-named Bounder, it should have been called Blunder, for that is certainly what it was.

As an attempt to build a big, fast jet bomber it was an outstanding failure which revealed an embarrassing lack of understanding of the problems of high-speed flight. Although Myasishchev and his design bureau had won a Lenin Prize in 1957 for

Realise that by that time, Convair had been flying the B-58 for a couple of years, breaking records. The French were well along with their supersonic Mirage IV bomber, and were flying it when Myasishchev probably was watching his prototype take form.

It might not have been too late, even then, to have learned something from the Convair and Dassault designs, but Myasishchev obviously could not read the handwriting on the wall, even though it was in large Cyrillic letters.

Bounder flew, probably in 1960, and the Russians decided to show it at the 1961 Tushino display. The aircraft that performed that day used afterburners on its inboard engines, but not on the outboard ones. That might have been one last attempt to get the M-50 to accelerate a little faster through the speed of sound.

So little is known, and so much has been conjectured, about the Bounder that there is no more to be said about it at this point. It was never much of a threat, although it was made to seem real enough and threatening enough at the time.

But Bounder has not been heard of since, and neither had Vladimir Myasishchev.
21 September 1964:
North American XB-70A Valkyrie
The gleaming white XB-70A, first of two prototypes built and flown, stands today in the Air Force Museum at Wright-Patterson AFB, Dayton, Ohio. In the mid-1950s, it was conceived at Wright-Patterson in a requirement for a new weapon system. And if the original schedule had reached reality, the B-70 would, about now, be leaving service with Strategic Air Command, and most likely one of them would be earmarked for display at the Air Force Museum.

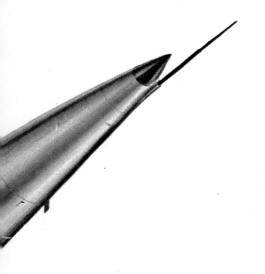

Tupolev Tu-22 (Blinder B)
Crew: 3 *Powerplant:* 2 afterburning turbojets,
26,000 lb thrust each (est) *Span:* 90·88 ft
Length: 132·96 ft *Weight:* 185,000 lb *Bombload:*
1×AS-4 (Kitchen) stand-off bomb *Armament:*
1×23-mm cannon *Speed:* Mach 1·4

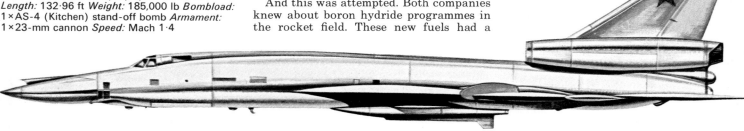

But that is not the way the story went. Instead, it encompassed policy changes, technical problems, financial cutbacks and restorations, and a spectacular fatal accident that helped speed the end of the programme.

In late 1954, Strategic Air Command was looking for a bomber to follow the B-52, and to use the same bomber environment that SAC had developed – runway requirements, ground facilities and crew composition. By mid-1955, SAC's needs had been translated into a requirement for Weapons System 110A, a bomber with subsonic cruise and maximum possible penetration speed, able to carry thermonuclear bombs over long ranges.

Boeing and North American responded, submitting their designs in October 1956. But the designs were stretched to the outer limits of technology. There seemed to be no way to meet the WS-110A requirement without repealing the laws of aerodynamics and thermodynamics.

And this was attempted. Both companies knew about boron hydride programmes in the rocket field. These new fuels had a heating content, per pound, about twice that of the hydrocarbon fuels. They promised rocket combustion performance of a new order, and they looked adaptable to turbojet designs. There was enough push behind them to set up pilot production plants for fuels, and to start developing turbojets to burn what would become known as 'zip' fuels.

The laws of aerodynamics were a little harder to repeal. But North American found an obscure technical note published by the National Advisory Committee for Aeronautics (NACA, the predecessor of today's NASA, the National Aeronautics and Space Administration). It described a phenomenon which would become called 'compression lift' as one way of improving the lifting efficiency and reducing the drag at supersonic speeds. Armed with that knowledge, North American laid out their re-studied

A Tu-22 leads a formation of Su-11 interceptors in a fly-past at Domodedovo, July 1967

Novosti

115

concept of WS-110A, and in December 1957 were awarded a contract for development of their design.

But the 'zip' fuels had been oversold and under-investigated, and that programme was cancelled. A funded programme at North American for the F-108 long-range interceptor, which was sharing some of the high costs of supersonic research and development, was also cancelled; the whole developmental cost burden then shifted to the B-70 programme. In December 1959, because of escalating costs, the B-70 programme was cut to the design and flight tests of a single prototype. In October 1960 it was re-instated as a complete weapon system, after a lot of forceful arguments by the Air Force. In April 1961 it was cut back to three prototypes. In March 1964 it was cut to two prototypes, its final form.

That is no way to run a development programme. The original USAF schedule had projected that the bomber would be entering service with SAC in 1965. One year from that date, the airplane still had not flown, and the programme was going to produce only two prototypes.

But what prototypes they were! Their unique features were many, from the downward-folding wingtips to the brazed structure of honeycomb panels.

To get compression lift, the shape of the fuselage was critical. So all six of the big General Electric J93 turbojets were laid out side by side in a single underwing body, contoured to trigger a shock wave at a key location. That shock wave was confined by swinging the wingtips downward through 65° in flight, boxing in the flow so that the B-70 would ride on the compressed mass of air. The top of the wing was flat; paired vertical surfaces were located just outboard of the engine body, but above the wing. The fuselage projected ahead of the wing, and

was shaped in a curving set of contours that gave the plane the nickname of 'Cecil, the Seasick Sea Serpent', after a TV puppet character of the 1950s.

The purpose of the flight test programme was to achieve the predicted performance, which included a cruising speed of Mach 3 at altitudes between 70,000 and 80,000 ft. The prototypes were heavily instrumented, the second much more intensively than the

first. Almost every aspect of the proposed flight envelope was a new one, with altitudes and speeds reached previously only by special research aircraft. The two prototypes were flight research vehicles, never intended to be bomber prototypes. Crew stations were different, and there was none of the many features that transform an experimental aircraft into a service bomber. That had been reserved for the third prototype, cancelled in March 1964.

Both prototypes flew. Towards the end of their first phase of flight tests, the second prototype led a formation of aircraft for an air-to-air photograph. There was a mid-air collision; the second XB-70A and its co-pilot, Major Carl Cross, were lost, as was a Lockheed F-104 flown by NASA pilot Joe Walker, also killed in the collision.

The fiery spiral of the stricken Valkyrie was its funeral pyre. The programme went downhill from there. The first prototype had

to be extensively instrumented to replace the test equipment lost with the second, and it required much modification. By then, the plane had been handed over to NASA for research on the supersonic transport programme. By the time they retired the test airplane, it had logged only a few hours of flying time at Mach 3, hardly enough to have made any difference to the knowledge required for a supersonic transport design.

Now the XB-70A first prototype is a museum piece, the bomber that never was. And neither its compression lift concept, nor its general layout, nor 'zip' fuels have been used again.

25 September 1969:
General Dynamics FB-111A
The FB-111A variable-sweep medium-range bomber originated as a tactical fighter-bomber which was the centre of a swirling political controversy for more than seven years. But out of all this came a highly praised weapon for Strategic Air Command,

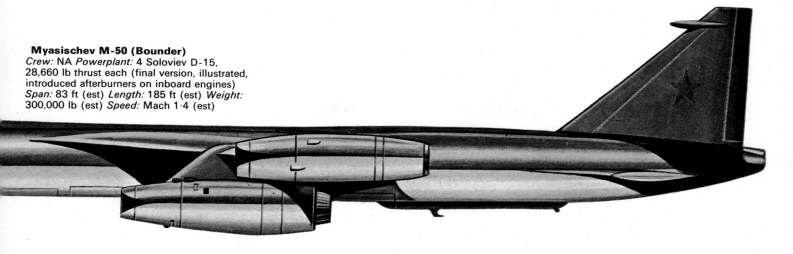

Myasischev M-50 (Bounder)
Crew: NA *Powerplant:* 4 Soloviev D-15,
28,660 lb thrust each (final version, illustrated,
introduced afterburners on inboard engines)
Span: 83 ft (est) *Length:* 185 ft (est) *Weight:*
300,000 lb (est) *Speed:* Mach 1·4 (est)

and, in the words of one SAC pilot, 'The only people who knock this airplane are the ones who haven't flown it!'

One reason for choosing the FB-111A as an SAC bomber was its ability to get right down to the ground in a high-speed terrain-following ride that was automatic and that left the crew free to concentrate on other problems. Armed with up to 50 Mk 117 bombs, which weigh nominally 750 lb each, or with up to six nuclear weapons including SRAM missiles, an FB-111A is a formidable force by itself.

It currently equips two of SAC's bomber wings and it is not likely to see any wider service. Only 76 of the bomber version were built, and the Air Force has no further plans or funds for more.

The variable-sweep wing is the key to the performance of the FB-111A. Wings spread, it can take off and climb; add a little sweep for high-speed cruise, more sweep to go supersonic, and nearly all the sweepback for those on-the-deck dashes.

They began to enter service with an SAC training wing in the autumn of 1969. In May 1970, two of them went to the RAF's bombing and navigation competition, to which SAC had been invited. An FB-111A

was leading the field in the navigation event after three days, but finally lost it to one of the B-52s. But in November that year, in SAC's own competition, an FB-111A crew carried off the individual bombing trophy.

It is equipped for in-flight refuelling, a standard SAC requirement. But it is classed as only a medium-range bomber because of its unrefuelled range, and it has been assigned to targets near the enemy borders, rather than far into the interior. On its low-level penetrations, it can fly at about 660 mph just 200 ft above the ground.

Aside from the terrain-following radar which gives the FB-111A this capability, the plane has an inertial navigation system

North American XB-70A Valkyrie
Crew: 2 *Powerplant:* 6 General Electric YJ93-GE-3, 31,000 lb thrust each with afterburning
Span: 105 ft *Length:* 185 ft *Weight:* 525,000 lb
Speed: Mach 3

which is so accurate that it can be used to taxi and position planes on the ramps. They start all missions from a surveyed mark on the ramp where the aircraft has been pre-positioned, and from which the inertial system measures all future displacements.

For defence, there are on-board electronic countermeasures and infrared detectors mounted at the tail to warn of fighters or missiles to the rear. Automatic jammers, chaff and flares will further confuse the enemy radars and weapons.

On a typical bombing exercise mission, three FB-111A aircraft will take off and climb to 30,000 ft, rendezvous with a tanker and top their tanks. Then just before they

The massive propelling nozzles of the Valkyrie's six J93 turbojets, designed to propel it at Mach 3 on a compressed mass of air – now an expensive exhibit at the US Air Force Museum

John Batchelor

General Dynamics/Convair FB-111A
Crew: 2 *Powerplant:* 2 Pratt & Whitney TF30-
P-7, 20,350 lb thrust each with afterburning
Span: 70 ft (wings spread)/33·9 ft (wings fully
swept) *Length:* 73·5 ft *Weight:* 81,537 lb
Bombload: 37,500 lb or 6 Boeing AGM-69A
SRAMs *Speed:* Mach 2·5

An F-111A folds back its wings from fully extended to fully swept in preparation for an on-the-deck dash. The FB-111's wings are larger, and are those originally designed for the cancelled US Navy F-111B

reach the target area – low-level runs surveyed in barren and remote country in the western United States – they refuel again. They drop down to the 200-ft level and, with wings swept to the 55° or 60° mark, they blast along the run at about Mach 0·65. For the actual simulated bomb run or weapon launch, they accelerate to Mach 0·75.

Four targets are 'hit' during a typical mission by each bomber, and then they climb back to altitude and the cruise home. *1970(?):*

Tupolev variable-geometry bomber 'Backfire'

Proving the principle of parallel invention, the USSR has a large variable-geometry bomber in development, production and perhaps in early operational deployment. In size, shape and performance it compares to the Rockwell International B-1. But there is a major difference: the timetable.

The B-1 had only flown a handful of times by mid-1975. Backfire, as NATO calls the new Russian bomber, was observed via satellite in mid-1970, and was expected to become operational with the Soviet air force during 1974.

Given the general knowledge of aircraft design and the state of the art, plus a few – even one good example – satellite or SR-71 photographs, some fairly accurate estimates can be made of Backfire's weights and performance. Pentagon data credit it with dash speeds between Mach 2·2 and 2·5 at altitude, low supersonic speed in low-level dashes, and a combat radius close to 4000 miles.

Tupolev's design bureau has long been a leader in the design and development of big Russian jet aircraft, both civilian and military. By Russian standards, they have been very successful aircraft. But on the military side of the ledger, Backfire is an outstanding technical achievement, by any standard. Assuming that there are no troubles during early deployment, the Russians should have their bomber in operational units by now.

The Russian concept of variable-geometry designs differs from that of the US. The Soviet teams, typically, have started their

General Dynamics

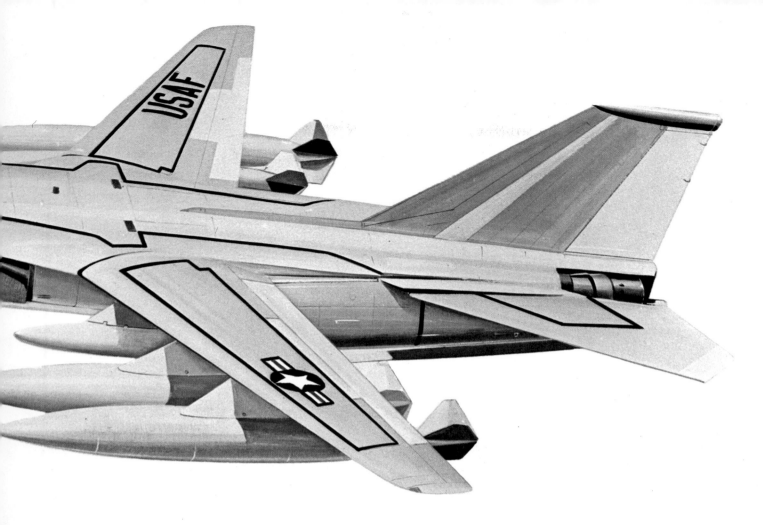

variable-geometry portion of the wing well outboard, much farther along the span than in Western designs. This feature of Backfire's design may result from Tupolev's commitment to the landing gear, retracted aft into a wing pod, and almost a Tupolev trademark. Part of it may be the desire, or the need, to keep structural loads on the wing pivot lower than the loads that Rockwell International find acceptable.

Backfire's weapons load is the usual Russian range of iron and thermonuclear bombs, plus a pair of new air-to-surface missiles which are believed to have been developed as part of the Backfire weapon system and to have a range of more than 450 miles.

21 December 1974:

Rockwell International B-1A

Currently America's most controversial weapon system development programme, the Rockwell International B-1A jet bomber is intended to replace late-model Boeing B-52G and B-52H aircraft in the SAC fleet.

The genesis of the B-1A lies in the basic argument for a bomber fleet as part of a balanced deterrent force. The opponents argue that missiles can and should do the job. But a missile is an all-out weapon, not subject to recall, and targeted best against enemy cities and strategic complexes. Hardened point targets are another matter indeed, and it seems that the only way to get them is to go in with a bomber and drop the thermonuclear weapon accurately right on top of the target.

That is what the B-1 was designed to do.

And more. The B-52 fleet is geared to a quick reaction time measured in terms of only a few minutes. But even that short a time can be too long, in the event of a real

crisis, and an airborne alert – maintaining a portion of the bomber fleet constantly aloft – is a quick way to national poverty, if not bankruptcy.

What is needed is a bomber that can take off in less than a minute after receipt of the early warning, that can operate from dispersed fields rather than the known and targeted SAC bases, that can carry a huge load of nuclear weapons and that has a penetration range of many thousands of miles, unrefuelled.

That is the B-1A.

Currently, three prototype aircraft are being built to fly, and a fourth will be completed to the extent necessary to perform static tests. Originally, there were to have been five flying prototypes and two static test articles. That reduction is one that has hit the B-1A programme hard as the real costs of research and development begin to mount.

The only layout that would meet all the requirements for performance was a variable-sweep geometry. With its wings spread to the fullest, the B-1A can take off, fully loaded from a runway of the order of 6000 ft long, and there are hundreds of runways that length in the US. Further, its tyres of relatively low pressure mean that the footprint of the big bomber will be light enough to use the average 6000-ft runway, which was not designed to bear SAC heavyweights in the first place. The B-1A will cruise at high altitudes with its wings partially swept, for maximum efficiency in cruise. The extreme sweepback will be reserved for the low-level penetration, when the B-1A will be slashing along a few hundred feet above the terrain just under the speed of sound.

The B-1A will carry up to 24 SRAM

missiles internally, and another eight externally. Additionally, it will be equipped with electronic countermeasures and penetration aids, designed to fool the enemy, decoy his attacks, and raise havoc with his defences.

The crew will include pilot, co-pilot, defensive systems officer and offensive systems officer.

As of mid-1975, the B-1A programme was moving slowly but efficiently. There is much test data to be gathered and analysed before the next flight can be undertaken, to avoid repetition of data or to repeat a portion of the mission if some data were missed on the previous flight.

After seven months on flight status, the first B-1A has flown ten test flights for a total of a little over 41 hours in the air. It has reached a top speed of Mach 1·25, and a maximum altitude of 29,500 ft, both well below the desired maximum speed above Mach 2 and flight altitudes of about 60,000 ft.

If the programme proceeds as planned, there will soon be a decision on whether or not to order production. The cost of doing so has been estimated widely, but in current dollars it seems like a $20,000 million programme just for procurement of the B-1A itself. Other figures for supporting and flying the B-1A over its projected 30-year life span exceed $90,000 million.

The deciding factor will finally be whether or not such a bomber is judged as a necessary programme for the defence of the US. If it is, then it will cost what it will cost.

The story of the B-1A is still to be written. It will be interesting to look back from, say, 1980, and review the programme again from that vantage point.

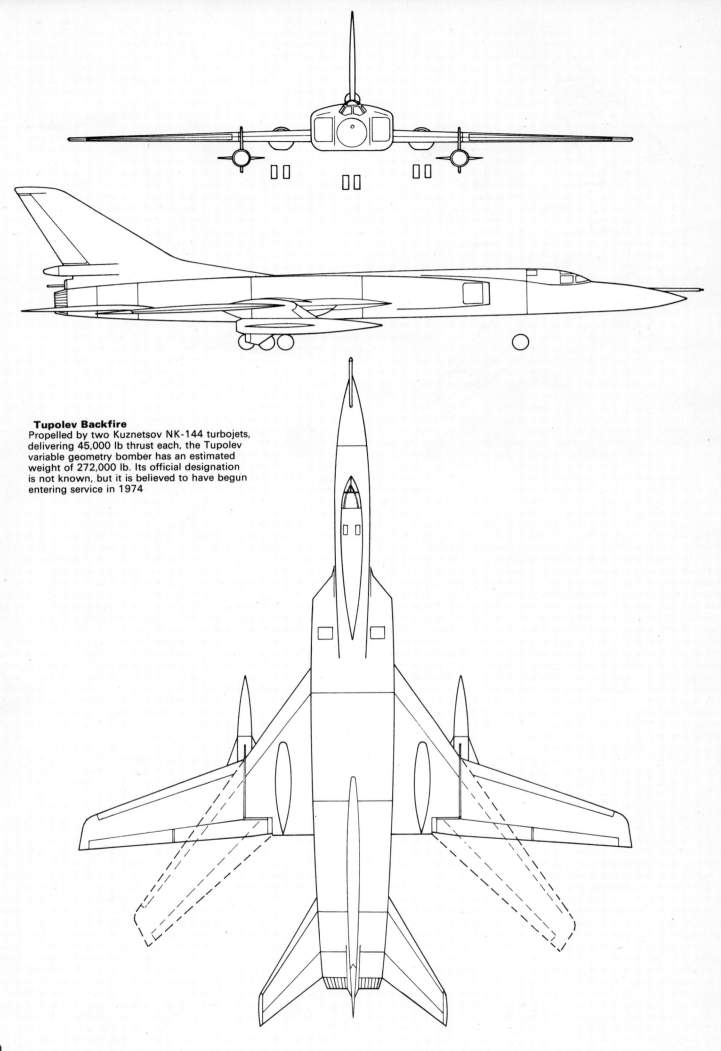

Tupolev Backfire
Propelled by two Kuznetsov NK-144 turbojets, delivering 45,000 lb thrust each, the Tupolev variable geometry bomber has an estimated weight of 272,000 lb. Its official designation is not known, but it is believed to have begun entering service in 1974

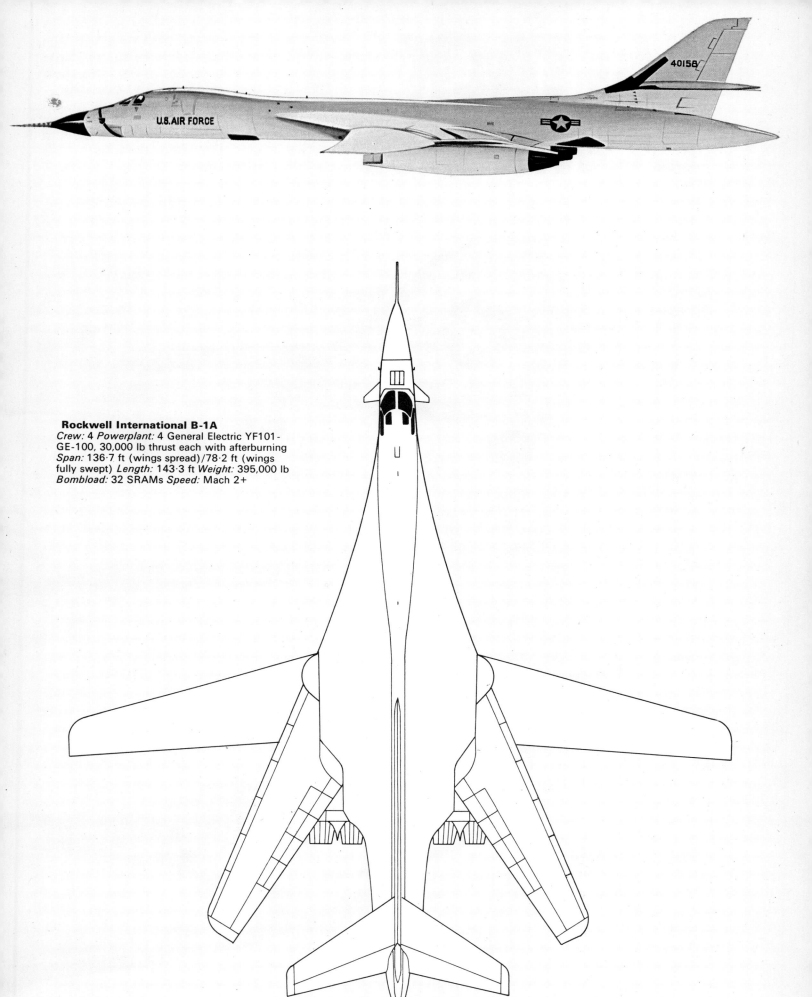

Rockwell International B-1A
Crew: 4 *Powerplant:* 4 General Electric YF101-GE-100, 30,000 lb thrust each with afterburning
Span: 136·7 ft (wings spread)/78·2 ft (wings fully swept) *Length:* 143·3 ft *Weight:* 395,000 lb
Bombload: 32 SRAMs *Speed:* Mach 2+

ATTACK BOMBERS

Wars since 1945 have not seen much demand for heavy strategic bombers to perform their designed role, and over the years the fighter-bombers of the Second World War have evolved into specialised ground-attack and close support aircraft

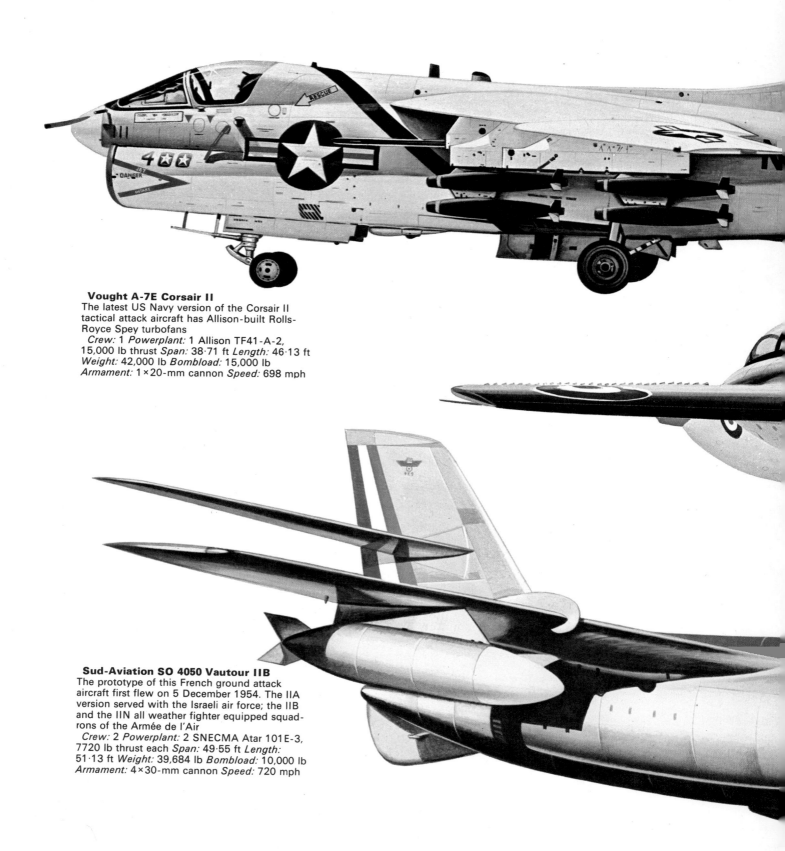

Vought A-7E Corsair II
The latest US Navy version of the Corsair II tactical attack aircraft has Allison-built Rolls-Royce Spey turbofans
Crew: 1 *Powerplant:* 1 Allison TF41-A-2, 15,000 lb thrust *Span:* 38·71 ft *Length:* 46·13 ft *Weight:* 42,000 lb *Bombload:* 15,000 lb *Armament:* 1×20-mm cannon *Speed:* 698 mph

Sud-Aviation SO 4050 Vautour IIB
The prototype of this French ground attack aircraft first flew on 5 December 1954. The IIA version served with the Israeli air force; the IIB and the IIN all weather fighter equipped squadrons of the Armée de l'Air
Crew: 2 *Powerplant:* 2 SNECMA Atar 101E-3, 7720 lb thrust each *Span:* 49·55 ft *Length:* 51·13 ft *Weight:* 39,684 lb *Bombload:* 10,000 lb *Armament:* 4×30-mm cannon *Speed:* 720 mph

Blackburn Buccaneer S Mk 1
XK 486, first of 20 development aircraft, flew on 30 April 1958. Originally built for the Royal Navy, Buccaneers now serve as low-level high-speed strike aircraft with the RAF
Crew: 2 *Powerplant:* 2 Bristol Siddeley Gyron Junior 101, 7100 lb thrust each *Span:* 44 ft *Length:* 63·42 ft *Weight:* 62,000 lb *Bombload:* 16,000 lb *Speed:* 720 mph

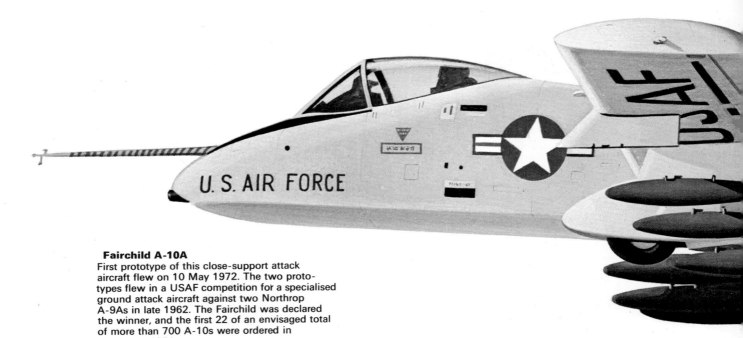

Fairchild A-10A

First prototype of this close-support attack
aircraft flew on 10 May 1972. The two prototypes flew in a USAF competition for a specialised
ground attack aircraft against two Northrop
A-9As in late 1962. The Fairchild was declared
the winner, and the first 22 of an envisaged total
of more than 700 A-10s were ordered in
December 1974
   Crew: 1 *Powerplant:* 2 General Electric
TF34-GE-100, 8985 lb thrust each *Span:* 55 ft
Length: 52·65 ft *Weight:* 44,547 lb *Bombload:*
18,500 lb *Armament:* 1×20-mm Vulcan cannon
(production aircraft to have 1×30-mm GAU-8/A
cannon) *Speed:* 500 mph (est at sea level)

Northrop A-9A

The loser in the USAF's A-X close-support
aircraft competition first flew on 30 May 1974
   Crew: 1 *Powerplant:* 2 Lycoming ALF502,
6000 lb thrust each *Span:* 57 ft *Length:* 53·5 ft
Weight: 39,570 lb *Bombload:* 18,500 lb
Armament: 1×30-mm GAU-8/A cannon

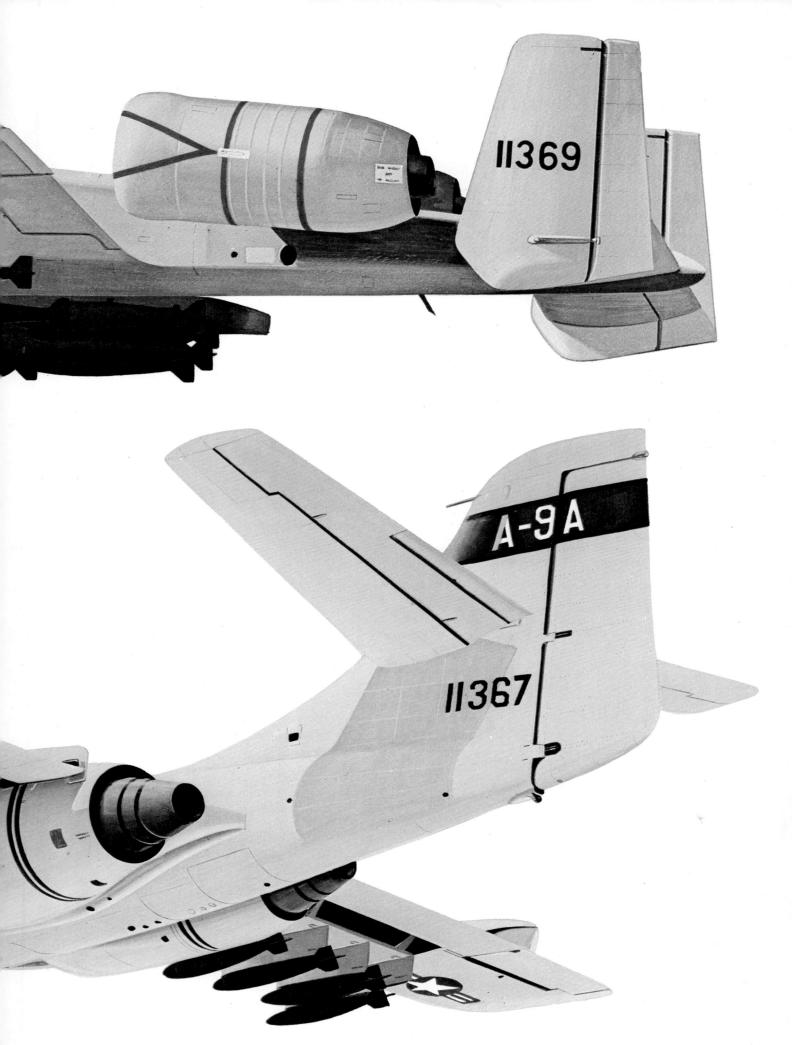

PLUTONIUM TO IRON

US Air Force

Bombing strategy divides itself neatly into two problems: one for the attacker, one for the defender. The attacker must get the bombs on the target; the defender must prevent that from happening. On these two commandments hang all the offensive and defensive systems discussed below.

The practical jet bomber arrived on the scene soon after the atomic bomb. The general concept then was that nuclear

Low Approach Bombing System
To evade anti-aircraft missiles, the bomber approaches the target in a low-level dash, pulls up into a loop and releases the bomb on the upward zoom. The bomb is thrown up and towards the target, while the bomber rolls out of the top of the loop and breaks for safety

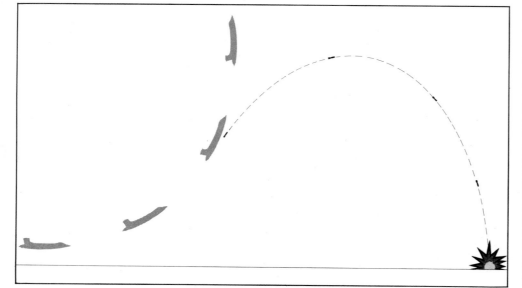

weapons were the be-all and end-all of bombing, and all jet bombers were designed to carry atomic bombs. That was easier said than done for two reasons: advances in weapons design, and security.

The former kept the shapes and weights changing, as well as the requirements for bomb-bay heating and for electrical power. The latter kept anybody from knowing about the former. Consequently, designers actually were planning bombers and missiles around weapons and warheads whose exact dimensions and weights they did not know. Nor did they know where such weapons might be grabbed, or fastened, or supported. They did not know where the fuses would be, where the centre of gravity would be located, how the bombs were to be

Boeing B-52 with Hound Dog stand-off cruise missiles. Powered by a J52 turbojet and weighing 1100 lb, Hound Dog has a range of 600 miles and a speed of Mach 1.6 carrying a thermonuclear warhead

armed or what kind of clearances would be needed in the bomb bay.

So early bombers tended to have big bomb bays. For one thing, the bombs were big. For another, the bomb design was so fluid that designers assumed the worst and chose bigger than usual dimensions for the bomb bays.

This choice provided later bonuses, although at first carrying all that extra weight and space didn't do anything for performance. Later, that big bomb bay was used to carry much smaller thermonuclear weapons, bombs of a more reasonable size. The space behind or ahead of them could be used for an extra fuel tank, or for something else to make the bomber a bit more of an adversary.

One of the ideas for doing this developed a series of decoy missiles, of which one – the Quail – saw service with USAF's Strategic Air Command. The idea is simple: you build a tiny airplane with the speed and other performance of the bomber that carries it. You build in some special electronic reflectors so that it looks just like the big bomber to enemy radars. And then you take it along on your ride to the target. As you approach you release the decoy, which soon appears as a second bomber to the enemy radar operator. Now it starts to turn away from the mother ship and the enemy has two tracks to follow. Are both bombers? He has no way of knowing, and by the time he finds out it may be too late.

Suppose that by luck the enemy picks out the bomber instead of the decoy, and he calls the warning to his anti-aircraft section. They are ready for action when the bomber gets within range. The bomber knows this, and he goes upstairs, heading for as much altitude as he can get. For one thing, he can get above the range of artillery-type anti-aircraft fire. For another, he can get some time warning of anti-aircraft missiles fired at him, and maybe take evasive action or decoy or destroy the missile.

But missiles kept getting better, and faster, and they had a greater range, and it was going to be suicidal to try to sail in undisturbed above the level of the effective fire. That level was invariably going to be several miles above the best bomber altitude.

That leaves two choices. The bomber can try to put up an elaborate electronic screen, jamming and confusing the enemy search and guidance radars to the point where their chances of success are very low. The risks are going to be acceptable in such a case, and the bomber goes in high.

Alternatively, the bomber can get out of the whole mess by heading down instead of up, heading for the protective cover of low altitude. There, he is below any effective anti-aircraft missile fire, and if he is really low he only exposes himself to the fire of automatic heavy machine-guns or light cannon for the briefest instant before he is out of range again.

He may have other missiles to deal with, fired by fighters or other aircraft flying above him and able to look down with their radars and see him against the clutter of the ground. The bomber still has some options remaining; he may be carrying, in addition to the electronic jammers, some window or chaff, tiny aluminium foil ribbons which, when dropped, make a huge bright spot on any radar system and tend to make the missile home on the cloud of foil rather than on the plane. If the on-board detectors tell the bomber that an infrared guided missile is coming his way, he may fire a flare, whose hot burning will attract the missile more strongly than the infrared signature of the bomber, and the enemy is fooled again.

This cat-and-mouse game describes the defensive counters that the bomber can use in a passive sense. Active defences include the conventional gun turrets, which in the early days of jet bombers were manned, and which now are almost universally remotely controlled by semi-automatic radar and a gunner. A further development is the bomber defence missile, proposed but never adopted, which would give the bomber a complement of air-to-air missiles that could be fired from turrets or launchers against enemy fighters or missiles.

But there is more and more reliance on using electronic means to counter the enemy defences, and the B-52 provides one outstanding example. One electronics warfare officer sits at a console surrounded, as far as the hand can reach and the eye can scan, by black boxes, their faces covered with knobs, dials and switches. Each of these can do something very well; each is a specialised bit of defence, able to jam an enemy radar, or overload a locked-on guidance system or fool a homing device. All over the bomber are antennae, reaching out with their electronic eyes to detect something other than empty air around and the ground below. Once those antennae spot an incoming missile or fighter, or detect and pinpoint an operating radar, the

Concrete Dibber Bomb
The Israeli bomb that was reported to have wrecked Egyptian airfields in 1967 and 1973. Three-tenths of a second after its release (at about 330 ft) form Vautour or Mirage aircraft, the four solid-propellant outward-angled retro rockets fire, and 0·6 seconds later a cruciform drogue parachute opens, stabilising the bomb at an attack angle of 60°–80°. Finally, 4·7 seconds after launch, four booster rockets ignite, accelerating the bomb to 525 ft per second, ploughing its 365-lb explosive charge into the runway

electronic countermeasures go into action.

But that is not the end of the defensive system. The electronics warfare officer is a walking tape deck and reel, with memorised sounds of radars catalogued in his memory. An early-warning radar of a certain type buzzes. A height-finder radar produces a beeping sound. Search radars for anti-aircraft missiles play an interrupted tone while on the lookout; when they find something, the tone shifts to a higher note. The missile radar is higher still. Radar fire-control systems also screech. And a data link sounds like a touch-telephone tone.

All these chirps and buzzes and squeaks have to be heard, identified and acted upon in split seconds. Some of this is done automatically by electronic systems, but an amazingly large part of it can only be done by the electronics warfare officer.

Meanwhile, bombs have been augmented and in some cases replaced by newer families of weapons. Most bombers are equipped with one or more types of stand-off bombs, so-called because they are fired while the bomber is still well out of enemy reach, outside his borders and far from his defences. They can be used to saturate a defensive zone, or to strike at targets en route to the main objective.

They generally started as rocket-powered winged bombs, looking much like miniature aircraft. In the early days of their development, they were too big for the bomb bays, which could hardly squeeze in an unadorned bomb, let alone one to which wings, tail surfaces and a powerplant had been added. Later versions were submerged in the fuselage, their smaller size reflecting later technology. The latest are concealed completely within the bomb bay, or slung underneath the wings on pylon racks.

These air-launched missiles have been of two basic types: the boosted ballistic, and the cruise. The former, like the ill-fated Skybolt, was an attempt to combine ballistic missile performance with the advantages of launching from a position of speed and altitude. This would reduce the initial requirements for launch thrust, and reduce the size of the weapon. The cruise missiles, like the Hound Dogs carried under the wings of the B-52s, are miniature aircraft, jet powered like their carriers, and generally able to perform over a much wider range of parameters because they are pilotless, and small, and can be designed to be much stronger than the bomber.

The Hound Dog, for example, can streak along the ground with its belly practically scraping the earth, at speeds that would demolish the average bomber. And it is a safe bet that the Hound Dog carries some electronic trickery so that it could double as a decoy for its B-52.

One of the newest of the current crop of bomber weapons is the Boeing/USAF SRAM, which stands for Short-Range Attack Missile, and is pronounced as if it were spelled SHRAM. These missiles are rocket-propelled, carry nuclear warheads, and are endowed with amazing performance and manoeuvrability. Once launched from the B-52 or the FB-111A, the SRAM is inertially guided to its target. It can turn to hit targets abeam or even somewhat behind the position of the carrier aircraft, lending an element of suspense to the defence problem. It can operate along a variety of mission flight profiles, from low to high altitude. Because of its inertial guidance system, which does not need any external signals from electronic systems once launched, no electronic countermeasures can be applied to it, to jam its guidance, or to decoy it. Further, its radar and infrared signatures are so small, because of its size, that it is unlikely to be detected until it is much too late. SRAM is as sure of getting through to its target as you are of reading to the end of this sentence.

SRAM can be mounted in a rotary launcher, much like the chamber of a revolver. Installed in the bomb bay of a B-52, the launcher will index one of its eight SRAMs every five seconds, release it and start the launch sequence. After a brief free-fall to clear the aircraft, the solid-propellant motor fires: SRAM is on its way.

Development work continues on such weapons, as adjuncts to the gravity-propelled bombs that bombers now carry, and the other forms of weapons they employ.

But SRAM and its generation may be the last of the bomber missiles, because if there are no more bombers, there will be no more need for bombs and such weapons.

But this is the real world, isn't it? Shall we look at jet bomber history again, say, in ten years?